FRENCH CINEMA SINCE 1946
VOLUME ONE
by Roy Armes
Above: Jacques Tati

In the same series
produced by THE TANTIVY PRESS
and edited by Peter Cowie:

Roy Armes

FRENCH CINEMA

since 1946

VOLUME ONE: THE GREAT TRADITION

> *Man is dependent less on his race than on
> the soil which nourishes him, the conditions
> of life which shape his body and brain, the
> landscapes which, all day long, pass before
> his eyes ... A Frenchman living in France,
> drinking red wine and eating Brie cheese
> before the greyness of Parisian perspectives
> can only create a work of quality by resting
> on the traditions of people who have lived
> like him.*

> *JEAN RENOIR*

A. ZWEMMER LIMITED, LONDON
A. S. BARNES & CO., NEW JERSEY

Acknowledgements

I SHOULD like to thank the following organisations and individuals
for their help with this book: the British Film Institute and the
Cinémathèque Royale de Belgique for showing me films I should not
otherwise have been able to see; the Information Department of the
B.F.I. for providing facts; B.F.I., Connoisseur, Gala, Mondial and Se-
bricon Films, and Mme. Camus of Unifrance for help with illustrations;
and Peter Cowie for his encouragement.

COVER STILLS
Front: Ingrid Bergman and Mel Ferrer in
Renoir's ELENA ET LES HOMMES.
Back: Jacques Tati in his own PLAYTIME.

First Published 1966
SECOND ENLARGED EDITION 1970
Copyright © 1966, 1970 by Roy Armes
Library of Congress Catalogue Card Number: 77-106379
SBN 498 07652 0   (U.S.A.)
SBN 302 00233 2   (U.K.)
Printed in the United States of America

Contents

For Anne

1. Introduction

In the commercial cinema it is fairly easy to discuss trends and genres, as films are made to fit neatly into set categories and any outstandingly successful film will give rise to a host of imitations. Where the cinema is an art, such discussions are more difficult, since important directors — whether they are creators or interpretative artists — forge an individual style and strive for new and distinctive forms of expression. Certain attitudes and stylistic features, however, recur so frequently in the French cinema that we can talk meaningfully of a French cinematographic tradition, though it must be understood that any definition offered can be neither all-embracing nor exclusive. It is easy to begin talking about a specifically French approach: some films — *Orphée* and *L'Année Dernière à Marienbad* for instance — could hardly have been made anywhere but in France and certain directors like René Clair and Jean Cocteau are self-evidently part of the French cultural tradition. The best work in France of an alien like Max Ophuls can easily be fitted into the dominant pattern (perhaps because he was born in the Saar, a meeting place of French and German culture) but other film makers defy too rigid a classification. Jean Renoir in France and Luchino Visconti in Italy, for instance, have a greatness that goes beyond the boundaries of their native filmic traditions. While each has directed films that are among the purest examples of his own national cinema, both may be said to bestride two traditions: *Toni* and other Renoir films of the thirties prefigure Italian Neo-Realism, whereas Visconti's *White Nights*, despite its Russian source, Italian director and international cast, is best understood as a work in the French style.

With these reservations in mind, how can we define this French tradition? Firstly, it is the tradition of Méliès rather than that of Lumière, being concerned not with the recording of reality but with the creation of an illusion of reality and having its home therefore in the film studio. Despite Vigo and Renoir, this is the tradition that dominates the French cinema from the advent of sound, ranging from Clair's *Sous les Toits de Paris* (1930) through Feyder's *La Kermesse Héroïque* (1935) and Carné's

Le Jour se lève (1939) up to Bresson's *Les Dames du Bois de Boulogne* (1944-5) and the postwar era. Work within the studio inevitably brings with it a certain formalism, and the stylistic exercise is far more typical of the French cinema than the rough document with a hard ring of truth. Certain subjects (notably war) remain tabu, and the films intended as documents are, significantly, the ones that do not get made: Clouzot's film on Brazil, Becker's on Morocco, Malle's on Algeria. The characteristic features of studio film making — the planning of a film in detail before shooting and the adherence to a precise shooting script — are factors that unite the most disparate directors: Clair and Clouzot both plan every move in advance, Bresson and Tati both willingly spend years on the elaboration of a single film script, Carné and Resnais both shoot the scripts written for them without altering a word. A remarkable degree of control can be exercised when filming within the studio, and a concern with exact lighting and with photographic shades and textures runs through the whole history of French film making: Gance in the twenties, Carné in the thirties, Bresson in the forties, Clément in the fifties and Resnais in the sixties. Moreover from Clair to Bresson, Cocteau to Resnais there is the same opposition to naturalistic acting and search instead for refinement and stylisation of gesture. With the possible exception of Tati (who is himself a mime trained in the theatre), it is hard to find a single director who regards the recording of ordinary human behaviour in an everyday context worthy of attention. Abstract themes like fate (Carné), grace (Bresson), death (Cocteau) or memory (Resnais) are sought as being somehow more significant and take the place of a close analysis of social problems or political ideas.

It is as much from these stylistic preoccupations as from any limitations imposed by producers or censors that are derived the detachment from reality and corresponding isolation of the characters from the economic pressures of the actual world which can be sensed in so many French films. This impression is reinforced by the use of settings to create a world that totally reflects the film's mood and atmosphere. With the older directors this effect is attained, as in the prewar cinema, by the use of studio-constructed settings with a minimum of location work. Since the décor is fabricated it is as valid to draw inspiration from the world of painting as from the world of reality. So it is that Cocteau in *La Belle et la Bête* follows Feyder in drawing inspiration from the Dutch masters, while Renoir in his later colour spectacles continues to bring Impressionist paintings to life as he had done when shooting *Une Partie de Campagne* in 1936. With the younger directors the same effect of total unity of tone is achieved through sensitive handling of real settings, a striking example being the way in which Franju in *Le Sang des Bêtes* makes his location shots of the real Canal de l'Ourcq echo the constructed décor of Carné's films in the thirties. Location shooting is more common but often this entails photographing a "doctored" reality, as in Demy's *Les Parapluies de Cherbourg* or Varda's *Le Bonheur*. The essence of this approach being how a given setting is handled, the commonest outside sources of inspiration for the younger directors are other styles of film making and in this way we find Astruc imitating the angling and lighting techniques of German expressionism and Melville those of the American cinema of the thirties.

The lack of a French social or political cinema is most remarkable. In the case of some directors one finds a tendency to opt out of contemporary society altogether, either by retreating into a private world (the romanticised Parisian suburbs of Clair's *Porte des Lilas,* the fairytale Vienna of Ophuls, the proletarian wonderland of Varda's *Le Bonheur*) or by creating a dream world quite independent of reality (Cocteau's *Orphée,* Carne's *Juliette ou la Clef des Songes,* or Resnais's *L'Année Dernière à Marienbad*). Among the important directors, only Autant-Lara maintains a consistent and explicit attitude towards society, and his isolation is emphasised by the failure of the leftwing group of documentarists to establish themselves as feature film-makers in the late fifties. It is true that the situation is complicated by censorship restrictions, as Roger Vadim (something of an expert in these matters) reminds us: "The censor has been able to accept, though not without difficulty, the wedding breakfast scene in *Et Dieu créa la Femme* but he would never accept a scene with as much violence towards the social order as that sequence had towards the moral order." But this is only a partial and ultimately unsatisfactory explanation.

An equally important reason why so few films treating working class or peasant life are made is that the origins of French film-makers are uniformly bourgeois and their culture predominantly Parisian. Even as nonconformist a director as Godard feels this: "If I began by making bourgeois stories it is because I come from the bourgeoisie. If I were of peasant stock I would probably have filmed differently . . . For *La Femme Mariée* I would have preferred a couple with a lower class, more difficult social setting. But I risked what I reproach *Le Bonheur* for being: an artificial and an unintegrated idea." Against such isolated works as Becker's *Antoine et Antoinette* or Rouquier's *Farrebique* one must weigh the innumerable films which, if they analyse middle-class attitudes, do so from an exclusively middle-class standpoint. Even in the thriller, which could be a valid means of escape from class attitudes, the same tendency is found: the gangsters of Becker's *Touchez pas au Grisbi* or Melville's *Bob le Flambeur* have the air of particularly enterprising business men and Pierre Kast has justified a recent thriller by adapting Clausewitz: "Crime is the pursuit of commerce by other means."

Though there is plenty of independent film-making in France—Bresson and Tati, Varda's *La Pointe Courte* and Rivette's *Paris Nous Appartient,* the 16mm films of Rouch and Rohmer—none of it is political and, lacking a firm ideology, the French cinema focuses almost exclusively on the individual and his personal relationships. Rarely is the individual viewed as a microcosm, reflecting the working of social or political forces, or given a sense of oneness with nature or the universe (the idyll in Renoir's *Le Déjeuner sur l'Herbe* or Varda's *Le Bonheur* can be no more than temporary, a holiday from the pressures of life). The French cinema is predominantly urban and therefore confronts us with the problem of solitude: that of Monsieur Hulot in holiday resort or modern suburb, that of Bresson's Pickpocket amid the crowds he preys upon, of Ophuls's Lola Montès surrounded by a mocking audience in the circus that forms her gilded cage, and of Malle's film star heroine in *Vie Privée,* hounded by unfeeling press photographers. Often the solitude is depicted in specific urban terms: a battle is to be waged against a hostile city (Clément's *Monsieur Ripois,* Varda's *Cléo* or Rohmer's *Le Signe du Lion*) and if it is lost then the only outcome can be suicide (Malle's *Le Feu Follet*) or withdrawal into madness (Jessua's *La Vie à L'Envers*).

Lacking a firm ideology, the French cinema focusses almost exclusively on the individual and his personal relationships. Rarely is the individual viewed as a microcosm, reflecting the working of social or political forces, or given a sense of oneness with nature or the universe (the idyll in Renoir's *Le Déjeuner sur l'Herbe* or Varda's *Le Bonheur* can be no more than temporary, a holiday from the pressures of life). The French cinema is predominantly urban and therefore confronts us with the problem of solitude: that of Monsieur Hulot in holiday resort or modern suburb, that of Bresson's Pickpocket amid the crowds he preys upon, of Ophuls's Lola Montès surrounded by a mocking audience in the circus that forms her gilded cage, and of Malle's film star heroine in *Vie Privée*, hounded by unfeeling press photographers. Often the solitude is depicted in specific urban terms: a battle is to be waged against a hostile city (Clément's *Monsieur Ripois*, Varda's *Cléo* or Rohmer's *Le Signe du Lion)* and if it is lost then the only outcome can be suicide (Malle's *Le Feu Follet)* or withdrawal into madness (Jessua's *La Vie à l'Envers)*.

Thrown back on himself, the individual must search to establish his own identity. This leads the heroes of Clément's later thrillers, such as Tom Ripley in *Plein Soleil*, to murder, and the confused heroines of Astruc's *La Proie pour l'Ombre* and Godard's *Une Femme Mariée* to adultery. For others it may imply trying to rekindle a lost love — Resnais's *Muriel* or Colpi's *Une Aussi Longue Absence* — or even the merging of one's own personality into that of a fictional character (Leenhardt's *Le Rendez-Vous de Minuit*). True self realisation can only be achieved by establishing genuine contact with others, either through love or friendship. In the cinema the latter is less frequently portrayed but it forms the core of Clair's *Porte des Lilas*, Clouzot's *Le Salaire de la Peur* and Truffaut's *Jules et Jim*. It is noticeable how often friendship is between men opposed to society — in Becker or Melville — and often leads not to integration or freedom from solitude, but to death.

Love is the great theme of the French cinema but seldom is it as happy a relationship as in Becker's *Edouard et Caroline* or as pleasurable a one as in Vadim's *Et Dieu créa la Femme*. More commonly it is the final

11

refuge of a tormented soul (Bresson's *Pickpocket*), the temporary asylum of a fugitive (Clément's *Au Delà des Grilles*) or a complex individual's search for clarity (Resnais's *Hiroshima mon Amour*). French directors have probed love in all its manifestations, giving us particularly sensitive studies of the adolescent emerging into adulthood (Leenhardt's *Les Dernières Vacances*, Autant-Lara's *Le Blé en Herbe*), depicting "amour fou" both as morally destructive (Clouzot's *Manon*) and as a source of rebirth (Malle's *Les Amants*). Rarely is there the kind of interaction between lovers and society such as we find in Clair's *Les Grandes Manoeuvres*. Mostly the lovers live indifferent to society and their failure comes from personal weaknesses, not external social forces (Autant-Lara's *Le Diable au Corps*, Truffaut's *Jules et Jim*, Godard's *Pierrot le Fou*). Sometimes indeed society is totally non-existent, the lovers acting out their comings and goings in a vacuum (Resnais's *Marienbad* and Varda's *Le Bonheur*).

The preoccupation with the individual and his problems at the expense of interest in society is reflected in the formal patterns adopted by French film-makers. Since it serves better to depict man in society than man in isolation, the straight narrative consisting of a sequence of dramatic scenes leading to a forceful climax tends to be discarded by the more original directors. In its place comes a diversity of stylistic approaches: a "closed" pattern of repetitions and symmetry (Ophuls's *La Ronde*, Varda's *Le Bonheur* and Demy's *Lola*) or an "open" one of intentional ambiguity (Melville's *Le Doulos* and Colpi's *Une Aussi Longue Absence*); the inclusion of *temps morts* that contribute nothing to the advancement of the plot (Becker's *Touchez Pas au Grisbi*) and the abandoning of establishing shots and smooth links from scene to scene (Godard's *A Bout de Souffle*); the fragmentation of a single narrative (Resnais's *Muriel* and Godard's *Une Femme Mariée*) or the fusion of several levels of reality (Carné's *Juliette ou la Clef des Songes* and Leenhardt's *Le Rendez-Vous de Minuit*).

The handling of the flashback has progressed a long way from the "classical" pattern of Yves Allégret's *Manèges* or Autant-Lara's *Le Diable au Corps* to the complexities of Ophuls's *Lola Montès* and Resnais's *Hiroshima mon Amour*. Of great interest too is the way Demy, in *Lola*, uses secondary characters to show Lola as she once was (in the person of Cécile) and as she may one day be (Madame Desnoyers); and Resnais in *L'Année Dernière à Marienbad* includes scenes of varying degrees of reality, not only what *is* happening but also a hypothetical past and premonitions of a possible future. The critical attitude of the audience towards the characters is maintained in various ways: by dividing the narrative into tableaux (Godard's *Vivre sa Vie*), timing each small scene (Varda's *Cléo de Cinq à Sept*), or shooting largely in long-shot (Godard's *Les Carabiniers*). Keeping the characters at a distance from their settings serves the same purpose in the films of Tati, Bresson and Resnais, as does the deliberately theatrical dialogue in Varda's *La Pointe Courte* and the maintenance of the actor's own personality even in an alien part, such as one so often finds in Godard.

Another aspect of film structure that has undergone considerable development is the interaction of sound and image. It will be recalled that Bresson and Tati make subtle use of sound in their films (Tati has recently gone so far as to reissue *Les Vacances de Monsieur Hulot* with a new sound-track) and directors who come from the documentary, such as Franju and Resnais, often accord a great importance to musical accompaniment. With Cinéma-Vérité the concern with words reaches such a degree that the primacy of the image is denied and reliance placed on the interview rather than the visual evocation. More fruitful in every way is the use of a commentary to balance the images, a device which has been developed by many directors. In the documentary this is a common technique: Franju's text for *Hôtel des Invalides* probes the realities beneath the dull conventionality of the War Museum, and Cayrol's sober commentary for *Nuit et Brouillard* is a necessary concomitant of the often brutal images assembled by Resnais. The culmination of this comes with Chris Marker who, in works like *Lettre de Sibérie* and *Description d'un Combat*, accumulates images not as picturesque details but as signs that need interpreting. The commentary is of great importance in such works, for by capturing a particular tone of voice it gives the film its rhythm, and the full meaning is to be found only in the interaction of words with images. Grémillon, in his last documentary film, *André Masson*, spoke the commentary that gave his speculations on the nature of artistic creation and in a similar way, in feature films, we hear the voice of Cocteau in *Les Enfants Terribles*, that of Melville in *Bob le Flambeur* and of Godard in *Bande à Part*.

The definition we have given of the French tradition of film making is wide enough to contain considerable differences of approach. Although the individuality of any great director is something one must always bear in mind, it is nonetheless possible to discern certain trends and changes in the twenty years of film making from 1946 to 1965. By bringing the more important of the individual directors together into various rough groupings we can in fact obtain a fairly coherent pattern. If we adopt as our initial means of classification the date of a director's first film of note, three main groupings emerge. Firstly there are the veterans who had made their reputations before the outbreak of war. One would expect these men — many of whom were formed by the techniques and requirements of the silent film — to be traditionally minded and concerned more to reaffirm old values than to seek out a fresh approach, but in fact they are in many ways freer and more original in their attitude to the medium than their immediate successors. The second group comprises those who came to the fore during the Occupation or immediately afterwards. Despite the great events they had lived through and the changing society in which they found themselves these directors proved remarkably susceptible to the influences of the past. They are largely craftsmen, forming the culmination of a long tradition, rather than creators whose work marks the beginning of a new approach to the cinema. Their virtues are precision and elegance, not originality. No great and shattering event separates these men from the third group, but the years 1949 to 1955 form a convenient watershed, for between these two dates (the début of Tati and the début of Astruc) no new director of importance made a first feature film under commercial conditions. While the links between these new directors, who made their débuts in the late fifties, and the earlier directors are stronger than is generally realised, it is fair to see these newcomers as representing a radical change, the search for a fresh start which may not as yet have borne full fruit. There are a few individualistic directors who do not fit into these three categories but in general they provide a useful basis for analysis. We are concerned in this volume

14

with the veterans and the first postwar generation whose specific qualities now demand consideration in greater detail.

The war caused a break in French film production, for most of the men who had dominated the thirties had their careers interrupted, and many — Jacques Feyder, René Clair, Jean Renoir and Julien Duvivier among them — went into exile. Eventually these directors returned to France to continue their careers but the situation had changed and none of them again achieved the same dominant position. **JACQUES FEYDER** (b. 1888) died in Switzerland in 1948, having been unable to find a single directorial assignment in France. **JULIEN DUVIVIER** (b. 1896), who had for a while in the thirties given the illusion of being a great director, returned to purely commercial production after 1945 and his numerous films, though reaching a wide audience, have little lasting value. **RENÉ CLAIR** (b. 1898) and **JEAN RENOIR** (b. 1894) had both been markedly less successful in the films they had made in Hollywood but returned to something like their best form in Europe and their later films are not entirely unworthy of comparison with their finest work. By contrast there are two men of this generation whose reputation rests essentially on films made since 1945: **JEAN COCTEAU** (1889-1963) and **MAX OPHULS** (1902-1957). Each had established a reputation at the beginning of the sound era with a work of outstanding interest (Cocteau with *Le Sang d'un poète* and Ophuls with *Liebelei*). Then there is a gap until the war, Cocteau having spent the thirties largely engaged on playwriting while Ophuls directed commercial films all over Europe after the advent of Hitler had made it necessary for him to leave his native Germany.

Those who remained in France during the war years experienced varying fortunes. For two established directors, **MARCEL CARNÉ** (b. 1909) and **JEAN GRÉMILLON** (b. 1901) the Occupation years had been marked by brilliant works but after the Liberation both failed to get into their stride again. Marcel Carné has made on average a film every two or three years, but these postwar works have not the same value as his work in the thirties. Jean Grémillon, who died in 1959, was able to make only three feature films in fourteen years and most of his energies were devoted to short films. By contrast, the commercial directors whose only aim is to entertain moved unconcernedly through the war and postwar years: men like **HENRI DECOIN** (b. 1896) who directed one or two interesting thrillers in the fifties, **MARC ALLÉGRET** (b. 1900) who maintained his reputation as a discoverer of youthful acting talent, **CHRISTIAN-JAQUE** (b. 1904), director of some of the most successful of postwar spectacles, many of them starring his erstwhile wife, Martine Carol, and **JEAN DRÉVILLE** (b. 1906) who was responsible for the Franco-Norwegian documentary *La Bataille de l'Eau Lourde* (1948). Two highly successful dramatists who had also begun their film careers around 1930 when the advent of sound made them feel that they could secure wider distribution for their plays by filming them, likewise continued film making well into the postwar years. **MARCEL PAGNOL** (b. 1895) and **SACHA GUITRY** (1885-1957) had both produced works of more than average interest in the thirties but neither achieved comparable results after 1945, though Guitry did win great commercial success with a series of star-studded costume spectacles.

There were also survivors of an even earlier generation, the men whose reputations were made in the early twenties or before. **JACQUES DE BARONCELLI** (1881-1951) had begun his career during the first world war and continued directing until 1947 though producing nothing of great interest in his later years. **JEAN EPSTEIN** (1897-1953), an important figure in the French silent cinema, produced only two short films, *Le Tempestaire* (1947) and *Les Feux de la Mer* (1948) in the last fifteen years of his life and was, at his death, a neglected and forgotten figure. His contemporary **MARCEL L'HERBIER** (b. 1890), the founder of the IDHEC, continued as a feature director until 1953, his later films including a version of *Gli Ultimi Giorni di Pompei* made in Italy in 1949, but then turned to television. **RAYMOND BERNARD** (b. 1891), who had once directed Max Linder in *Le Petit Café*, made a string of unimportant films including the Resistance melodrama *Un Ami Viendra ce Soir* (1945), a version of *La Dame aux Camélias* (1953) and a group of light comedies, two of which starred Edwige Feuillère. The most vigorous and enthusiastic of these real veterans was **ABEL GANCE** (b. 1889) who had been a dominant figure in the French cinema during the years of the first world war and in the twenties. Most of his time after 1942 was spent on projects that were never realised or experiments in wide screen techniques (notably the collection of shorts shown under the title of *Magirama* in 1956). Amid innumerable frustrations he did manage to find a new lease of life in the sphere of period spectacle, scripting a version of Alexandre Dumas's novel *La Reine Margot* (1953) and directing three features: *La Tour de Nesle* (1954), *Austerlitz* (1960) and *Cyrano et d'Artagnan* (1964).

With men of such a wide variety of approaches, survivors of so many past movements, it is impossible to talk of any sort of stylistic unity. What is of interest, however, is the scope and ambition which these men reveal. None of them is interested in the simple reproduction of reality and only the openly commercial directors among them are content to adapt existing works. Among the creative men of this generation one finds a passion for history, together with a rare willingness to tackle great themes and to confront directly the literary giants of earlier times. Thus René Clair gave variations on a plot of Molière's in one film and tackled the Faust theme in another. Abel Gance, obviously fascinated by that other legendary figure, Napoleon, made him the subject of two of his films and innumerable projects, and ranged freely through the seventeenth century in *Cyrano et d'Artagnan*, drawing inspiration from the whole wealth of Classic and Romantic literature (especially the latter, from Dumas to Rostand). Jean Grémillon showed a similar ambition in the late forties though none of his great plans came to fruition. Again, in the case of many of these veterans we find a delight in the possibilities of spectacle, a revelling in the joys of colour and dimension, which is most evident in Gance, but apparent too in the visual exuberances of Renoir's *French Cancan* and Ophuls's *Lola Montès*. On a more commercial level we have the spectacles directed by L'Herbier, Guitry and the prolific Christian-Jaque. Alongside this fascination for history runs an interest in fantasy. "Realist" is not a term one would apply to any of the great survivors of this generation. With them one finds rather an interest in illusions, dreams, myth and fairytale, a common factor shared by works otherwise as different as *Juliette ou la Clef des Songes* and *Orphée, Les Belles-de-Nuit* and *La Belle et la Bête*.

The reasons for this particular approach are not far to seek. The members of this generation were all formed by influences outside the cinema which only grew to maturity as an art form in their lifetime.

Their literary and, especially, theatrical interests never left them, and reassert themselves whenever the freedom to choose subjects presents itself. Guitry (author of some 120 plays), Pagnol and Cocteau were all men of the theatre before becoming film directors. If the first two limited the artistic success of their work by remaining suspicious of the potentialities of the film medium, Cocteau at least saw the need to recreate his material in film terms and produced films to equal his plays. Ophuls was for six years a theatrical producer and his last creative work was a production of Beaumarchais's "Marriage of Figaro" at the Schauspiel Theater in Hamburg. Clair is very much a man of letters: he wrote poetry in his youth, a novel in the twenties. as well as a couple of stories in the fifties, and his commentaries on his published film scripts show clearly his concern with the principles of classical drama. Gance too, in many ways Clair's opposite, was formed by the theatre, in his case the plays of Edmond Rostand. His first work was a verse tragedy "La Victoire de Samothrace", written for Sarah Bernhardt, and his latest film has a dialogue in rhymed alexandrines. Renoir has also felt the lure of the theatre and has several times abandoned film making to write or translate plays for the Parisian stage. Carné, of course, being so much younger, does not share this attitude. He was trained in the cinema, as assistant to Feyder, but through his work with Prévert he too felt the fascination of the theatre and gave it expression in *Les Enfants du Paradis*, made during the Occupation but released in 1945. This pioneer generation was the last to be formed by such outside influences. The men who came to the cinema in the forties were predominantly men trained as film craftsmen and technicians, while the new directors of the fifties were largely film critics. Both therefore lack this added breadth of vision.

The men who are the dominant force in the French cinema in the first dozen or so years of the postwar period are those who established themselves as directors in the forties. The forceful new men of this generation were mostly in their late thirties when the war ended and their early careers give a clue as to their later styles and attitudes. Almost all had come to the cinema in a conventional way in the early nineteen thirties and served apprenticeships as assistant directors. This might be a lengthy process and even as gifted a man as Becker worked for over seven years in this subordinate capacity before being given a directorial assignment. The majority of the new men (including as austere a figure as Bresson) had also worked in some other capacity as well: as scriptwriters, directors of the French versions of foreign films or as short film makers. They were thus highly trained professional film makers who possessed a craftsman's approach to the medium, more technicians and interpreters of the work of others than creative personalities bursting with ideas they needed to express on celluloid.

Most of the men of this group made their feature débuts during the Occupation years. Although his first film was made in 1938, **JEAN DELANNOY** (b. 1908) belongs with **HENRI-GEORGES CLOUZOT** (b. 1907) and **JACQUES BECKER** (b. 1906) among those who proved themselves to be important directors with feature films made between the collapse of France and the Liberation. **CLAUDE AUTANT-LARA** (b. 1903) had a connection with the film industry dating back to the début of René Clair (he was art director for Marcel L'Herbier in the years 1919-23 and subsequently Clair's assistant) but he too achieved full freedom over his work only during the Occupation years. **ANDRÉ CAYATTE** (b. 1909), **YVES ALLÉGRET** (b. 1907) and **LOUIS DA-QUIN** (b. 1908), all of whom were to make interesting films in the late forties and early fifties, had also made a start with commercial works during the war years. Together with **RENÉ CLÉMENT** (b. 1913), whose first film appeared in 1946, these men were the ones who set the patterns of French film making after 1945. But there were others who stood aside from the mainstream of the French cinema and these include perhaps the major talents. **ROBERT BRESSON** (b. 1907) and **JACQUES TATI** (b. 1908) created only a small number of works but these are all of the greatest artistic importance. **GEORGES ROUQUIER** (b. 1909) and **ROGER LEENHARDT** (b. 1903) each made one outstanding feature film but commercial failure limited their opportunities and they returned, like Grémillon, to short film production. Even so they are perhaps more fortunate than **GEORGES FRANJU** (b. 1912) who belongs by age and temperament to this group but was unable to make a feature until 1958, after nine years work in the documentary. By contrast, **JEAN-PIERRE MELVILLE** (b. 1917) made his début in 1947 and continued with a film every two or three years but is, in outlook and style, far closer to the younger men of the fifties.

These last two directors form a link with the subsequent generation in the same way that Carné forms a bridge between the veterans and the men of the forties. If we ignore them for the time being we are left with a number of directors who, since they made their débuts at about the same time and share the same origins, do constitute a definite group to which can be ascribed a distinct style and approach. It would be going too far, however, to say that the forties generation constitutes a "school" in the manner of the Italian Neo-Realist directors. Rather the definition of their approach is a definition of limitations. Collectively this dominant group made few innovations in film technique and virtually no revolutionary changes in subject matter. The new directors did not abandon the studio and seek inspiration in the streets, nor did they, in general, attempt to get beyond the conventions of the well-constructed film adapted from an existing work of literature. They are basically craftsmen working within a tradition against which they do not rebel. Their films are meticulously planned and carefully constructed, exploiting to the full the great wealth of experienced acting talent available in France. Their greatest works, made largely between 1946 and 1954, constitute a solid and varied body of work, but there is no great outburst of creative energy akin to that in Italy in 1946 or Poland in 1956. Almost imperceptibly these directors become victims of their own success and move towards directing expensive international co-productions, filmed in colour on a large budget, the pretensions of which are commercial rather than artistic.

With all of these directors the script-writer is the key collaborator on whom the success or failure of a film largely depends, for great reliance is placed on dramatic construction and dialogue. The limitations of the great majority of this generation can be ascribed to this dependence on script-writers. Apart from Bresson and Tati, only Clouzot writes his own scripts and even he conceives his films in terms of suspense and dramatic build-up. The other directors lean heavily on the new script-writers whose emergence parallels their own. Jean Aurenche and Pierre Bost have been Autant-Lara's regular scenarists throughout the postwar period and have contributed also the script-adaptations of some of Clément's and Delannoy's greatest successes in the years 1946 to 1956. When these latter directors parted from Aurenche and Bost they moved, significantly enough, to mere stylistic exercise (Clément's later thrillers) or pretentiousness (Delannoy's spectacles). Other scriptwriters made equally important contributions, Jacques Sigurd, for instance, working on the scripts of Yves Allégret's best films and Charles Spaak writing the legal series with which Cayatte made his name. Jacques Becker is perhaps least dependent on scriptwriters but even in his case the contribution of Annette Wademant to a film like *Edouard et Caroline* cannot be overestimated, and many of his later films fail precisely because of deficiencies in their scripts. On the purely commercial level the same applies: it is to the dialoguist Michel Audiard, not to his various directors, that Jean Gabin owes his most characteristic successes of the fifties.

There is a marked lack of creative expressiveness among film makers of this first postwar generation. The output of the two great stylistic innovators, Bresson and Tati, is very small (only seven films between them in twenty years) and this can only partially be attributed to commercial conditions. Those more commercial directors who do feel strongly the need to communicate their ideas, such as Autant-Lara and Cayatte, use conventional vehicles for their views and rely heavily on the verbal adroitness of their scriptwriters. In the case of the others there is frequently a lack of deep involvement in their material, the dangers of which are most apparent in the career of Jean Delannoy, who had won a very high reputation for himself with his direction of Cocteau's *L'Eternel Retour* in 1943. Surrounding himself with skilled and experienced technical collaborators, Delannoy continued after the war to direct ambitious works: scripts derived from Gide and Sartre, for instance, and films treating religious and social problems. Three films scripted by Aurenche and Bost — *La Symphonie Pastorale* (1946), *Dieu a besoin des Hommes* (1950) and *Chiens Perdus sans Colliers* (1955) — may be taken as showing Delannoy at his best and representing one aspect of the work of this whole generation. All three films won international awards and are carefully and tastefully directed, but the very smoothness and beauty of the images gives these films a "coldness" that prevents their characters from coming to life. In retrospect, these works and the dull, overelaborate period films

21

that followed them epitomise the academicism which haunts many of the more ambitious enterprises of the forties and early fifties, and against which a later generation was rightly to rebel.

French film producers were reluctant in the forties to face up to the changed circumstances of postwar France and film makers sought inspiration instead in the artificial world of the Jean Gabin films of the thirties, works like Duvivier's *Pépé le Moko* (1937), Renoir's *La Bête Humaine* (1938), the Prévert-Carné films: *Quai des Brumes* (1938) and *Le Jour se lève* (1939). The result was a naturalistic type of film making — the "Film Noir" — which while nowhere near as important as the Italian Neo-Realist movement is of considerable interest in that it characterises French film making in the late forties and early fifties. The theme of doomed lovers, the setting of urban backstreet squalor and an all-pervading air of fatalism remained the dominant features of the French cinema in these years. Julien Duvivier, for example, on his return from Hollywood in 1946, made *Panique*, a work very much in the prewar tradition. If, by 1952, Duvivier had got round to parodying the conventions of the "film noir" (in *La Fête à Henriette*), Carné, by contrast, is inextricably bound up throughout his career with the moods and themes of the thirties. His first postwar work, *Les Portes de la Nuit* (1946) owed nothing to the forties but its setting, and even this was studio reproduced. His 1953 version of Zola's *Thérèse Raquin* reduced this novel to a script indistinguishable in themes and settings from his work with Prévert in the thirties and even as late as 1963 he was hopefully describing a new work, *Du Mouron pour les petits Oiseaux*, as being "like *Drôle de Drame* in the décor of *Hôtel du Nord.*" Traces of the same influence are to be found in films like Marcello Pagliero's *Un Homme marche dans la Ville* (1950) and Yves Ciampi's *Les Héros sont Fatigués* (1955), in Clément's *Au Delà des Grilles*, where Gabin again appears as a fugitive from justice, and in the films of Clouzot: the squalid background of *Quai des Orfèvres* (1947), the doomed lovers of *Manon* (1949) and the sense of fatalism in *Le Salaire de la Peur* (1953).

The qualities and defects of the "film noir" are best seen, however, in the work of Yves Allégret and his scriptwriter Jacques Sigurd whose first three films together — *Dédée d'Anvers* (1948), *Une si Jolie Petite Plage*

(1949) and *Manèges* (1950) — reveal them as the successors of the Prévert-Carné team of the thirties. Allégret here shows clearly his technical mastery and ability to draw performances of high quality from his actors, but these gifts are applied to themes and subjects taken unchanged from the prewar period. One finds in these three films the same insignificant characters, extreme and hopeless predicaments. The increasingly static nature of the films' basic situations again leads to experiment with narrative methods, particularly flashback technique. It is their lack of connection with the mood of France in the forties rather than any technical limitations that makes these films seem artificial. Carné and Prévert attained a similar degree of blackness in *Le Jour se lève* but were able to strike out afresh and apply their talents to more positive themes in at least two further masterly works. Allégret and Sigurd failed to achieve this renewal and their decline parallels that of the "film noir" tradition into a welter of gangster films and petty little works on prostitution.

The man who, briefly, revived interest in the "film noir" and succeeded in bringing it back into contact with reality was the ex-lawyer and novelist, André Cayatte, whose first work of real value was his tenth film, *Les Amants de Vérone* (1948), made, significantly enough, from one of Jacques Prévert's last scripts. The films on which Cayatte's reputation largely rests are of a somewhat different kind however. In four films — *Justice est Faite* (1950), *Nous Sommes Tous des Assassins* 1952), *Avant le Déluge* (1953) and *Le Dossier Noir* (1955) — Cayatte and his scriptwriter Charles Spaak tackled a variety of social and legal problems, such as euthanasia, the death penalty and juvenile delinquency, in a mood of black accusation. Carefully realistic settings, unknown young players and solid character actors together with sober if unexciting camera work are used to focus the audience's attention on the film's argument, which is expounded with all the explicitness of a legal testimony. The films themselves are sincere, forceful and courageous but as art they suffer from the sacrificing of all to polemics, and Cayatte's inability to evolve a visual style to encompass adequately his savage insight into the workings of society. With Cayatte's decline into routine commercial work in the late fifties the interest of the "film noir" as the characteristic product of the first postwar generation of film makers comes to an end.

In this Introduction we have been concerned with generalisations about trends and generations which, if they are necessary aids for obtaining a picture of French film making as a whole, nevertheless carry with them the danger of distortion. They minimise the contributions of those directors who work in opposition to the trends of their time and tend to reduce all directors and all films to the same level of importance. Great films are sometimes those which crystallise the attitudes and assumptions of their period but equally they may owe very little to their age. Certainly the greatest directors are individualists who stand aside from trends and fashions and oppose the accepted ideas of their contemporaries. For these reasons we turn now to examine in detail the careers of the most important directors of the early postwar years.

2. Veterans

IN THIS chapter we shall be dealing with five directors who had all made their reputations before 1945 but were able to continue film making with a fair degree of freedom in the postwar years. They vary widely in age, experience and attitudes. If we look for differences we may note that Jean Cocteau was twenty years older than Marcel Carné or recall that René Clair achieved international fame with the series of films beginning in 1927 with *Un Chapeau de Paille d'Italie*, while Max Ophuls was little known and not very highly regarded until he made *La Ronde* in 1950. As far as achievement is concerned, it is generally agreed that Clair, Carné and Jean Renoir all had their best work behind them by 1946, whereas Cocteau and Ophuls both reached new heights in the postwar years. If we turn to consider their approach to the film medium, it is easy to contrast the amateurism of the poet Cocteau with the professionalism of the technician Carné, or the restrained classicist Clair with the exuberant baroque Ophuls. Renoir has always loved improvisation, while Clair and Carné both plan their work fully in advance. In their later work some of these veterans have developed in opposite directions: René Clair's characters have deepened from mere puppets to beings whose emotions are treated with respect, whereas in Jean Renoir's films one can trace an increasing schematisation of character.

How then can we justify treating them together in this chapter? Firstly, all five entered the postwar years with their artistic maturity fully proved, though in Cocteau's case this experience had been gained largely outside the cinema. By 1946 all had made at least one work that figures in the histories of the cinema, and three had already made quite a number. All of them could therefore be expected to treat the cinema as the means of expression for their own personal vision of life and have the command of the medium necessary to make their notions clear.

These five veterans are clearly within the French film making tradition by virtue of the manner in which their films rely on a studio-created atmosphere. It is by their settings that we recognize the characteristic works of Clair and Carné. The décor of a René Clair film is of vital importance and as he worked with one designer, Lazare Meerson, on the works of his greatest period from *Un Chapeau de Paille d'Italie* (1927) to *Quatorze Juillet* (1932), so Léon Barsacq has been responsible for the settings of virtually all his films since 1945. The pattern of Marcel Carné's films is similar. Much has been made of Carné's dependence on the scripts of Jacques Prévert, but this should not make us overlook two other men whose contribution has been of supreme importance: Alexandre Trauner, who worked on the settings of every one of his films from *Drôle de Drame* in 1937 to *Juliette ou la Clef des Songes* in 1951, and Paul Bertrand, who has designed most of the subsequent films. Something of the same tendency is to be found in the films of Ophuls and Cocteau. The tracking shot was Max Ophuls's trademark, but Jean d'Eaubonne, who was responsible for the sets, and Georges Annenkov, who designed the costumes, were essential members of the team that Ophuls formed in 1950, and the deliberately artificial world of his films is that of the studio. Likewise Jean Cocteau has made clear the vast debt he owed to the designer Christian Bérard, who was the artistic director of three of his films — *La Belle et la Bête*, *L'Aigle à Deux Têtes* and *Les Parents Terribles* — and who was working on *Orphée* at the time of his death in 1949. Jean

Renoir, being more eclectic, has been less at the mercy of his designers and in fact the names of five different art directors appear on the credits of his six postwar European films. Frequently he has taken his camera into the open air, and such works as *The River* and *Le Déjeuner sur l'Herbe* are essentially hymns to Nature. But even he has directed films, such as *The Golden Coach*, *Elena* and *French Cancan*, which depend as much on studio atmosphere as any work of Clair or Carné.

These veteran directors use their constructed sets to create a new artistic reality that may have very little to do with realism. Two works of the postwar period may stand comparison with *Les Enfants du Paradis* as investigations of illusion and reality: Renoir's *The Golden Coach* (technically an Italian film) which meditates on the life of the actress Camilla, torn between love and the theatre; and Ophuls's *Lola Montès*, a critique of the world of spectacle set in a New Orleans circus. In a lighter vein Clair's *Le Silence est d'Or* touches on the same theme, this time in the setting of a Parisian film studio at the beginning of this century. Other films turn further still from realism to deal with the world of dreams. Carné's *Juliette ou la Clef des Songes*, Clair's *Les Belles-de-Nuit* and Cocteau's *Orphée* are all in their very different ways unreal, for they gain their effects from the juxtaposition of dream world and reality. Nor are the worlds of fairy tale and myth neglected: Cocteau filmed the tale of Beauty and the Beast in *La Belle et la Bête* while Clair tackled the Faust theme in *La Beauté du Diable*. Not all of these films are wholly successful but they are works of fantasy and imagination, qualities too rarely found in the postwar French cinema.

RENÉ CLAIR returned to France in 1946 to make his first film there for thirteen years. **Le Silence est d'Or** (1947), though described by Clair himself as a comedy, reflected the new and changed mood which was to dominate all the director's postwar work. The youthful exuberance of the early thirties is replaced by a more serious attitude to life and though humour is never absent greater depth is given to the characters who are no longer the simple marionettes of *Le Million*. For *Le Silence est d'Or* Clair drew inspiration from Molière's "L'Ecole des Femmes", treating the predicament of a middle-aged film producer who gives lessons on life

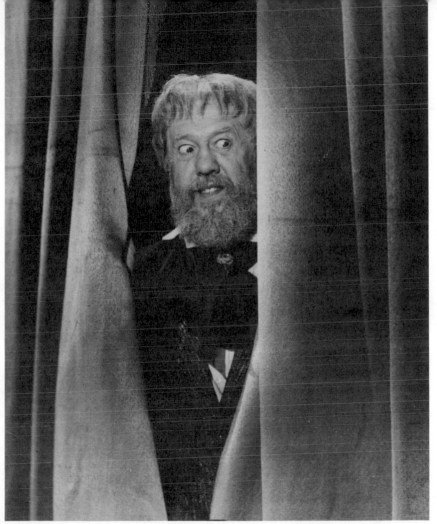

Michel Simon in René Clair's LA BEAUTÉ DU DIABLE

to his timid assistant, only to watch the latter profit by his teaching to the extent of winning the young girl with whom the producer has himself fallen in love. The film exploits to the full the ironies of this situation and is built around a series of repetitions: the café where Monsieur Emile and his assistant Jacques each in turn take Madeleine and where they meet again after their quarrel; the sentimental tune played there which serves as the film's theme tune, cropping up again and again; and, most strikingly of all, the helpful advice given by M. Emile which helps Jacques to win the girl and subsequently rebounds on M. Emile. As so often in René Clair's films the men are more sharply characterised than the women and Maurice Chevalier, who brings all his elegance and debonair charm to the role of M. Emile, is outstanding. The film is set in the Paris of 1906 and is an explicit homage to the directors of those days whose pupil Clair acknowledges himself to be. The period background is lovingly recreated by Léon Barsacq's settings and Clair includes a number of tiny film dramas of the kind made in those pioneer years. There are also many of those characteristic touches one remembers from Clair's films: the imperturbable card players who continue their game whatever may be happening around them, and two scenes where reality and theatricality coincide: the second meeting of Madeleine and Jacques who, all unsuspecting, come face to face as princess and explorer in one of M. Emile's oriental epics, and the final scene in the film studio where M. Emile gives the young couple his blessing under the pretext of directing them in a further film scene.

In **La Beauté du Diable** (1949), written in collaboration with the playwright Armand Salacrou and filmed in Italy, Clair broke new ground by tackling the Faust legend. The particular aspect of the story which attracted the authors' interest was how Mephisto manages to trick a man as intelligent as Faust into selling his soul for worldly power. The solution devised in this very free version of the legend is characteristic of Clair's interest in dream and reality: Mephisto gives Faust youth and love, power and success without asking anything in return and then reduces Faust to insignificant poverty again, so that he begs for the return of what he has lost. This idea is ingenious and gives rise to some sharp interplay of character but makes the story stray away from the central notions of good and evil, salvation and damnation. Having signed away his soul for power, Faust rejects it when shown a vision of his future life as a brutal if well-meaning despot. This scene, one of the dramatic highlights of the film, affords Clair an opportunity to include an indictment of science which is seen as aiding totalitarian governments and reducing the world to a wasteland of concentration camps. The acting of Gérard Philipe and Michel Simon is sound and the film is full of fine touches, like the notion of giving the devil the form of the aged Faust, but it remains curiously unsatisfying. It is not helped by its ill-defined seventeenth century Italian setting or the not very skilful inclusion of Marguerite into the story. Weakest of all are, as Clair himself has recognised, the scenes of Mephisto's overthrow in which the Devil's power is ignored and the film given an arbitrary and unconvincing happy ending.

Les Belles-de-Nuit (1952) marked Clair's return to pure comedy. The film's initial idea was that of a comic version of *Intolerance* (interweaving stories of several epochs so that they build up to simultaneous climaxes) and Clair also drew inspiration from one of Pascal's "Pensées" concerning the possibility of dreams acting as compensation for sufferings endured in everyday life. The film's hero, Claude (played by Gérard Philipe), is a music teacher in a small provincial town who seeks refuge in his dreams from a noisy world that refuses to recognize his talents. At first these dreams are satisfying and excitingly filled with romantic conquests, but as his real life improves under the sincere if often misguided efforts of his friends, so his dreams turn to nightmares from which he tries, unsuccessfully at first, to escape. The film is neatly constructed and the balance between dream and reality always held: all Claude's dreams grow out of his everyday life and all the women in them are romanticised versions of women he meets every day, for example, the cashier in the café becomes a voluptuous harem beauty (Gina Lollobrigida). The various periods in which Claude's dreams are set — Paris in 1900, Algeria in 1830, the reigns of Louis XVI (the Revolution) and Louis XIII (the Musketeers) — are linked by the recurring figure of an old man who constantly reminds the hero of the superiority of the "good old days", and thus heralds a new jump back in time. Music and sounds are very important in *Les Belles-de-Nuit*. The music of Georges Van Parys (who also worked with Clair on *Le Million*) helps to maintain the lighthearted tone and includes theme tunes for each of Claude's dream conquests. The sounds of the garage beneath Claude's windows are the source of many of the hero's troubles and obsess him so much that in one of his nightmares he finds himself conducting a cacophonous symphony of noisy implements, such as pneumatic drills and vacuum cleaners. There is an echo of the earlier Clair of the silent days in the climax of Claude's dreams which is a riotous comic chase back to the present from the Stone Age in which he has landed up.

With **Les Grandes Manoeuvres** (1955) Clair returned to a more serious dramatic mood. The film is a love story with near-tragic overtones and its setting, a provincial garrison town in the summer of 1914, recalls Clair's own childhood near Versailles and gave plenty of scope for experiment in the use of colour, which the director employed here for the first time. The hero, Armand de la Verne (again played by Gérard Philipe) is a handsome young cavalry officer who enjoys the reputation of being an irresistible Don Juan. At a party with his friends he nonchalantly agrees to seduce any woman in the town, chosen by lot. When the choice falls upon Marie-Louise (Michèle Morgan), a divorced Parisienne, Armand is delighted, but in fact she proves more than a match for him. As an outsider she has a somewhat equivocal position in town society and she is contemplating marriage with the dull but worthy Duverger. Their marriage is opposed by his two spiteful spinster sisters but would give Marie-Louise an accepted place in the community. She cannot remain unmoved by Armand, however, and he does win her love, though only at the price of succumbing himself. Deeply in love for the first time, Armand finds himself the victim of his own past and reputation. As Marie-Louise gradually discovers, all the words he uses sincerely to move her, he has used frivolously before. She resists his advances and sends him away, but flies to him when she thinks he has been wounded in a duel. Only when it is too late does she learn the shattering news of his wager, and the film ends on a note of doubt as to whether she will ever be able to forgive him. The setting allows Clair to draw yet another portrait of bourgeois society and show its underlying hypocrisies and deceits, while the romance of Armand's friend Félix (Yves Robert) with a pretty

"*A portrait of bourgeois society.*" Yves Robert, Brigitte Bardot, Gérard Philipe and Michèle Morgan in René Clair's *LES GRANDES MANOEU-VRES*.

little photographer's daughter (Brigitte Bardot) provides balance and a light relief to the main theme. The numerous scenes of background detail and the large number of subplots are not gratuitous, for society plays an important role in determining the romance of Armand and Marie-Louise and most of their meetings take place under the keen eyes of those around them and give scope for malicious tongues. Yet it is the figures of Armand and Marie-Louise that stand out and they are the most deeply drawn of Clair's lovers, beautifully played in their very different styles by Gérard Philipe and Michèle Morgan.

Porte des Lilas (1957) was based on a novel by René Fallet from which Clair, in his adaptation, has removed all the harsh realism. Rewritten in terms of Clair's own philosophy it stands as perhaps his major treatment of the theme of friendship, just as *Les Grandes Manoeuvres* was his most revealing analysis of love. *Porte des Lilas* tells of a middle-aged good-for-nothing, Juju, whose only friend is a melancholy musician, L'Artiste, and whose only pleasure is drink. Juju finds a new sense of self-respect when he shelters a gangster on the run from the police but his efforts soon prove to be misguided. When Juju discovers the extent to which the gangster has exploited him and more especially Maria, the girl he ineffectually loves, he kills him. The tone of the film is generally fairly sombre (Clair described it as a "comédie dramatique") and comic highlights are rare. As the central character, Juju, Pierre Brasseur gives a beautifully judged and quite uncharacteristic performance, the minor roles, including that of Maria (Dany Carrel) and l'Artiste (Georges Brassens), are adequately played, but the gangster himself (Henri Vidal) is less convincing. The violence associated with him — the shooting of the policemen and his own death at the hands of Juju — introduces too discordant a note into the gentle world created by Clair. The Parisian suburb that forms the background and gives the film its title has been lovingly constructed by Clair and his designer, Léon Barsacq, and the best scenes are those that grow out of it and share its air of slight stylisation: the muted scenes between Juju and Maria or those among the regulars in the bistrot owned by Maria's father.

In 1960 Clair directed one short episode in the composite film *La Française et l'Amour*, **Le Mariage**, which dealt with the little problems and uncertainties experienced by a young couple before they reach their honeymoon hotel. Two years later Clair participated in another collective work, *Les Quatre Vérités* (1962), for which he directed the episode **Les Deux Pigeons,** illustrating a fable by La Fontaine and dealing with two strangers who by chance get locked together in a flat.

Between these two sketches, Clair directed a further feature film **Tout l'Or du Monde** (1961) in which he went back once more to pure comedy. The idea for this film dated from the time of *Le Million* and *A Nous La Liberté* and it shares with the first the primary aim of arousing laughter and with the second a satirical approach to certain aspects of the modern world. The story concerns a peasant family (a father and two sons, all played by Bourvil) who withstand all the pressures brought to bear on them by a property tycoon and his public relations officer who want their land for an ambitious development scheme. There is also an important sub-plot involving one of the sons, Toine Dumont, with a starlet, Stella, and exposing all the lies and exaggerations with which the private lives of entertainers are treated by the popular press. The film is one of Clair's weakest from the point of view of construction: the two halves of the plot do not really hold together and by about three-quarters of the way through the film, everything seems to have ground to a halt, only to be started again by the introduction of a further sub-plot with a South American setting. Unlike Clair's previous work, the film was shot largely on location but does not really gain in credibility or liveliness. Despite Bourvil's playing, Toine Dumont and his father remain stereotyped caricatures, of a kind the actor has played in numerous insignificant rustic farces. Much more convincing are the tycoon and his assistant, very smoothly played by Philippe Noiret and Claude Rich. Though the film fails to satisfy as a whole, it will no doubt be remembered for a number of little touches worthy of the very best Clair, such as the scene where Toine confesses his love to the girl he thinks is standing just around the corner but who is, in fact, running happily down the hill, far away and out of earshot.

In 1965 Clair directed a Franco-Rumanian co-production, **Les Fêtes Galantes,** which while very different in tone from the previous work, displays much the same shortcomings. In the kind of literary terms of which Clair is so fond, this film is designed as a Voltairean tale, chronicling the absurdities of war in an elegant eighteenth century setting. The plot rests on the broad contrast between the antics of the starving defenders of a fortress and those of their gluttonous beseiegers and traces the efforts made to resolve the situation and restore peace. Though the mood is basically farcical there are moments of seriousness and Clair, who described his film not as a comedy but as "un conte héroï-comique," flirts with the underlying reality of death so that his hero (Jean-Pierre Cassel) is saved from execution only at the very last minute. Despite the intentions of the author, however, and the talents of his team of collaborators— which included the photographer Christian Matras, designer Georges Wakhévitch and composer Georges Van Parys—*Les Fêtes Galantes* shows the same mixture of laboriousness and slightly hollow joviality as Clair's other works of the sixties.

RENÉ CLAIR is one of the cinema's rare creators. Since his début in 1923 he has developed a distinctive vision of the world and perfected a unique and highly personal style to which he has constantly kept. The films he has made since 1946 form a continuation of the works of his greatest period, from *Un Chapeau de Paille d'Italie* (1927) to *Quatorze Juillet* (1932). The opposition to science in *La Beauté du Diable* and the attack on modern society in *Tout l'Or du Monde* recall the attitude behind *A Nous la Liberté* (1931). The Parisian suburb of *Porte des Lilas* irresistibly calls to mind *Sous Les Toits de Paris* (1930), while the social satire of *Les Grandes Manoeuvres* echoes *Un Chapeau de Paille d'Italie*. The group of friends who try to help the hero of *Les Belles-de-Nuit* and the studio workers in *Le Silence est d'Or* have the same function as the "chorus" of tradesmen in *Le Million*. The themes of love and friendship present in all Clair's early sound films find their fullest expression in *Les Grandes Manoeuvres* and *Porte des Lilas*.

The chief characteristic of Clair's film style had been his reliance on studio-built exteriors from which he distilled his own particular brand of poetry and in this respect too he remains faithful to his beginnings, finding in Léon Barsacq a worthy successor to Lazare Meerson. Discussing *Porte des Lilas* Clair expressed distrust of location shooting: "The connection we establish between a real image and its photographic reproduction exists only by virtue of a convention to which we are accustomed. Through the play of this convention the real loses its privileges. Cinema technicians know that a studio-constructed and artificially lit street can create a more striking impression of reality than a real street, whose photographic translation presents excessive or arbitrary contrasts. This is true for sounds and words as well as for images." Clair has remained unmoved and unaffected by current trends in the cinema and did not use location shooting on any real scale until *Tout l'Or du Monde* which remains one of his lesser works.

The sense of continuity in style and vision in Clair's work is very strong but the later films do have their distinctive tone and mood. The most successful works of the period since 1946 are the dramatic comedies — *Le Silence est d'Or, Les Grandes Manoeuvres, Porte des Lilas*. The happy ending of *La Beauté du Diable* is out of tune with the logic of the fable as a whole and increasingly Clair's work tends towards the tragic. This tendency even threatens at times to destroy the delicate balance of his world which is not really robust enough to encompass death. The logic of *Le Silence est d'Or* points to an unhappy ending which is avoided only thanks to Monsieur Emile's humour and resignation (cf. his last words: "You like happy endings, Mademoiselle? So do I"). It would seem that Clair shot an alternative ending for *Les Grandes Manoeuvres* depicting the suicide of Marie-Louise but rejected it when giving the film its final form. In *Portes des Lilas* the ending is one of violence and this is one reason why the film is only a partial success. The principal cause of this new seriousness is that the characters have been given greater depth. In the thirties the loves and friendships of Clair's heroes had been only lightly sketched in while the background figures were either mere types (the succession of characters played by Paul Olivier). In the later Clair the background figures are still of the same pattern, but the leading characters and their emotions have greater weight. Of the three figures played by Gérard Philipe only one, Armand de la Verne, is developed into a character giving full scope to the actor's talents, but the older men are more richly drawn: M. Emile (Maurice Chevalier), Mephisto (Michel Simon) and Juju (Pierre Brasseur). Again most of the women in Clair's films are rather pale figures, Madeleine (Marcelle Derrien) in *Le Silence est d'Or* for instance or Gérard Philipe's dream conquests in *Les Belles-de-Nuit*, but Marie-Louise (Michèle Morgan) in *Les Grandes Manoeuvres* is a far profounder study, idealised but completely believable. There are, however, distinct limits to Clair's range: he remains an ironist unwilling to commit himself too deeply. There is very little passion or sensuality in his work, despite his employment of Martine Carol, Gina Lollobrigida and Brigitte Bardot, and he is clearly less at home with the deeper impulses of his characters than when depicting muted feeling or the frustration of passion.

René Clair has always been a complete author, writing his own scripts and dialogue as well as directing. His films are entirely his own, though he does often use a collaborator on whom he can try out his ideas while elaborating his scenario. His scripts increasingly reflect both his own nostalgia and his literary interests. When, in *Les Belles-de-Nuit*, Clair satirizes those who believe in the superiority of the "good old days" he is dealing with a tendency in himself. *La Beauté du Diable* does not bring the Faust legend up to date, but retains instead a period setting. *Le Silence est d'Or* and *Les Grandes Manoeuvres* are set respectively in 1906 and 1914, and *Les Belles-de-Nuit* and *Porte des Lilas* owe nothing to the present. Even *Tout l'Or du Monde* which does attack modern city life does so by contrasting it with a largely mythical image of rustic peace and contentment. The commentaries which Clair has written to accompany his published scripts show too his great preoccupation with literature, particularly with that of the Classical period, and he has written his own versions of "L'Ecole des Femmes" and the legends of Faust and Don Juan. He elaborates his scripts with enormous care and diligence, for he regards this stage of film making as the vital one, to which the actual directing is subordinate, and backs up his belief with what are in fact false analogies with the theatre (comparing the writing of a film with the work of a playwright and the direction with that of a theatrical producer.) Clair has the true director's eye that enables him to make his points visually but he takes great pains with the overall structure of his films, favouring particularly a method of repetition of key phrases and musical themes, each time in a different mood or context. One thinks immediately of the repetitions of the waltz tune in *Le Silence est d'Or* or the themes connected with the dream figures in *Les Belles-de-Nuit*, the use made of M. Emile's little phrase "Je pourrais être votre père" or of the way we hear Armand's words of love successively recited in jest to his fellow officers, spoken sincerely to Marie-Louise and parodied, in Marie-Louise's hearing, by an ex-mistress.

This elaborate preparation allows Clair to adopt methods of shooting which are inconceivable with any other great director. After stating, in his commentary on *Les Grandes Manoeuvres*, that the prime quality of an "auteur de films" is invention, he continues: "But the shooting script? you may ask. The proportions of the shots? The camera movements? All the rubbish taught in schools of film technique which allows the filmologists of the little reviews an opportunity to show their knowledge? At one time I myself attached a certain importance to the preparation of the direction itself. Today I think that this can be carried out in a more or less improvised manner, provided one has a little knowledge of the craft." In *Les Belles-de-Nuit* and *Les Grandes Manoeuvres* Clair adopted the method of shooting just the key scenes himself while his assistant directed the minor ones: "So far as the physical side of production is concerned, I have always been in favour of the method called "double team". In *Les Belles-de-Nuit* I made use of this method all the time . . . I used the "double team" system also in *Les Grandes Manoeuvres* where there is a great number of settings and a very great number of second characters. Therefore while I was directing the key scenes, someone else was directing another team. On location, the assistant goes out alone, then shows me what he has shot and if I do not like it he goes out again. This saves time . . . and time is more expensive than anything else in film-making."

Despite this apparent contempt for what most critics would regard as the essence of the film art, Clair remains one of the great directors. Perhaps it is simply his enormous talent and visual sense that allow him to have his film completed before he enters the studio. Certainly it does not imply any failure to give full weight to the visual aspects. The things that one remembers from a Clair film are what one sees: the constructed settings to which such care is devoted and those scenes where Clair's sense of humour and his irony fuse completely: the scene where M. Emile and Jacques, both deeply involved with Madeleine, carry on their private inner dialogues, one each side of the angle of a studio wall; that where Armand's walk with Marie-Louise is commented on and dialogued by a succession of interested onlookers; Toine's confession of love in *Tout l'Or du Monde;* or the small boys seen through the window of the bistrot in *Porte des Lilas* who mime the gangster's acts as the newspaper report of them is read.

*   *   *

JEAN RENOIR had left France for the United States in 1941 and did not film again in his native land until 1954. The last two films of his exile, however, mark the beginning of a new period in his work and are therefore included here. **The River** (1950), an English language film made with American backing in India, was Renoir's first film in colour and the director has managed to make colour an integral part of the film, being particularly successful in his handling of the specifically Indian part of the film, the shots of the Ganges itself and the native festivals. The source of the film is a novel by Rumer Godden telling of the first awakening of love in three teenage girls growing up in India. Along with this study of adolescence we have a vision of India as it is seen by an outsider. It remains a marvellously picturesque but essentially tourist India and it was left for Satyajit Ray to show what lies behind the colourful façade of Bengal. Improvisation played a large part in this film, as in most of Renoir's work. The script grew up from the director's contact with India and the acting reflects the presence in the mixed cast of a number of amateurs, most notably Harriet, the eldest of the girls and the central figure in the film. Renoir's approach was particularly appropriate here as it allowed both a touching picture of the uncertainties of adolescence and the gradual absorption of the atmosphere of India. In the thirties Renoir had held strong left-wing political views and had been led as far as to make *La Vie est à Nous* in 1936 for the Communist Party, but now under the influence of India his views changed. From his contact with the Hindu religion he developed a new philosophy characterised by a total acceptance of all that the world has to offer by way of experience of joy or sorrow. The death of Bogey, Harriet's younger brother, exemplifies this attitude. Having visited the bazaar he spends his time with a flute trying

JEAN RENOIR: "The only thing I can bring to this illogical, irresponsible and cruel universe is my love."

*Jean Gabin and Françoise Arnoul
in Jean Renoir's FRENCH CANCAN*

to charm cobras. One day, as everyone in the house is asleep, the sound of his flute breaks off suddenly: Bogey is dead. The house is filled with sorrow, Harriet driven almost to suicide; but then another child is born and life flows on, like the Ganges.

The Golden Coach (1952) was made in Italy, again in colour with an international cast. It exists in three language versions, French, Italian and English, of which the latter is, Renoir tells us, the original. Set in eighteenth century Peru, *Le Carrosse d'Or* (as it is known in France) deals with the three transient loves of the tempestuous actress Camilla: Felipe, the young soldier who finally abandons civilisation to live among the primitive Indians, Ramon, the proud bullfighter who proves to have the intelligence of the bulls he fights, and the Viceroy himself who loves Camilla sincerely but is too weak to hold her. The Golden Coach of the title is one ordered by the Viceroy for his own use, coveted by the Council of Ministers, given to Camilla as a gift and finally donated by her to the Church to save the Viceroy from humiliation. As in *The River* the colour is pleasing, costumes and objects acquire a symbolic value (the coach itself and the Viceroy's wig that prevents him from being a man), and the music, this time by Vivaldi, is an essential element. In this film, which was completely studio-made, Renoir gives the clearest expression of his love for actors and the theatre generally, extracting a memorable and forceful performance from Anna Magnani as Camilla. The theme is summed up in one of the speeches of the leader of the troupe when he asks where the theatre ends and life begins and wonders whether the characters on the stage are not more real than the people off it. Renoir's methods of direction reflect the Commedia dell'arte of Camilla's troupe, particularly in the improvisation of dialogue and action in a set pattern of scenes. The director is at home satirizing the hierarchic world of the Court and probing the pretensions, ambitions and weaknesses of the rich (the performance of Duncan Lamont as the Viceroy is particularly revealing). Much of the comedy comes from the intrusion of the actors into this world and there is plenty of the slapstick farce that is to become characteristic of the later Renoir.

French Cancan (1954) which marked Renoir's return to the French studios after an absence of fourteen years is a further homage to the theatre. Set in the Paris of the 1880's it is also an evocation of the world of the director's father, the painter Auguste Renoir. The film's visual qualities were perhaps the director's prime concern: "When saying that we have just made a film we are not exact; it is rather a piece of tapestry, a composition in colours. The music is not only used as an accompaniment and commentary, but rather as counterpoint." The plot itself is no better than that of the average backstage musical, dealing as it does with the founding of the Moulin Rouge by Danglard (Jean Gabin), an impoverished but amorous middle-aged impresario. He takes a pretty laundress Nini (Françoise Arnoul) and trains her to lead the troupe of Cancan dancers who are to be the new show's special feature. He makes her into a star, takes her as his mistress and breaks her heart. But the show must go on and she leads the final triumphant dance. The characters in *French Cancan* hardly count. They exist to provide roles for the chosen stars or extravagant little cameos for bit players, but in neither case do they have any depth. Like *The Golden Coach* this is a studio-made film, with the street scenes carefully designed to recall paintings of the Impressionists. The colour is again inventively handled, particularly in the scenes at "La Reine Blanche", and the music of Georges Van Parys, with its pastiche of period melodies and recurring dance rhythm, serves to set the tone. The whole film, building up to a twenty minute Cancan climax, leaves an impression of intense vitality.

Elena et les Hommes (1956) has much in common with the previous films and was described by its maker as "une fantaisie musicale." It also bears some resemblance to *La Règle du Jeu* in that it is a comedy of manners with château-set scenes of amorous interchange of partners among the rich and their servants. The basis of the film is serious enough, being inspired by General Boulanger's bid for dictatorial power in the 1880's, but the original aim of historical authenticity was soon abandoned in favour of a freer and more lighthearted approach. The centre of the film is now the Princess Elena, played with engaging warmth by Ingrid Bergman, who meets the elegant Henri de Chevincourt (Mel Ferrer) during the celebrations to mark the Fourteenth of July and is introduced by him to General Rollan, the Minister of War (Jean Marais). Attracted by the latter, Elena dreams for a while of using her charm to drive him to seize power, but at the last moment she returns to Henri, the General abandons his ambition and love conquers all. This film has left even Renoir's most sympathetic critics in considerable perplexity. The characteristic elements of the later Renoir are all here: colour and movement, good humour spilling over into awkward farce and a wildly satirical look at the rich and ambitious, but the ultimate value of the film as a whole remains in question.

Le Testament du Docteur Cordelier, made in 1959 but not released until two years later, marks a fresh departure in Renoir's work. After a series of films that were basically spectacles, depending largely on colour, music and stars, Renoir virtually abandoned the cinema in favour of the theatre for three years and when he did return he sought inspiration from television methods. *Le Testament du Docteur Cordelier* was produced in collaboration with the French television service and it was its dual identity as television drama and feature film that aroused so much controversy and delayed its release. The story is not an original one, being a version of Dr. Jekyll and Mr. Hyde set in contemporary Paris and starring Jean-Louis Barrault in the double role of Cordelier-Opale. The film as originally planned was to have been transmitted live, but though this proved impossible (largely because of Barrault's make-up), Renoir clung to his idea of spontaneity. *Le Testament* was filmed scene by scene (not shot by shot) and only ten days were needed for shooting, after a fortnight's rehearsal. Each scene was played only once and recorded by up to eight cameras and twelve microphones. From the resulting mass of material Renoir and his editor pieced the film together, adding a musical score by Joseph Kosma. *Le Testament du Docteur Cordelier* is not one of Renoir's best films. The visual style is insufficiently interesting for projection on a cinema screen, the theme of opposition to science too schematised to convince and the whole film has the air of being a rough draft rather than a completed work. Barrault shows his versatility in his double role — the pale austere figure of Dr. Cordelier contrasts with the dark, contorted silhouette of Opale — but his performance lacks discipline. Opale never achieves the necessary stature of a personification of evil and his Chaplinesque antics provoke laughter rather than horror.

Le Déjeuner sur l'Herbe (1959) was shot in the same semi-improvised

43

manner as *Le Testament* and this is clearly evident in the finished film, although rather more time was spent on rehearsal and shooting. It is more typical of Renoir than the previous film in that it mixes its genres — farce and poetry, satire and hymn to Nature — and again recalls the director's origins and his benevolent philosophy of life. The hero, Etienne Alexis (Paul Meurisse), is a scientist specialising in artificial insemination and future president of a United Europe. He meets and falls in love with a peasant girl Nénette (Catherine Rouvel), but their idyll is destroyed by his former colleagues and only chance brings them together again just as he is about to marry his fiancée, a German Princess and enthusiastic girl-guide leader. The underlying theme of the film is serious — Renoir's distrust of science, and indeed of all human progress, and his compensating belief in the power of Nature — but the treatment is deliberately farcical and the characters mere puppets. Several scenes show a failure to realise fully the intended effect, as for instance the key scene of the picnic which brings the two lovers together for the first time, when solemn formality is turned to pagan orgy by the influence of the mysterious flute-playing Gaspard and his goat Cabri. Renoir shows an insufficient grasp of the technique and timing of farce and too often overacting and frenetic movement take the place of genuine comic invention. The film's message that happiness lies in submission to Nature is clearly communicated, however, and the film's most successful shots are those of the woods and fields of Provence. The film was shot on location, partly at "Les Collettes" which was once the home of Auguste Renoir, and its most memorable scenes are those inspired directly by the landscape and the great painter, such as Nénette's bathe or her lovemaking with Etienne.

After a break of three years Renoir was tempted back to the studios to make **Le Caporal Epinglé** (1962) for which he had director Guy Lefranc as collaborator. Inevitably this prisoner of war story invites comparison with *La Grande Illusion* but its whole tone and range are different. It is intentionally lighthearted (often perilously near to standard army farce) and its emphasis is on friendship and solidarity rather than suffering. Renoir's benevolence and warm humanity lead to an underplaying of the horror of war and captivity and make the use of authentic newsreel shots of the war in progress seem a little out of keeping. The corporal of the

Catherine Rouvel in Jean Renoir's LE DEJEUNER SUR L'HERBE

title succeeds in escaping from the camp only at his seventh attempt and the film consists almost entirely of his unsuccessful attempts, doomed by lack of planning or sheer bad luck. Jean-Pierre Cassel gives a lively performance in this major role but gives the character little depth. Of his friends Pater (Claude Brasseur) accompanies him on most of his attempts and eventually escapes with him, while Ballochet (Claude Rich) a coward tempted by the easy life that is his in the camp, makes amends with a foolhardy escape bid that is virtually an act of suicide. An air of good humoured charade pervades the film, emphasised by the dressing up, the chases and the ingenuity used fooling the stupid Germans. Only Ballochet's escape strikes a different note, but even this gives a theatrical effect with its initial three blows of a broomstick (sign that the curtain is going up in the French theatre), its lighting effects and rhetorical acting. *Le Caporal Epinglé* marks Renoir's return to orthodox shooting methods and is one of his most disciplined, as well as one of his funniest works.

The career of **JEAN RENOIR** spans forty years of film making and the works that fall within the scope of this book represent only a small portion of his output. His reputation rests essentially on the films he made during the thirties, from *La Chienne* to *La Règle du Jeu*, but the more controversial works made since 1950 do form a fairly unified whole and illuminate one side of his character and development. Renoir has himself characterised the change undergone between *La Règle du Jeu* in 1939 and *The River* in 1950: "Before the war my way of participating in this universal concert was to try to bring a voice of protest . . . Today, the new being that I am realises that it is no longer time for sarcasm and that the only thing I can bring to this illogical, irresponsible and cruel universe is my 'love.'" All seven of his works since 1950 are marked by an all-embracing sympathy and affection, with the rich and powerful turned into figures of farce and the acute problems of the poor lost beneath the play of colour and movement. Inevitably Renoir proves incapable of creating a really evil character; even Opale repents and seeks help to save his soul at the end. Never do the conflicts become more than a passing problem: the scientist intellectual in *Le Déjeuner sur l'Herbe* offers no reply to the priest's impassioned if woolly attack on science, and the punishments undergone by the corporal in Renoir's last film are treated as farcical. Life itself, like film making, is enjoyed and savoured by Renoir and all his films of this last period convey his sense of enjoyment in friendship and love, art, beauty and nature. The subjects he chooses are often serious, depressing or even potentially tragic but the over-riding mood is one of benevolence and humour.

Jean Renoir was fifty-six when he made *The River* and sixty-eight when he directed *Le Caporal Epinglé*. It is therefore not surprising that the films of this period are so strongly marked by nostalgia. *The River* is set in a dream India of happy understanding between colonists and Hindus where sorrow and tragedy are swallowed up in gay, colourful native festivals. *The Golden Coach* takes us to an eighteenth century colony and presents a picture from which the underprivileged are noticeably lacking. *French Cancan* and *Elena et les Hommes* both give a very romanticised view of Paris in the 1880's, while *Le Caporal Epinglé* would appear to see the early forties as a period that brought out the best in men and united them in brotherhood and solidarity. *Le Testament du Dr. Cordelier* and *Le Déjeuner sur l'Herbe* are both ostensibly set in the France of our own day but both hark back to an earlier age: the former containing echoes of Stevenson's late nineteenth century London and the latter recalling the vanished world of Renoir's father.

Jean Renoir has always had a hierarchic view of society, seeing it divided sharply into masters and servants, officers and other ranks. Much of the impact and the comedy of his best work derives from the inter-action of two worlds. This vision of two separate but adjoining and often intermingling halves of society is as characteristic of the later works, as of *La Règle du Jeu*. We find colonists and natives in *The River*, actors and courtiers in *The Golden Coach*, the rich and their servants in *Elena et les Hommes*, the intellectual and the peasant in *Le Déjeuner sur l'Herbe*, warders and prisoners in *Le Caporal Epinglé*. The fusion of these two worlds, where it does occur, happens through the medium of love: the Viceroy falls in love with Camilla, Etienne Alexis seduces the beautiful peasant girl. But if love knows no boundaries it remains a transient emotion and these relationships are just part of the eternal changing of partners that characterises Renoir's view of love. In the end order and social propriety usually win; where they do not, we wonder what can

47

possibly become of so ill-matched a couple as Etienne Alexis and Né-nette. This same principal of duality is also used with regard to ideas. *The Golden Coach* is a meditation on the conflicting loyalties of theatre and life, *Le Testament du Dr. Cordelier* is a treatment of the problem of good and evil. Too often this gives rise to the easy use of types instead of the construction of characters. The Viceroy is both a comic figure and a rounded human being with a real personality but subsequently the urge to caricature has not been resisted. Danglard, Etienne Alexis and the Corporal are all types, lacking in depth, who exist as props to sustain the action, not individual human beings about whom we can care.

If the schematisation of character and the paucity and superficiality of ideas — as exemplified in the character of Etienne Alexis and the whole anti-scientific argument of *Le Déjeuner sur l'Herbe* — are the principal weaknesses of Renoir's later work, its real impact comes from the director's handling of what we might call the elements of spectacle. Only two of his films since 1950 have been shot in black and white, the others rely for their effect on the interweaving of colour, movement and music. In his handling of colour, especially in *The River* and *Le Déjeuner sur l'Herbe* Renoir reveals a painter's eye and the influence of his father's work. All these films were made in conscious opposition to the natural-istic and pessimistic conception of life that is dominant in the French postwar cinema. Two of these works, *French Cancan* and *The Golden Coach* exalt the theatre as an antithesis to life, more real it seems than dull reality itself. In others nature is contrasted with human society. The Indian background of *The River* provides consolation for Harriet and an ever-present illustration of the philosophy of acceptance; nature and the primitive life of the South American Indians offer a refuge for the soldier Felipe in *The Golden Coach;* and in the two works of 1959 the sanctity of Nature becomes an explicit message. *Le Testament du Dr. Cordelier* shows the dark world of those who tamper with God's creation while *Le Déjeuner sur l'Herbe* celebrates the glories of nature, source of love and true reverence.

Renoir's methods of film making have evolved and changed during the dozen years that separate *The River* and *Le Caporal Epinglé* but a concern with actors remains central to all his work. Technique, in the sense of the carefully planned lighting and angling of shots, is of secondary importance. As he said after *Le Testament:* "What remains for me from this experience, what I have believed for a long time moreover, is that one must not be a slave to technique. I detest technique, it invades everything and destroys the vitality." Film making for Renoir centres on the human element, the actors, whose mystique he celebrates explicitly in two of his films. A Renoir film evolves as it is being made. Interviewed while making *Le Caporal Epinglé* he said in reply to a question: "In any case I can hardly talk of my film before it is finished because I change everything during the making. In the cinema I am the opposite of René Clair." The film grows as a result of Renoir's contact with the actors, constantly rewritten and partially improvised: "I believe in improvisation but it is only of value when it is built on a firm basis." Renoir was particularly happy making *The River* for actors and technicians lived as a group and a school of acting was formed for the benefit of the inexperienced. For his two films using television methods the director founded the "Compagnie Jean Renoir" to unite all in a co-operative effort. Renoir's loose method of construction makes his films of this period rely heavily on their stars — Magnani, Gabin or Bergman — whose personality serves to hold together the disparate elements. Even more responsibility was thrown on the actors of the two films in which Renoir used television methods, for the rehearsals were followed by shooting scene by scene, with only one take. Perhaps because of insufficient rehearsal or lack of adequate preparation both these films seem overacted, Barrault as Opale and Paul Meurisse as Etienne Alexis both being guilty in this respect. The use of several cameras here makes the editing a key part of the film making process, but even earlier, in *The River* for example, Renoir had favoured shooting extensive footage, the use or rejection of which was decided only at the editing stage. Music plays an important part in the establishment of the all-important rhythm. Renoir has said that the music of Vivaldi was decisive when he was giving *The Golden Coach* its final form; the recurring cancan rhythm and hectic finale by Georges Van Parys contributed much to *French Cancan*; while Joseph Kosma's music with its themes for the principal characters is vital to *Le Testament du Dr. Cordelier* and *Le Déjeuner sur l'Herbe.*

49

The films of Renoir's later period may not be the unbroken series of absolute masterpieces that certain French critics like to imagine but they do form a vital and varied sequence of works. The affectionate humour, zest for life and warm humanity that they show would rank Renoir high among film makers, even if he had not made an even greater succession of films twenty or so years before.

* * *

MARCEL CARNÉ was at the height of his fame in 1945. His collaboration with the poet and script writer Jacques Prévert had culminated in two of the greatest films made during the Occupation period — *Les Visiteurs du Soir* and *Les Enfants du Paradis* — and the director seemed destined to achieve still further successes. In fact, Carné's postwar work has nowhere near the same interest as his earlier films and his reputation has declined steadily during the last fifteen years. In 1946, however, Carné was able to make a film of his own choosing and enjoy the advantages of a large budget. Though given a contemporary setting, **Les Portes de la Nuit** (1946) had as its source a ballet which Jacques Prévert had written the previous year with music by Joseph Kosma and choreography by Roland Petit. The weaknesses of the film stem largely from this hybrid conception: on the one hand it was an ostensibly realistic film treating the immediate postwar problems of the black market and the aftermath of the Occupation, on the other, a "poetic" work with a melodramatic plot involving a character who personifies Fate and introduces the hero to "the most beautiful woman in the world". The film also suffered from certain inadequacies of interpretation, attributable partly to the fact that Jean Gabin and Marlene Dietrich refused the parts written for them and had to be replaced at the last moment by a less experienced pair (Yves Montand and Nathalie Nattier). Carné remained faithful to the pre-war studio tradition, the exteriors being reconstructed in the studio, at considerable expense, by his designer Alexandre Trauner. The film was technically sound, with at least one bravura passage (the suicide of Serge Reggiani, who played Nathalie Nattier's brother), but completely out of touch with current taste.

Les Portes de la Nuit was a resounding commercial failure and for a time Marcel Carné underwent considerable difficulties. Three years passed before another film of his was released, for the next film on which he worked with Jacques Prévert, *La Fleur de l'Age* in 1947, was interrupted because of financial difficulties and never resumed. It is on this low note that the long collaboration of Carné and Prévert, one of the most famous writer-director teams in the history of the cinema, came to an end. Prévert is said to have made a small and uncredited contribution to Carné's next film but his career as a scriptwriter comes virtually to an end in 1948.

In his subsequent films Carné has collaborated with quite a number of reputed scenarists but never fully recovered his old touch. In the late forties he worked on several projects, all of which were turned down by producers and when a new film of his did appear it was by intention and execution a minor work. **La Marie du Port** (1950) was an adaptation, written with Louis Chavance, of a Simenon novel set in Normandy. It is the story of a hard and calculating young girl, excellently played by Nicole Courcel, who succeeds in replacing her more elegant sister (Blanchette Brunoy) as mistress, and ultimately no doubt wife, of the wealthy restaurant owner Châtelan, played by Jean Gabin. All Carné's enormous technical skill is brought to bear on this simple realistic subject which lacks the fatalistic overtones of his most characteristic work. Carné succeeds in capturing the authentic Simenon atmosphere and extracts good performances from all his players, particularly Jean Gabin, who here sets the pattern for his subsequent postwar career. René Clément's *Au delà des Grilles* was the last film in which he appeared in the type of part that had made him famous in the thirties: the defeated fugitive from justice. In *La Marie du Port* he played for the first time the sort of role he was to appear in throughout the fifties: a powerful and successful character who, despite a possibly criminal past, remains master of his life and environment.

After the success of this film Carné was again free to tackle a more ambitious subject and significantly he left the humdrum world of reality to make **Juliette ou la Clef des Songes** (1951) which had been a cherished project of his since 1939. The film adaptation written by Carné and Jacques Viot consists largely of a young prisoner's dream of a journey to

51

a mysterious land where time and memories do not exist in search of the beautiful Juliette (Suzanne Cloutier). He finds his beloved, clad radiantly in white, but loses her to the elegant Bluebeard (Jean-Roger Caussimon) who dominates the village with his massive castle, his black carriage and his hounds. Then the film switches back to reality: the dream turns out to be no more than a simple transposition of the hero's situation. He is released from prison but having lost the real Juliette for ever he prefers to return, through suicide, to the land of dreams. The film is impeccably photographed by Henri Alekan, and notable contributions are made by the designer Alexandre Trauner and the composer Joseph Kosma who here work with Carné for the last time. But despite an interesting opening the impression left by the film is one of coldness and, ultimately, banality. What is lacking is any real sense of poetry in the handling of Carné's favourite themes of fatalism and impossible love, and even Gérard Philipe's engaging personality cannot overcome the film's air of exaggerated defeatism.

Thérèse Raquin (1953) marked a return to reality and though imperfect is perhaps Carné's most accomplished postwar film. In the adaptation of Emile Zola's novel which he made with Charles Spaak, Carné brought the story up to date and set it in present day Lyons. In so doing he deliberately sacrificed the social pressures of nineteenth century provincial bourgeois life which Zola had seen as decisive in shaping the heroine's life, attempting instead to invest the story with an aura of fate or destiny, of the kind to be found in all his most characteristic work. Throughout Carné's version of the story the lovers are the prey of forces beyond their control: their first meeting, their liaison, even the death of the husband are more the result of chance than planning and the accidental death of the blackmailer that finally destroys them is simply the ultimate blow of a malignant fate. The weaknesses of *Thérèse Raquin* derive almost entirely from this deterministic conception of life which fails to motivate adequately the conduct of the characters, particularly when the modernisation of the work entails a number of disturbing inconsistencies (for example, a modern Thérèse would not feel herself bound in the same way to her husband, nor would a modern husband think of locking up his wife in order to make her forget a lover). There is still much to admire in

52

A coldly beautiful universe, dominated by fate: Suzanne Cloutier and Jean-Roger Caussimon in Marcel Carné's JULIETTE OU LA CLEF DES SONGES.

the film. Most of the acting is of a high standard, with the central trio of husband, wife and lover well contrasted and played by Jacques Duby, Simone Signoret and Raf Vallone. The part of the mother-in-law, however, played by Sylvie is largely gratuitous in this free-ranging adaptation and by far the most interesting character is the ever smiling but tenacious blackmailer, played by Roland Lesaffre, who has appeared in virtually all Carné's films since *La Marie du Port*. The studio-built exteriors (here by Paul Bertrand who succeeded Trauner as Carné's regular designer) emphasise the link with the past, and Carné's handling of composition and editing is as assured as always and nowhere more strikingly displayed than in the death of the blackmailer which forms the film's ironic climax.

Marcel Carné's next two films are not generally considered to rank among his best. In **L'Air de Paris** (1954) he returned to a Parisian setting and assembled a cast that included Jean Gabin and Arletty, but little of significance emerged from this story of a retired boxer and his attempts to make a champion of his young protegé (played by Roland Lesaffre, himself an ex-boxer). **Le Pays d'où je viens** (1956), the director's first colour film, was a further departure from realism, being a tale of mistaken identity set in a snow-filled little town at Christmas time. The popular singer Gilbert Bécaud appeared in the double role of vagabond and shy pianist, while Françoise Arnoul played the girl whom the pianist loves and, indeed, wins thanks to the vagabond.

Carné achieved commercial, if not critical, success two years later with his study of contemporary youth, **Les Tricheurs** (1958). This film is one of the first attempts on the part of the older French directors to come to terms with youth, anticipating René Clément's *Plein Soleil* and Henri-Georges Clouzot's *La Vérité*. *Les Tricheurs* has a number of superficial contemporary touches: its players — Pascale Petit, Jacques Charrier, Laurent Terzieff and Jean-Paul Belmondo — are young and talented, its musical backing is a lively mixture of recorded jazz and at times the camera even ventures out into the streets of Paris, though the director is obviously much more at home with the sequences filmed in the studio. Technically the film is impeccable but conventional and there is no originality in construction to match the new subject matter. Throughout it is the set-pieces that succeed best — the "truth" game, with its huge culminating close-ups or the final car chase, superbly edited to a piece of climactic jazz drumming. Little insight is shown by Carné or his script writer Jacques Sigurd into the motives and feelings of their rebellious young characters and the story is told through the eyes of the most sober and decent of the youths, the bourgeois outsider who for a short time joins up with the gang and who is left with a few regrets for his lost innocence at the end. Little sympathy is shown for the other members of the group and the film's treatment of the two girls is particularly revealing: the rich young nymphomaniac suffers an improbable crisis of conscience on discovering herself pregnant and agrees to a marriage of convenience arranged by her father, while the heroine, who contravenes the gang's rules by unwittingly falling in love with the hero, suffers the conventional cinema's fate for heroines who sleep with more than one man and dies to give the film a specious air of tragedy.

Since *Les Tricheurs* Carné has fared badly. With works like **Terrain Vague** (1960) and **Les Jeunes Loups** (1968) he attempted to repeat his 1958 success by dealing with young people and their problems but with only limited results. In the sixties he has conceived a number of ambitious projects of a literary kind, including versions of "La Dame aux Camélias" and "Germinal", but none of these have come to anything and he has been compelled to make fairly routine films: **Du Mouron chez les Petits Oiseaux** (1963), a comedy-thriller set in a studio-constructed boarding house and unsuccessfully attempting to revive the glories of an older period of the French cinema, and **Trois Chambres à Manhattan** (1965), a simple and realistic adaptation of a Simenon novel in the same minor vein as *La Marie du Port*.

It would have been difficult in 1945 to foresee the almost complete eclipse of **MARCEL CARNÉ's** reputation within fifteen years. When the war ended he appeared to have behind him an unassailable body of work and to be still at the very height of his powers. His most ambitious film, *Les Enfants du Paradis*, on which he had worked for two years, was released in 1945 and universally hailed as a masterpiece. Carné was still comparatively young. Born in 1909 he was younger than many of the men who were to dominate the postwar scene: Autant-Lara, Becker, Bresson, Clouzot, Tati. He was able in 1946 to reassemble a team including his favourite collaborators: Jacques Prévert, Alexandre Trauner and Joseph Kosma, and though the members of this team have gradually been replaced, Carné has found talented successors for them, and has been able to call on a succession of brilliant directors of photography, Roger Hubert, Henri Alekan and Claude Renoir among them. All his work shows a fine command of the essentials of composing and editing a scene, his continued technical mastery being clearly revealed in those scenes of violent death with which most of his films culminate. His gift with actors is maintained too, as the performances of Gabin in *La Marie du Port*, Simone Signoret in *Thérèse Raquin* and the young actors of *Les Tricheurs* show.

On the surface at least Marcel Carné has much in common with the dominant and highly successful group of postwar directors. Like them he is not a complete creator: he shares their predilection for a well constructed film, always working in close collaboration with a scriptwriter, but imposing his own vision of the world on his material. This vision, fundamental to which is the notion that love is impossible in this world, is no blacker or less valid than that of, say, Henri-Georges Clouzot. He has proved too, in a work like *La Marie du Port*, that he can work well within the purely realistic tradition. The fundamental difference that separates him from Clouzot or Clément is that his own inclination is to turn his back on realism as soon as the opportunity presents itself and continue to aim at the kind of philosophical, fate-dominated and essentially fantastic spectacles he made in collaboration with Prévert during the Occupation.

There is no doubt more than a grain of truth in the classic view of the Carné-Prévert partnership whereby Prévert was deemed responsible for the poetry and Carné for the sense of realism, and perhaps it is the Prévert touch that is lacking from such a work as *Juliette ou la Clef des Songes*. But in Carné's case at least the definition needs careful qualification. His first film, *Nogent, Eldorado du Dimanche* (1929) was a piece of realistic reportage made in natural settings and without actors, but since then he has turned his back on reality, substituting for it the lessons of Jacques Feyder and René Clair whose pupil he was. He remained convinced that the only way of creating a film is within the studio and if his name is associated with a succession of works, from *Quai des Brumes* to *Thérèse Raquin*, which have a nominal setting in the everyday world, Carné, with or without Prévert, has never shown the slightest interest in the details of day to day life. The vital elements in Carné's work are the unrealistic ones: the constructed exteriors that are never quite real streets, the characters who tend to become abstractions with a symbolic function, the dialogue which is elevated and deliberately non-naturalistic. Behind the cold beauty of the images one finds an interest in the workings of fate, not an exploration of society. Since he has moved against the current of the contemporary cinema and remained fascinated by notions that most of his juniors would regard as outmoded, his most ambitious work has failed to make much of an impact and he has been driven to direct purely commercial films which he is too much of an artist to do successfully. Fashions in the cinema have a habit of changing rapidly and perhaps Marcel Carné will some day be rehabilitated, but today at least he is a director whose last film of real importance was made when he was thirty-five, back in 1944.

* * *

MAX OPHULS returned to France in 1949. One of the most widely travelled of directors, this German-born film maker had directed films in Germany, Italy and Holland as well as in France which was his home from 1933 till 1940. The war years he had spent in the United States, unable to find work until 1947 when he made the first of his four American films. Like so many of Ophul's projects, the one which brought him back to France — a version of Balzac's "La Duchesse de Langeais" to star Greta Garbo — was never realised. Instead Ophuls made **La Ronde** (1950), his most widely distributed film and one of his greatest successes. It opened the series of works on which his reputation chiefly rests and with it he formed the team of collaborators that remained virtually unchanged until his death. *La Ronde* was adapted from the play "Reigen" by one of Ophuls's favourite authors, Arthur Schnitzler. In collaboration with Jacques Natanson, Ophuls has idealised this work, setting it in a fairytale Vienna of 1900. In this film the view of love as a regular interchange of partners (which Ophuls shared with Renoir) is developed into a ring of encounters linking the characters, each of whom passes from one lover to another. The film is full of cynicism and worldly wit and Ophuls takes an apparent delight in the manipulation of his characters, exploiting to the full the irony of their situation: the fact that their partners change but their gestures remain the same, that they are in turn deceivers and deceived, involuntarily echoing each other's words and sentiments. The film is episodic, amounting in effect to ten variations on the same theme and great ingenuity is shown by the authors in varying the routine of encounter, seduction and desertion. To link the episodes Ophuls used the famous waltz written for the film by Oscar Straus, the recurring image of the roundabout, and the very important character played by Anton Walbrook, that of master of ceremonies or *meneur de jeu*. He is a sort of personification of the director himself, manipulating the characters and making them dance to the tune of the waltz. The freedom of the *meneur de jeu* contrasts with the captivity of the other characters. He can choose a new identity at will and range freely through time, while they are prisoners of their own personalities, unable to escape from the crowded present. The fact that the circle is never broken gives a sense of fatality to the coupling of the characters and the dialogue is littered with epigrams about the impossibility of love and happiness, but only in the eyes of the most fervent admirers of Ophuls does this lighthearted work contain a tragic demonstration of the futility of man's quest for pleasure.

After this resounding success Ophuls turned to Guy de Maupassant, choosing three of his stories for adaptation to make up **Le Plaisir** (1952). The three episodes are by no means given equal weight and the middle story tends to overshadow the other two. The first, *Le Masque*, contrasts pleasure and old age, telling the rather gruesome tale of an old man so addicted to dancing that he keeps to it despite his age and has a mask made to hide his wrinkles. His story is told by his wife to the doctor who treats him after he has collapsed on the dance floor. The second and longest story, *La Maison Tellier*, opposes pleasure and purity. The inmates of a brothel attend the first communion of the madame's young niece. Their appearance causes quite a stir in the remote village and in church the tears brought to their eyes by the thought of their own fate prove contagious and soon all are weeping. After one of them, Rosa (Danielle Darrieux), has enjoyed a brief idyll with their farmer host (Jean Gabin), the girls return home and resume work again. For the final episode Ophuls wanted to contrast pleasure and death in "La Femme de Paul" but had to replace this with *Le Modèle* at the producer's insistence. This episode now deals with pleasure and marriage, seen as opposites. A young painter who has had an *affaire* with his model marries her after she has thrown herself out of the window because of her love for him and devotes his life to caring for his crippled wife. Despite the unifying theme, that the search for happiness is not gay, *Le Plaisir* is the most disjointed of Ophuls's films. He has striven to give it unity and shape by balancing the humorous central story with two shorter ones, both more serious in mood. In the first story we see a woman who sacrifices herself to the man she loves, in the third the roles are reversed and it is the man who makes the sacrifices. In the final version the stories are linked tenuously by the voice of a narrator but originally the link was to have been tighter, for Ophuls planned to set the stories in a framework of conversation between the author (Maupassant) and the cinéaste (Ophuls). As in all his films Ophuls indulges his passion for tracking and crane shots. Typical in this respect is his treatment of the Maison Tellier: although the interior of this was built in the greatest detail and at great care and expense, the camera never enters it, contenting itself with circling the exterior, climbing the walls and peering through the windows at the activity within. Apart from the ingenuity with which Ophuls and his team have solved the technical problems which he set, the film's main delight is the humour extracted from the ironies of the central story's situation of a brothel "closed because of first communion."

For the subject of his next film, **Madame de . . .** (1953) Ophuls turned to a shortish story by Louise de Vilmorin which he adapted with two new collaborators, Marcel Achard and Annette Wademant. His attitude to the subject is clear from his own description of it: "The only thing that tempts me in this slight story is its construction: there is always the same axis around which the action continually turns, like a roundabout. A tiny, scarcely visible axis: a pair of earrings." These earrings pass from hand to hand. Husband and wife, his mistress and her lover all own them at some time until they complete the circle to give the husband proof of his wife's infidelity. Among the changes made is the inclusion of a duel at the end between husband and lover, presumably added to give greater weight to the story. It is in perfect keeping with the film's turn of the century setting, as is the conception of the heroine dying of a broken heart. Décor and costumes play a vital role in the film. The camera tracks and whirls amid the curtains, mirrors and chandeliers, catching all the glitter of the sumptuous dresses of the women and the uniforms of the soldiers and diplomats, pursuing the characters as they move to theatre, dance or reception and return again. As so often in Ophuls one is struck by the vanity and frivolity of the lives of the main characters interpreted here by Charles Boyer, Danielle Darrieux and Vittorio de Sica. The freedom with which Ophuls handles his marionettes and subordinates them to his aesthetic design is perhaps best shown in the dance scenes where shots of Madame de . . . and her diplomat lover move to and fro, from long shot to close-up, to trace the development of their relationship, the successive changes of clothing with each new shot indicating that this sequence is a condensation of a number of meetings. The unifying function of the waltz tune here is typical of the use of music throughout the film.

Lola Montès (1955), the last film Max Ophuls made before his death at the age of fifty-five, is in many ways a fitting culmination to his life's work. The producers' aim was a block-buster starring Martine Carol, then at the height of her fame, and based on a novel by Cécil Saint-Laurent, author of the celebrated and highly successful "Caroline Chérie". Ophuls was given the sort of resources normally available only to the tried commercial director, such as Martine Carol's ex-husband Christian-Jaque: a large budget and a thirty-three week shooting schedule, colour, cinemascope and a cast of international stars. When completed the film turned out to contain the very essence of the director's art and to be, at the same time, an enormous commercial failure, even after drastic cutting and re-editing by the producers, who as a result went bankrupt. The novel and its heroine were of little interest to Ophuls: "Lola Montès? That woman doesn't interest me: half-prostitute, mediocre dancer, pretty face, what else? It is the people who surround her that excite me. If the almost permanent presence of Lola on the screen

60

"*Half-prostitute, mediocre dancer, pretty face, what else?*" Martine Carol with Peter Ustinov in *LOLA MONTÈS.*

is indispensable it is not the same as saying she embodies the essential of the subject. Her role is roughly the same as that of our pair of earrings in *Madame de . . .*" The subject — the rise of Lola Montès from humble beginnings as a dancer to the heights as lover of Liszt and mistress of the King of Bavaria, and her subsequent fall to circus star selling kisses at a dollar a time — is not the major consideration. All the interest is in the treatment and here Ophuls is at his most elaborate. The film begins and ends with scenes in the circus, with flashbacks to her earlier life rising out of this, provoked by the ring master's account of her life and the audience's remarks. Ophuls was opposed to the use of the wide screen but has been able to mask part of it with pillars, draperies and arches. This was his only colour film and he has attempted to use colour both dramatically (contrasting the blackness of the auditorium with the vivid colours of the performers) and symbolically (in the garishness of the circus). The costumes of the performers are in violent colours, often contrasting ones, and the revolving circus settings are frequently bathed in coloured light. The main flashbacks have been given a dominant colour scheme corresponding to a season: black blue and grey for Lola's youth (spring), red and gold for her affair with Liszt (autumn), white, blue, silver and gold for the Bavarian episode (winter). The camera is never still. It pivots and circles restlessly through the extravagant décor crammed with grills and stairways, performs arabesques within the ever changing scenery of the circus ring, sweeps after the characters as they move in their brightly coloured costumes from setting to setting, up and down stairs or from trapeze to trapeze, and peeps through windows, curtains and doorways. What is there beneath this surface? Hardly a human being for Martine Carol is wooden and inexpressive in the main role, while the men around her are little more than caricatures or puppets. Technically, however, the result is awe-inspiring. All the features of Ophuls's style, all his favourite situations and love of opulence and intricacy are here. *Lola Montès* seems at times a synthesis of his life's work of twenty-one films. But what is lacking is depth: the whole tour de force is dazzling but ultimately quite remarkably hollow.

MAX OPHULS is virtually a test case of one's approach to the cinema. For those whose concern is purely visual and whose ideal is an abstract symphony of images, Ophuls has the status of one of the very great directors. For spectators and critics who demand in addition to the images the sort of human insight and moral depth that a play or a novel can give, he is merely a minor master, maker of exquisite but rather empty films. Whether he is regarded as a major or a minor figure in the history of the film there is, however, no denying that he is an artist of considerable sensitivity and possessor of an incredible technical command of his chosen medium.

Ophuls came to the cinema at the age of twenty-eight after six years activity as a theatrical producer. He has explained his changed approach on abandoning the theatre with a typical Ophuls simile: "I was no longer concerned with anything but the image. The camera, this new means of expression which I had at my disposal for the first time, turned me irresistibly from words, rather as a young mistress turns a man from his wife." He has always had an enormous respect for technical achievement, realising that a lifetime can be spent mastering all the intricacies of film making, but for him technique is only a beginning, not an end: "I believe that the aim of all technique is to allow itself to be mastered. One should dominate it so well that it becomes transparent, that beyond the reproduction of reality it becomes the instrument of thought, play, enchantment and dream." A knowledge of technique is important so that one can break the rules and do the impossible. He was ready to admit that the film is a collective art form to which many people contribute: "I do not believe there is *one* creator in a film: I think, and it is practically an axiom for me, that there are as many creators in a film as there are people working on it. My job as director is to make these people into a chorus . . . I can only arouse the creative force in each of them." On the four films with which we are concerned here he assembled a highly gifted team of collaborators who have never surpassed their work with him: the writers Jacques Natanson (principal scriptwriter on three films) and Annette Wademant (who worked on the last two); the director of photography Christian Matras who was responsible for lighting all but the third episode of *Le Plaisir;* and the team of Jean d'Eaubonne and Georges Annenkov who designed respectively the sets and the costumes of all four films. But Ophuls knew also that he was ultimately responsible for his films and that the work of these collaborators was of value only if it translated his vision into film terms: "I believe that the real aim of the artist is to give a new vision of the world. Fundamentally all subjects end by resembling each other. It is the personal vision which we have of a milieu or of a person, and the form which we communicate to them, that differentiate them."

The image was for Ophuls the only possible beginning to a film: "The argument, the subject of a film begins to exist for me only when I can "represent" it to myself by a succession of images . . . In a film the text, the technique, the logical development must come *after* the image — the latter bearing the artistic truth in the cinema and revealing in itself innumerable marvels." Max Ophuls was a man of wide cultural interests and had a deep respect for literature, yet the characteristic of his subject matter is its triviality. It is not by chance that his last film in the U.S.A. was from a Ladies' Home Journal story, for Ophuls's subject matter is the beautiful but unhappy woman. The themes of the transitoriness of pleasure and the precariousness of happiness recur again and again, their reappearance emphasised by the continual use of a dream-world turn of the century setting with beautifully gowned women and elegant top-hatted gentlemen or uniformed officers. The same images — the lovers' meeting in the snow and the duel for instance — tend to crop up continually in films made over a period of twenty-five years in five countries and give his work its striking stylistic unity. The stories of Ophuls's films are slight, tending to be episodic, and a great deal of care is expended by director and writers on the shaping of this material: the perfect roundabout of meetings in *La Ronde*, the peregrinations of the earrings in *Madame de . . .*, the balancing of the three stories in *Le Plaisir* and the pattern of the flashbacks in *Lola Montès*.

Above all Ophuls is concerned with details: "Details, details, details! The most insignificant, the most unobtrusive among them are often the most evocative, characteristic and even decisive. Exact details, an artful little nothing, make art." The sets and costumes of his films from *La Ronde* to *Lola Montès* are all elaborate evocations of the nineteen hundreds, with the detail chosen not for historical accuracy but for picturesque value. These settings are the source of the heaviness that many critics have found in Ophuls's work despite its slight themes and agile camera-work. Ophuls brought from his stage career a genuine affection for his players ("I love all actors") and he would spend hours rehearsing them on the set, guiding them to the exact effects he wanted, but nevertheless he allows them to be dominated by the décor and his visual preoccupations. As Peter Ustinov, who was the ringmaster in *Lola Montès*, put it: "The actor was often reduced to a cloistered being on tiptoe who could hardly breathe for fear of blowing away some precious cobweb which had its vital symbolical meaning." The feeling that the characters are not people but mere puppets is increased in some films by the presence of a figure representing the omnipotent author putting the other characters through their paces: the *meneur de jeu* in *La Ronde* and the ringmaster in *Lola Montès*.

For Ophuls the essence of the cinema lies in the play of light, the juggling with surfaces. His camera tracks, turns and zigzags in virtuoso fashion to catch every facet of the intricate settings and costumes of his films. Not content with filming straightforwardly, he multiplies the difficulties, shoots round pillars or through curtains or grills, making his characters move the whole time so that his shots grow in length and complexity. But never does he use his camera to probe beneath the surface. His director of photography Christian Matras explained this by saying: "The reality which he glimpsed was so fragile that too direct a penetration would have destroyed it. That is the justification for those innumerable spiral staircases or long tracking shots which skirt or caress reality without ever damaging it." Perhaps it is truer to say, however, that in fact there is a void beneath the elaborate surface of Ophuls's films. He described Danielle Darrieux's task in playing Madame de . . . as that of "incarnating a void, non-existence. Not filling a void, but incarnating it," and described Madame de's life as "non-existence copiously fed and richly dressed." If one accepts this void as a yawning abyss looming beneath those who base their lives on the search for pleasure, it is possible to see Ophuls's films as a critique of elegant society and to regard him as a baroque poet in the full sense of the word. If not Ophuls remains an amiable, entertaining guide to a world of frivolity and pleasure, rather like the *meneur de jeu* of *La Ronde* who introduced himself with the

Max Ophuls directing LOLA MONTÈS: "My job as director is to make these people into a chorus."

words: "I am the incarnation of your desire ... of your desire to know everything. Men never know more than a part of reality. Why? ... Because they see only one aspect of things. As for me, I see everything, because I see things in the round."

*   *   *

JEAN COCTEAU began his connection with the cinema in 1930 when he made *Le Sang d'un Poète*, an entirely personal work for which he was given a completely free hand by his private backer. Cocteau has characterised this work as anti-surrealist but when it is reseen today the similarities in manner which it shares with Buñuel's masterpiece *L'Age d'Or*, made at the same time and for the same patron, are more apparent than the divergences. Cocteau had no desire to establish himself as a commercial director and over fifteen years passed before he directed another film. During the Occupation years, however, he did work as scriptwriter on a number of films and indeed continued this activity intermittently into the sixties. The films on which he has worked as scenarist or dialoguist range from insignificant melodramas like Serge de Poligny's *Le Baron Fantôme* (1943) and Pierre Billon's *Ruy Blas* (1947) to Robert Bresson's second film *Les Dames du Bois de Boulogne* (1944) and Jean Delannoy's cold and polished version of the Tristan and Isolde legend, *L'Eternal Retour* (1943). But all these — apart from the Bresson film — are overshadowed by the series of films which Cocteau himself directed in the years after the war.

La Belle et la Bête (1946) was an adaptation of the fairy tale by Madame Leprince de Beaumont and told of the courage of the beautiful young Belle who sacrifices herself in her father's place after he has enraged the powerful Beast by plucking a magic rose from his garden. Gradually Belle is won over from fear to affection by the Beast's kindness which extends even to granting her permission to visit her sick father. Belle breaks her promise by staying longer than the stipulated week, and when she returns the Beast is already dying of a broken heart. Meanwhile Avenant, a dissolute friend of her brother who loves Belle, has resolved to rescue her and steal the Beast's treasure. He dies in the attempt and is transformed, as he expires, into the corpse of the Beast, while the latter

67

is miraculously transformed into a princely version of Avenant after Belle has looked at him for the first time with loving eyes. The childlike innocence which Cocteau demands of his audience in his brief introduction to the film is not at all apparent in his own approach. Visually, the film is most sophisticated: the costumes (by Christian Bérard, who was also artistic director) and the camera style (by Henri Alekan, under the technical supervision of René Clément) are decorative rather than functional and have their origin in Dutch painting, particularly the work of Vermeer. The legend is handled in a variety of styles. The home life of Belle's family is parodied and is often broadly farcical in tone (as, for instance, in the use of cackling ducks to accompany the shots of Belle's two sisters). By contrast, the departure of Belle for the Beast's castle and her entry there are stylised, Cocteau employing slow motion photography to obtain a dreamlike effect. The fairytale world of the Beast's castle is given great solidity for Cocteau aimed at giving a "realism of the unreal" and it is arguable that in fact the setting has been given too much weight: there is a degree of ponderousness about the film which Georges Auric's music serves only to emphasise. In evoking the magical qualities of the castle Cocteau has made strangely little use of the film's trick shot possibilities; the living faces of the statuary and the disembodied human arms that act as the Beast's servants are essentially theatrical devices. One of the great difficulties facing Cocteau was that of making the oversimplified and unpersonalised figures of a fairytale into characters capable of sustaining interest in a film lasting some ninety minutes. The solution found for the minor characters was caricature and an often humorous approach. As far as the two principal characters are concerned, the make-up of Jean Marais as the Beast emphasises his bestial nature in a number of ways, as do such scenes as that of the Beast drinking and that where he scents game. But Belle remains a rather dull figure, despite the beauty of Josette Day. The film does, however, constantly open up odd perspectives — particularly through the ambiguities of Belle's attitude to the Beast — and the double use of Marais as Avenant and Beast-cum-Prince Charming avoids the danger of too easy an explanation of the film's symbolism.

After this appropriation of a fairytale to his own personal mythology,

"Belle is won over from fear to affection by the Beast's kindness." Josette
Day and Jean Marais in Jean Cocteau's LA BELLE ET LA BÊTE.

Cocteau turned to the adaptation of his own works. He directed film versions of two of his plays and also collaborated closely with Jean-Pierre Melville on a film transcription of his novel *Les Enfants Terribles* (1950). The first of Cocteau's own adaptations was **L'Aigle à Deux Têtes** (1947). Like the play (which had been written two years previously) the film is an attempt to revive the type of Romantic drama associated with Victor Hugo and is thus a kind of reworking of *Ruy Blas*, on the script of which Cocteau had worked the previous year. In *L'Aigle à Deux Têtes* Edwige Feuillère appeared as a (vaguely Bavarian) Queen and Jean Marais as her lederhosen-clad assassin, Stanislas, who bears an uncanny resemblance to the Queen's dead husband. When Stanislas bursts into her apartment on his mission of hate, the Queen welcomes him as the death she is seeking. The pair fall in love, plan for a while to oppose the machinations of a largely hostile court but then die together. The work contains much that is characteristic of Cocteau, particularly the fusion of love and death. Again working in close collaboration with Christian Bérard, Cocteau enlarged the physical scope of the play and experimented with the use of the camera to obtain a fresh view of its action, but the result was not very favourably received.

Much more successful was **Les Parents Terribles** (1948) which was adapted from a work Cocteau had written for the stage some ten years earlier. It is a tragi-comedy of tangled family relationships, filled with melodramatic confrontations, incorporating deliberately shocking elements (incest and suicide) and a plot of vaudeville complexity. Cocteau has himself admirably defined his objectives in this film: "I had set out to do three things: firstly, record the acting of an incomparable cast; secondly, walk among them and look them straight in the face, instead of contemplating them at a distance on the stage; thirdly, peep through the keyhole and catch my wild beasts unawares with my tele-lens." The film includes three members of the original cast, as well as Yvonne de Bray, for whom the central role of the mother had been written but who had been prevented by illness from appearing in it on the stage. The only real newcomer is Josette Day (Beauty in *La Belle et la Bête*) as Madeleine, the girl whom both Michel and his father love. The power of the actors is decisive in a film of this nature and Cocteau has succeeded admirably in drawing outstanding performances from his cast and co-ordinating them into a credible if totally artificial family. Yvonne Bray is superb as the devouring mother whose life revolves around her son. Emotional and domineering, she refuses to emerge from her cluttered, untidy apartment to admit that at twenty-two her son may be a man. She is the magnet holding the others together and it is evident that even after her death her spirit will continue to hold sway in these gloomy rooms. Gabrielle Dorziat as Aunt Léo is the perfect foil, revealing a true spinster's dedicated opposition to disorder and drawing her satisfaction from manipulating the lives of others. Marcel André captures effectively, if less strikingly, the harassed defeatism of a man constantly pushed aside by life, replaced by his son first in the affections of his wife and then in those of his mistress. Jean Marais (already thirty-five when the film was made) vividly captures the youthful innocence and impetuosity of Michel, while Josette Day fills the least demanding role with grace and beauty.

Realising that his characters are monsters, inconceivable outside the closed walls of their apartment, Cocteau has limited himself to just two settings — the family home and Madeleine's flat. The combination of close-ups and non-naturalistic acting emphasises the intense theatricality which is so essential to the work. The exact sequence of speeches (with only a few tiny cuts) and the three act structure are also preserved from the play and nothing is done to make the plot more realistic. The film opens with a shot of a curtain rising to reveal the actors, and the plot follows a highly artificial pattern, opening and closing in the family apartment, beginning with a fake suicide and ending with a real one, and containing a succession of dramatic revelations and "coups de théâtre". The young follow in the footsteps of the old. Michel, having taken his father's place in the affections of his mother, further emulates him by seeking escape in the arms of Madeleine. When the mother dies, Madeleine is on hand to take her place, so that the film's ending is no more than a fresh beginning.

The film **Orphée** (1950) is undoubtedly Jean Cocteau's major achievement in the cinema. It depicts the love of the poet Orphée (Jean Marais) for the Princess (Maria Casarès) who is "one of the innumerable functionaries of death" and whose constant journeying between this world and

71

the next has made her susceptible to human emotions. She returns Orphée's love, just as her chauffeur Heurtebise (François Périer) is moved by the beauty of the poet's neglected wife (Marie Déa). When, after the jealous Princess has had Eurydice killed, Orphée goes into the "Zone" — the no-man's land that lies behind the mirror — it is as much to see the Princess again as to fetch back his wife. Finally, after Orphée has again lost Eurydice and himself been killed in a brawl, the Princess and Heurtebise use their power to restore him to life and happiness, before going off to face some nameless punishment.

Orphée makes full use of the trappings of this world. The Princess's leather-clad executioners carry machine guns and roar by mysteriously on their motorcycles. She travels in a Rolls-Royce and it is on the car-radio that Orphée hears the mysterious messages from the other world (such as "The bird sings with its fingers", "Silence goes faster backwards", "A single glass of water lights the world" and "Mirrors would do well to reflect more") which unknown to Orphée are sent out by Cégeste (Edouard Dermit), the young poet whose death he has witnessed. Similarly it is the bombed ruins of Saint-Cyr which serve as the "Zone", while distant train noises are employed to heighten its strangeness. The solidity of this world is disturbed by the delight Cocteau takes in the conjuring potentialities of the film medium. The method of access to the other world, by means of mirrors, necessitated a number of trick shots for which Cocteau used such devices as mercury tubs, plain glass substituted for mirrors, duplicate rooms and doubles. He also included a flight scene which made necessary the construction of some décor in false perspective, while the resuscitation of Cégeste entailed reverse projection. All these subterfuges, while in no way particularly advanced technically, contribute to the disturbing impact of the film.

Orphée is a film set apart from the works of its time and inevitably its production involved numerous difficulties. It is an intensely personal work and its creator has described it as the orchestration of a theme which twenty years before, in *Le Sang d'un Poète*, he had played with one finger. The poet Orphée reflects Cocteau himself in many ways, adored by the public and hated by his fellow poets, even being admonished with the words: "Etonnez-Nous." Cocteau claims to have avoided symbolism and as with Resnais's *L'Année Dernière à Marienbad* it is doubtless naive to seek too exact an interpretation. The film embodies Cocteau's personal mythology and conception of the poet as an exceptional being who has a unique and intimate relationship with death. Eternally self-preoccupied, Cocteau regarded the myth of Orpheus as *his* myth, for he felt himself to be a man with one foot in life and the other in death. For him the conflict of life and death is not a contrast of light and darkness but a matter of degrees of greyness and twilight merging into one another. The boundaries between the two are never drawn with exactitude — the Princess comes to watch Orphée asleep and the poet moves from this world to the next without pain or anguish. For a work dealing so largely with death *Orphée* is remarkably idyllic in tone. There is no sense of terror here, for death is a beautiful princess who can return the poet's love. There is no sign of physical struggle or decay, for Orphée remains handsome in death and his love for the Princess is never expressed on a physical level. Nor has death any irrevocability or awesomeness: the dead can be revived and the servants of death are often bungling and inefficient.

It is on the level of its mythology that *Orphée* must be judged. In his handling of the film medium Cocteau remains an amateur in the best sense of the word. The film is not without its defects: the transitions of mood are not always adequately handled (the farcical comedy of Eurydice's return from the Zone sits oddly in the film), the integration of Aglaonice and the Bacchantes into the modernisation of the myth is poor, and the whole handling of Eurydice's pregnancy is very weak in its use of dialogue clichés and facile symbolism. But despite these blemishes *Orphée* is a most remarkable and independent work which remained unique in the French cinema until Resnais and Robbe-Grillet created their no-man's land between life and death in *Marienbad* a dozen years later.

Orphée virtually completed Cocteau's work in the cinema and nine years passed before he returned to the studio to make **Le Testament d'Orphée** (1959) which is in many ways a summing up of his whole career. In this fable Cocteau himself appears as a traveller in time who enters our world to be met by a mysterious centaur and led to a gipsy cave where a picture of Cégeste is conjured from the flames. When the fragments of this are thrown into the sea, Cégeste himself emerges, carrying a flower which he gives to Cocteau. After trying unsuccessfully to paint it, Cocteau destroys the flower, then reassembles the fragments and at Cégeste's command sets off to take it to Minerva. After numerous encounters, including one with the Princess and Heurtebise from "Orphée" at a tribunal where he is accused of innocence and of meddling in a world where he does not belong (and incidentally is sentenced to life), Cocteau reaches Minerva who scorns his gift and transfixes him with a spear. He rises from the dead, however, and continues on his wanderings, finally vanishing into thin air with Cégeste. *Le Testament d'Orphée* abounds in allusions to Cocteau's earlier work and life. The references to the film *Orphée* will be clear from the above summary. Cocteau also meets the Sphinx and Jean Marais in the role of Oedipus and travels on the same boat as Isolde, while the smoke which comes from his mouth as he lies "dead" before Minerva recalls the statuary in *La Belle et la Bête*. On his travels he passes in front of his own mural of Judith and visits the Eglise St. Pierre which he decorated. Cocteau's adopted son Edouard Dermit reappears as Cégeste and others of his acquaintances ranging from Picasso to the bullfighter Luis Dominguin and Yul Brynner put in brief appearances. Jean Cocteau also reveals here to the greatest extent his delight in the conjuring possibilities of the cinema, the ability to move freely through time and space, or to perform (by means of reverse projection) such impossible feats as making a picture appear by rubbing it out or reassembling a shattered flower or creating a photograph from the flames. While the mythology of the film is sometimes obscure, there is no mistaking the poet's serenity and good nature, here emphasised by his own slightly awkward performance. The film abounds in quirky humour, such as the air hostess voice admonishing the waiting poet to fasten his safety belt (in four languages), or the intellectual lovers jotting down their thoughts and feelings between embraces.

JEAN COCTEAU occupies a unique position in the cinema. In a world peopled on the one hand by technicians with no need of self-expression and on the other by creators whose vision is expressed solely in film terms, Cocteau is an isolated figure, a man with impressive achievements in a wide range of media. The bulk of his work falls outside the scope of

Jean Cocteau appeared as the Poet who visits Minerva (Claudine Oger) in his own LE TESTAMENT D'ORPHÉE.

this study and here we are attempting to assess not the man in all his diversity but simply the films. The unevenness and variety of Cocteau's work as a whole is reflected in his work in the cinema: he has been connected with some of the cinema's masterpieces, such as *Orphée* and *Les Dames du Bois de Boulogne*, and also worked on films that are bad by any standards; he has directed films exploiting to the full the cinema's ability to treat what he once called "the frontier incidents between one world and another", and used the film camera simply to record versions of his own plays. While working as a scriptwriter he shared the common fate of all writers: dependence on the director for the success or failure of the film. His film adaptations of his own works vary according to the intrinsic worth of the originals, and his reputation as a film-maker rests essentially on three films, all of them original cinematic creations: *Le Sang d'un Poète* (1930), *Orphée* (1950) and *Le Testament d'Orphée* (1959). In these films Cocteau reveals his true status as a film-maker entirely free from the limitations of a conventional approach. These are personal works, filled with the director's own ideas, views and obsessions, but Cocteau is not an uncompromising hermit-like director in the manner of Robert Bresson. His art is wide enough to embrace stars and trick photography, not in the sense of concessions to the routine, but as essential elements in the spectacle: "It is not up to us to obey the public which does not know what it wants, but to compel the public to follow us. If it refuses we must use tricks: images, stars, décors and other magic lanterns, suitable to intrigue children and make them swallow the spectacle." It is this enthusiasm for devices to enchant an audience (visible in his early plays as much as in his films) that has given him a reputation of being a mere showman and led to criticism of his work as empty and pretentious.

Characteristic of Jean Cocteau's work, in the film and in the theatre, is the fusion of contrasting, even opposing elements. We find in his films a unique combination of the real and the unreal, seriousness and farce, personal obsession and antique myth. One of the reasons why Cocteau succeeded in creating an acceptable and absorbing fantasy world was his ability to make myth and reality intermingle. The description which he gave of the approach of Christian Bérard, his principal collaborator, is equally applicable to himself: "Bérard's death is irreparable. He was the only one to understand that vagueness is unsuitable to the world of the fairy-tale and that mystery exists only in precise things. He knew too that nothing is easier in film making than false fantasy. He avoided it with unerring grace." So it is that *La Belle et la Bête* is given an added dimension by the solid reality of the merchant's house and that in this film, and even more in *Orphée*, poetry is shown to derive from the ordinary and everyday. This applies as much to the visual style of these films as to their content. It was indeed the craftsmanship inherent in film making that attracted Cocteau to it: "My great discovery is that the cinematograph (Cocteau's term for the film as art, as opposed to the film as industry) is the refuge of craftsmanship." This was important for him because he senses in himself an "incredible indifference to the things of this world" and the cinema is a way of maintaining contact with the world of everyday reality: "The more manual work I have the more I like to think I am participating in worldly things and the more I work unceasingly at it, as a drowning man clings to a straw. That is why I entered the cinema whose work occupies every moment and retreat from the void where I am lost."

Cocteau was able to make films as naturally as he wrote plays or poems because he had always been an artist as well as a writer: "I am a draftsman. It is natural for me to see and hear what I write, to give it plastic form. When I make a film the scenes which I direct become for me animated pictures, a painter's arrangements." (In this connection it is interesting to note that *Le Sang d'un Poète* was originally to have been an animated cartoon). Cocteau has evolved his own theory of the film image, which as might be expected is the complete antithesis of that developed by the anti-theatrical Robert Bresson: "The cinematograph demands a syntax. This syntax is only obtained by the connection and impact of the images among themselves . . . My first concern, in a film, is to prevent the images from flowing, to oppose them, embed them and join them without harming their relief." Contrast and change are the recurring features of Cocteau's films. Never is one allowed to adopt a single way of looking or remain in one mood. In *La Belle et la Bête*, for instance, he adds farce and beauty, tragedy and trickery to the original

77

ingredients of bestiality and love. Cocteau followed the same principle in his treatment of the music Georges Auric has composed for his films. He rejects the conventional approach: "Nothing seems to me more vulgar than musical synchronisation in films. It is a further pleonasm . . . The only synchronisation that I like is accidental synchronisation, the effectiveness of which has been proved to me by innumerable examples." By this Cocteau means juggling with the musical score so that passages written for one scene in fact accompany another. Of *Orphée* Cocteau says "I used the most disrespectful liberties in relation to my collaborator. I recorded his music without the images and placed, for example, the scherzo written for the comic scene of the return home on the pursuit across the deserted town."

It is doubtless futile to attempt a rational interpretation of the symbolism in Cocteau's films. His whole approach defies logical analysis and much of his imagery is based on personal symbolism and private associations. This is a closed world to which one must surrender totally or not at all. If one is not to regard his whole work as a mere charade one must accept Cocteau's conception of the poet as a supreme being, living outside time and in proximity to death. To be moved one must accept too Cocteau's eternal self-preoccupation and his idyllic conception of life. Though death is the central theme of all his major films there is no sense of conflict or suffering. As the transformation of the Beast into a glorified version of Avenant removes all the emotional conflicts in *La Belle et la Bête*, so too the horror of death is masked by its depiction as a beautiful woman in *Orphée* (recalling Bérard's remark that "Death must be the most elegant woman in the world because she cares for nobody but herself"). Death in Cocteau's world has no finality: the poet in *Le Sang d'un Poète* commits suicide twice, Orphée is returned to life and humdrum happiness after being shot, Cocteau in *Le Testament d'Orphée* is raised from the dead after being slain by Minerva. All this is possible because the world of Cocteau is that of the dream. He has spoken of the importance of dreams in his life: "I begin to live intensely only when asleep and dreaming. My dreams are detailed and terribly realistic." Cocteau's films, for all their unevenness and reticence, are the cinema's most sustained attempt at capturing the reality of this unreal world.

3. Traditionalists

FOUR directors — Henri-Georges Clouzot, René Clément, Jacques Becker and Claude Autant-Lara — all of whom established themselves in the forties and have worked almost exclusively within the normal commercial framework of the film industry, may be said to dominate the French cinema in the first dozen years after the war and to set the trends which prevail. Each has stamped a clearly defined personality on his work and made a certain range of subject matter his own but in the works of their maturity they share a common dependence on scripts and script-writers. Clouzot, it is true, writes his own scenarios but, like Clément and Autant-Lara, he derives his material largely from adaptations of novels which may range from literary classics to detective stories but nonetheless emerge virtually indistinguishable from the scripting process. Only Becker worked extensively from original scripts (written, in his case, mostly with Maurice Griffe or Annette Wademant) but these, like the adaptations written by Clouzot and the prolific Aurenche and Bost, offer little that is revolutionary in dramatic form or construction. It is significant that two of these directors felt the need to escape from this type of film. During the last five years of his life Becker dreamed in vain of being given a little money, a cameraman and some Eastmancolor film which would allow him to emulate Flaherty and shoot what he called his "little Moroccan Nanook". Likewise Clouzot in 1950 turned down various offers in order to set out to make "Le Voyage au Brésil", which was to be an account of his discovery of Brazil (the homeland of his wife Véra), but this project too was never realised because of production difficulties.

René Clément ventured outside the studio to make the documentary *La Bataille du Rail* and capture the authentic settings of *Au delà des Grilles* and *Monsieur Ripois* but in general these four directors keep to the French tradition of studio work. Becker's comedies, for example, take place in an artificial, studio-contrived world, remote from the pressures of real life, and Clouzot rebuilds the settings of his films whether he is tackling the Paris of *Quai des Orfèvres* or the South America of *Le Salaire de la Peur*. Many of the finest films of these "traditionalist" directors have period settings which naturally entailed studio reconstruction: Clément's *Gervaise*, Becker's *Casque d'Or* and many of Autant-Lara's works, including *L'Auberge Rouge* and *Le Rouge et le Noir*. Settings are approached with a meticulous concern for detail and the aim is generally absolute authenticity, only Autant-Lara (himself trained as an art-director) experimenting with the symbolic use of deliberately unreal décor, most notably in *Marguerite de la Nuit*. For the other three it is realistic settings that are important: the hospitals and class-rooms of so many Clouzot films, the enclosed spaces for which Clément has such a predilection (the submarine of *Les Maudits* or the yacht in *Plein Soleil*), and the prison cell of Becker's *Le Trou*.

*　　*　　*

Craftsmanship is a constant feature of the work of all four directors but deep involvement with the characters is much rarer. Only Becker fills his films with real human warmth, for the preoccupations of the others — Clouzot's concern with suspense, Clément's with camera style, Autant-Lara's with the expression of his own idiosyncratic ideas — tend to give all but their best films a certain coldness which at times verges on academicism. This distance from the characters is not, however, accompanied by any critical concern with the state of postwar France. Only Autant-Lara is concerned with ideas and his targets are the traditional ones for a radical French intellectual — the Church, the Army and the Bourgeoisie — rather than specifically modern issues. In the late fifties the work of these four was less exciting as they succumbed to the temptations of colour, widescreen and international co-production. Hybrid works, like Clément's *Barrage contre le Pacifique* and Becker's *Aventures d'Arsène Lupin*, were produced which revealed all too clearly the conflicting demands of differing national audiences. But in the sixties there have been more encouraging signs. Shortly before his death in 1960 Becker completed *Le Trou*, one of his finest works, and in 1961 Autant-Lara finally contrived to make *Tu ne tueras Point*. Clément has achieved considerable success with the experiments in brilliant camerawork undertaken with the photographer Henri Decaë, and Clouzot's *L'Enfer*, so unfortunately abandoned in 1964, promised to be a work of great visual impact.

The future of the three survivors of this group is difficult to assess at this stage but it is likely that they still have some surprises in store for us.

*　　*　　*

HENRI-GEORGES CLOUZOT was virtually blacklisted at the end of the war because of the scandal surrounding his second feature film. After ten years of work as script-writer and assistant, and a feature début with a skilful but routine thriller, Clouzot had made *Le Corbeau*, without question one of his three finest films, but one which draws a very black picture of French provincial life. It was alleged, without foundation, that this film, produced by the Nazi-run Continental company, had been distributed in Germany as anti-French propaganda. As a result, the film was banned after the Liberation and its director was unable to find work until 1947.

The film which Clouzot made in order to re-establish himself after a four year break was in the same pessimistic manner as *Le Corbeau*, but this time the form chosen was the harmless one of a detective thriller, based remotely on a novel by S. A. Steeman, who had already provided material for Clouzot's first film. **Quai des Orfèvres** (1947) is remarkable above all for the masterful realism with which Clouzot sketched in the background of police station and shabby music halls. The film concerns a young couple (played by Suzy Delair and Bernard Blier) whose marriage is already precarious because of the wife's ambitions as a singer and is further threatened when both are unwittingly involved in a murder. The plot itself is not altogether convincing, but Clouzot handles the various threads in an adept fashion and a considerable amount of suspense is created. The dialogue throughout is witty and pointed. Louis Jouvet has one of his best parts as the detective who works, like Maigret, more by examining people than with conventional clues such as finger-prints. The atmosphere of the Quai des Orfèvres — the French equivalent of Scotland Yard — is beautifully caught, as in the small incident where the hero Maurice has to sign a statement which when translated into police jargon seems false since it lacks all the shades of meaning which are important to him. Clouzot knew from personal experience the music-hall background and was able to reproduce its atmosphere authentically in his studio-built sets. Despite the nominally happy ending, the picture Clouzot draws of this milieu is most depressing. The couple's surroundings are thoroughly sordid: Maurice has given up a serious musical training to become his wife's accompanist, only to find that she is prepared to make use of her charms to help her own career. Their friend Dora is an unhappy Lesbian photographer, and the murder victim, Brignon (played by Charles Dullin), is a rich old lecher with a taste for pornographic photographs of prostitutes. Moments like Maurice's attempted suicide are handled with pitiless realism, and typical of Clouzot's approach to his characters is the image used to represent the lovemaking of Maurice and Jenny: a pan of milk boiling over on the stove.

Manon (1949) is a much more ambitious work than *Quai des Orfèvres*. For one thing it is based on a classic eighteenth century novel by the Abbé Prévost, "Manon Lescaut", and not on a mere detective story. Clouzot, however, reveals in his approach as little real respect for the original as in his previous film and deliberately runs the risk of producing a hybrid work by bringing "Manon" up to date. The choice of parallels for the original settings is audacious and Clouzot gives us glimpses of a number of facets of recent history rarely shown on the screen (the Liberation, the Paris black-market, and the illegal emigration of Jews to Palestine). But this multiplicity of settings does in some ways detract from the impact of the film which is more diffuse and less gripping than most of Clouzot's work. Occasionally, however, the settings do come alive and make a positive contribution: the church that witnesses the birth of the very profane love of Manon and Robert, and the train that takes the couple as fugitives to Marseilles. *Manon* remains a key work in Clouzot's development for it is his most outspoken treatment of love. Manon and Robert Des Grieux are perhaps the least sympathetic couple in the history of the French cinema. Manon (played by the sixteen year old Cécile Aubry) is completely lacking in moral sense. She prostitutes herself to buy dresses and jewels without feeling in any way unfaithful to Robert. Her love is indeed the true centre of her life and when her lover is on the run she abandons everything without a second thought so as to be near him. Robert (ably played by Michel Auclair) is totally dominated by Manon. For her he leaves his post in the Resistance, condones her prostitution and becomes involved in the Black Market with her brother (Serge Reggiani) whom he eventually kills. The film's theme is summed up in the words of Manon when she comes face to face with Robert in the brothel where she works: "Nothing is sordid when two people love each other". For lovers like these, death is the true culmination and this they find in the deserts of Palestine.

After *Manon* Clouzot contributed an episode **Le Retour de Jean** to the film *Retour à la Vie* (1949) which contained other sketches by André Cayatte, Georges Lampin and Jean Dréville. His next work **Miquette et sa Mère** (1949) was adapted from a vaudeville farce by Flers and Caillavet but since Clouzot lacks the charm and delicacy which had ensured René Clair and Claude Autant-Lara success with similar material, the film remains one of his minor works. In 1950 Clouzot went with his young South American wife to Brazil, hoping to combine their honeymoon there with a new film, but his project "Le Voyage au Brésil" came to nothing. Clouzot did, however, produce a book, "Le Cheval des Dieux", from his experiences, and was no doubt helped in the creation of the setting and atmosphere of his next film.

The making of **Le Salaire de la Peur** (1953) was accompanied by numerous production difficulties, but the result was one of the director's finest and most successful films. It is set in a hot, squalid little South American town called Las Piedras, and revolves round a group of European layabouts trapped there. Their situation seems as hopeless as that facing Jean Gabin in the pre-war *Pépé le Moko* and *Le Jour se lève*, but then a means of escape is offered. The American oil company that virtually owns the town needs four men to drive two lorries loaded with nitro-glycerine three hundred miles to a burning oil well. The chances of success are slim, but the reward is high — two thousand dollars apiece. Under the strain of the nightmare journey which occupies half the film's time, the characters of the four men are laid bare. The horror and tension are maintained throughout, up to the last ironic crash on the mountainside when the sole survivor meets his death. The source of *Le Salaire de la Peur* was a best-selling novel by Georges Arnaud, but Clouzot has completely reshaped the material in cinematic terms. The construction is such that the film may be divided into two parts: the first hour or so which deals with the background of Las Piedras and the second half which is taken up almost entirely with the ride itself. The lounging, sponging group of polyglot outcasts is neatly characterised and the impossibility of escape for these men made clear. These early scenes are handled without undue exoticism and a very convincing semi-tropical atmosphere is built up, although the film was in fact shot near Nîmes in Southern France. The contrast between the helplessness of these men and the natives on the one hand, and the arrogant power of the oil company on the other, is a clear comment on U.S. policies in South America. During the ride itself the personalities of the four principal characters, all excellently played, are sharply differentiated. There is the blond narcissistic Bimba (Peter van Eyck), proud and completely fearless, whose last act is to shave. His partner, the ebullient Italian Luigi (Folco Lulli) manages to retain his good humour despite the danger. He has preferred the possibility of a quick death from the T.N.T. to the slow death which will be his fate in Las Piedras. These two, seemingly the more efficient team, are killed when success seems to be within their grasp. Greater attention is paid to the two Frenchmen who form the second crew. At first, Mario (Yves Montand) is taken in by the old man's tough act but when the tension rises it is Jo (Charles Vanel) who cracks up. Despite Mario's initial anger and contempt when his illusions are shattered, the two do find something like friendship during Jo's last agonised hours. It is this comradeship of men facing death that makes this film Clouzot's most favourable comment on human nature. Elsewhere the blackness of his view of life is complete; here there is even a touch of sentimentality in the two men's nostalgia for Paris. If the opening sequences show Clouzot's ability to fix his characters in their settings, the later scenes show an unrivalled mastery in the creation of suspense. By using the very simplest means with the utmost skill and concentration, he plays on the audience's nerves. Most of the time the camera is focussed on the faces of the characters as they tackle a succession of hazards — a rutted stretch of roadway, a rotting bridge, a huge rock that has to be dynamited and (for the Frenchmen) the oil-filled pool left by the explosion of the preceding lorry. In terms of sheer construction and vigorous narration the film is a

"Concentration on moments of horror and brutality": Charles Vanel in Clouzot's LE SALAIRE DE LA PEUR (above). The natural outcome of passion in Clouzot's world: Brigitte Bardot in LA VÉRITÉ (below).

masterpiece: its tension, relieved only by a few necessary touches of humour, is utterly unrelenting.

Le Salaire de la Peur marks the climax of Clouzot's career, and he has experienced difficulty in making further progress. Ill-health prevented him from directing his next script, *Si tous les gars du monde*, in which it is probable that the affirmative qualities of *Le Salaire de la Peur* would have been even more evident. This film, which shows the stricken members of the crew of a Breton Trawler saved by the united efforts of amateur radio enthusiasts throughout the world, was eventually directed by Christian-Jaque, but with so little conviction that the necessary tension was never built up.

Les Diaboliques (1955) is a difficult film to discuss or even to treat seriously, since unlike Clouzot's earlier work it is no more than a wholly artificial exercise in suspense and audience manipulation. The opening sequences, however, are admirably done: the setting of a shabby, provincial private school is thoroughly and methodically built up and the tensions between the three principal characters revealed. Michel Delasalle, the school's headmaster (Paul Meurisse), bullies all around him, and his forceful, business-like mistress (Simone Signoret), smarting under a final humiliation, persuades his rich and ailing wife (Véra Clouzot) to join her in murdering him. The committing of this murder and the subsequent dumping of the body into the school swimming pool are shown in the most convincing and realistic detail. Then, inexplicably, things start going wrong: a boy claims to have seen the dead man, the pool is found to be empty, his suit is returned from the cleaners. So far suspense has been created by happenings which are quite within the bounds of possibility, but the virtuoso display of plot-twisting with which Clouzot resolves the film in the last ten minutes (the whole thing turns out to be a plot by husband and mistress to kill the wife, who has a weak heart) destroys the credibility of all that has gone before. If the film is reseen after the ending is known, it emerges as a dishonest and misleading piece of work. As a mere empty shocker the film succeeds but such a facile success is unworthy of Clouzot's great talents.

Le Mystère Picasso (1956) forms an interlude in Clouzot's creative work, being an hour-long study, in colour, of the painter Pablo Picasso. By means of the use of special ink and semi-transparent paper we are able to view the development of Picasso's drawings and paintings from the reverse side without seeing either painter or brush. The result is fascinating: the pictures grow, change and multiply as Picasso pursues his inspiration, is sidetracked, retraces his steps or leads the work to a successful conclusion. Clouzot eschews camera tricks and commentary, relying entirely on the pictures themselves (beautifully photographed by Claude Renoir) and on Georges Auric's exceedingly expressive music.

Les Espions (1957), like *Les Diaboliques*, reveals a willingness on Clouzot's part to apply his talents to unsuitable themes. Like the earlier film it shows the intrusion of the unreal into a French provincial setting and its lack of success may again be attributed to the fact that the carefully documented shabbiness of its milieu (in this case a psychiatric clinic) is ruined by the absurdities of the plot. The characters, played by an international cast including Peter Ustinov, Sam Jaffe and Curt Jurgens, are openly caricatures and the dividing line between the spies and the insane is never clear. The film mixes real violence and torture with moments of pure farce and the result is unsatisfying in that it lacks both logic and tension.

In **La Vérité** (1960) Clouzot turned, as in *Manon*, to the problems of amoral youth, taking as his heroine this time a popular star and sex-symbol, Brigitte Bardot. The atmosphere of *La Vérité* is set in the ominous opening shots of the heroine's prison and the form of the film is a long murder trial into which are interspersed flashbacks of the accused's past. The construction allows Clouzot to employ one of his favourite plot devices: the contrast of two sharply distinct worlds, in this case the law courts and the coffee bars. In 1959 the director had reported a trial for a Parisian newspaper and the courtroom scenes have an authentic ring about them. The opposing counsel — Paul Meurisse as the prosecutor and Charles Vanel as the defence advocate — are beautifully conceived and well acted parts. Clouzot uncovers the mutual understanding and comradeship beneath the violent histrionics and drives home his point that all their arguments serve only to distort the truth about the heroine, Dominique. It is left to the flashbacks to show us what really happened. Dominique (Brigitte Bardot) attracts Gilbert (Sami Frey), her sister's

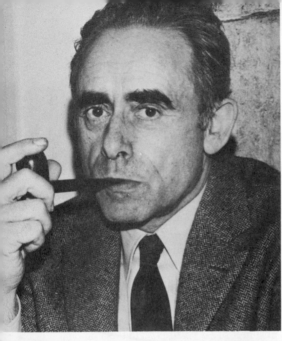

Henri-Georges Clouzot (left), and below, Laurent Terzieff and Elisabeth Wiener in *LA PRISONNIERE*, directed by Clouzot.

serious-minded boy friend, who has ambitions to be a conductor. Their mutual love does not give them lasting happiness for, while her love deepens, his affection dies as he is revolted by her casual attitude to sex. Eventually he makes it clear to her that their relationship means little to him. In despair and hardly aware of what she is doing, Dominique shoots him and finds herself on a charge of premeditated murder. As the trial nears its climax, she despairs of ever being understood and commits suicide. There is much that is characteristic of Clouzot in *La Vérité*: the insight into the workings of justice, the concept of love whereby each partner in turn humiliates the other, the violent deaths of the main protagonists and the claustrophobic atmosphere of the courtroom. But the film has serious weaknesses: the script, on which four writers collaborated with Clouzot, is too glib, the handling of flashbacks pedestrian in the context of the modern cinema, and there are a number of cases of over-emphasis (notably the thundering music that accompanies Dominique's last visit to Gilbert). If the performance of Brigitte Bardot is excellent, the whole conception of Sami Frey's part is weak and he never convinces either as lover or conductor. *La Vérité* restored Clouzot's commercial reputation but does not mark any advance in his artistic achievement.

In 1964, after many months of preparation, Clouzot embarked on a new film, **L'Enfer**, which was to be a study of jealousy and in which the director, intent on achieving unique visual effects, planned to employ no less than three directors of photography — Claude Renoir, Armand Thirard and Andréas Winding. But the production was dogged by misfortune. First the star, Serge Reggiani, fell ill and then, when shooting began, Clouzot himself was struck down by a heart attack, with the result that the whole project had to be abandoned. A further four years passed before he completed a new feature, **La Prisonnière** (1968), and even then, because of his ill-health, the film was interrupted for several months in the course of production. The subject is a characteristic one—the corruption of an avant-garde painter's wife by a perverted amateur photographer—and approached with all Clouzot's customary directness: "Perversion exists and to describe it in its most crushing and tragic form I had to go as far as possible without being afraid of traumatising the audience." From his actors, Laurent Terzieff and a newcomer Elisabeth Wiener, the director was able to obtain performances of great exactitude and power while the film's final sequence—seven hundred shots contained in a mere seven minutes of screen time—allowed him to experiment with photographic technique and visual effect in a virtually abstract way.

HENRI-GEORGES CLOUZOT is perhaps the most forceful of those directors who made their débuts in the forties. His personality is stamped on every aspect of his work — on the material, settings, acting and structure. The characteristics of his approach are an extremely pessimistic view of the world, a ruthlessness and significant lack of humour. It is this latter that differentiates him most strongly from his only serious rival as master of the thriller genre — Alfred Hitchcock. The world of Clouzot's films is one where beauty and tenderness have no place and even love and friendship are rare. It is not an unemotional world, but the passion is of a kind where one partner completely dominates the other. Whenever he probes the characters in his films, he uncovers some unsavoury truth: ambition, lust, hatred or cowardice. The natural outcome of all this is violence and all Clouzot's films contain scenes of murder, suicide or, at least, unnatural death.

Since Clouzot is interested above all in the violence of life, his typical mode of expression is the thriller. Most of his films are adapted from bestselling novels and it is significant that his one attempt at filming a work of literature, *Manon*, is only a partial success. Clouzot was a scriptwriter in the thirties and he is the principal author of all his scripts. This writing ability gives him the freedom to reshape the material he chooses, often in a drastic way. Normally he retains from the original novel little more than the central idea and the basis of the characters, conceiving his script entirely in cinematic terms. The combination of writing and directing makes Clouzot's films unmistakeably his own in style, but still one hesitates to call him a true creator. The nature of his material is a definite limitation and generally he makes no attempt to widen the scope and significance of his films. The traces of social criticism in his works — the attacks on U.S. colonialism in *Le Salaire de la Peur* and on the deficiencies of the French legal system in *Quai des Orfèvres* or *La Vérité*, for instance—remain marginal. Moreover the extreme pessimism of Clouzot's attitude to life and his willingness to sacrifice the truth of setting and character to suspense make his moral judgements suspect.

Clouzot's settings are the conventional ones of the thriller — Parisian music halls, South American slums and common-place provincial towns, the police station and the law court. To all of these he brings a fresh visual imagination and all he fills with enormous vigour and vitality. Normally he works within the studios; he built the Paris of *Quai des Orfèvres* just as he was to reconstruct, near Nîmes, the South America of *Le Salaire de la Peur*. His approach to this studio work is as minutely realistic and as meticulous as that of Jacques Becker. He has the gift of choosing the exact detail to establish a particular atmosphere and has never been concerned with what is merely picturesque or extraneous to the plot. Although the authentic and totally convincing description of a shabby location is one of his greatest talents, Clouzot has also a definite liking for the unreal, and this finds its clearest expression in *Les Diaboliques* and *Les Espions*. Of the latter he said: "For several years I have wanted to adapt a book by Kafka, either "The Trial" or "The Castle" but I have never been able to find a solution . . . There is an anti-logical strain in Kafka that attracts me enormously. Nightmares follow me in real life. I like to dream and remember my dreams."

The meticulousness Clouzot brings to his settings is matched by his ruthless treatment of his actors. He will go to any lengths to get precisely the results he needs. There is a story that to capture exactly the reactions of people forced to eat bad fish in *Les Diaboliques*, he obtained some, made his actors consume it and trained his cameras on them as they did so. Whether or not this is true, Clouzot is prepared to drive his actors to the limit, as their testimonies confirm. Gérard Séty's account of his first day's shooting for *Les Espions* (his first film) is typical: "He didn't say very much to me: and almost immediately we embarked upon a complex sequence. After I had said three words of one of my lines he shouted, "Cut". We started again: and again he stopped me. After ten starts and ten stops, I could no longer think straight and was a bundle of nerves. With a wry smile, Clouzot consoled me: "Now the way you feel at the moment is exactly the feeling I want you to get over on the screen." I wiped the perspiration off my brow, and *Les Espions* had started."

Simone Signoret, who has worked with many of the finest French directors, had this to say of Clouzot: "He is concerned with every detail, almost to an obsession. He cannot work in peace. He has to work in a constant *ambiance* of crisis. He has to be furious, he has to be depressed, he has to be sad. And he expects all his artists and technicians to share his sorrows completely. It is very tiring. Besides that he is tyrannical. He does not ask you to do things, he demands that you do things. It is no use your trying to explain that you would prefer to do something another way. He tells you, "Do what I tell you and shut up" . . . Clouzot does not really respect actors. He claims he could make anyone act." Clouzot is remarkably successful in this latter respect; almost all his films show a high standard of performance and a remarkable evenness of quality from actors of very varied talents.

The actual shooting of a Clouzot film is always preceded by a long period of preparation during which the details are worked out: "Every phrase is at first in my head. I have a fear, almost a panic, of the empty white page. I cannot write until I know everything. I think of the images and the dialogue together and then, when I have reached the end of the story, I make a copy of it and dictate the dialogue and then work over the typed copy." The improvisation favoured by some of the newer directors is the exact antithesis of Clouzot's approach: he works out virtually every movement of the actors and the camera before setting foot in the studio. By means of this preparation Clouzot is able to emphasise to the full the conflicts and contrasts that give his work its exceptional vitality. He has a taste for contrasting various milieux — the police station and the music hall in *Quai des Orfèvres*, the courtroom and Dominique's haunts in *La Vérité* — and different tones: for example, the real and the unreal, farce and tragedy are mixed in *Les Diaboliques* and *Les Espions*. The same principle of contrast is the basis of his photographic style: "For me, I repeat, the great rule is to push the contrasts as far as they will go, the dramatic highlights being separated by "neutral zones". To move the spectator I always aim at emphasising the chiaroscuro, opposing light and shade. It is for this reason that my films have been criticised as oversimplifications." Clouzot's visual style is bare and probing and has certain affinities with that of Luis Buñuel, particularly in the concentration on moments of horror and brutality, of which the suicide attempt of Maurice in *Quai des Orfèvres* is a fine example. Like Buñuel, Clouzot aims at making his shots telling rather than beautiful. He has found excellent support in this from his habitual director of photography, Armand Thirard, who in his work with Clouzot avoids the prettifying of settings which is so characteristic of his work with Roger Vadim.

The fact that his films are planned as a whole and almost all the details worked out beforehand allows Clouzot the opportunity to give his films that firm dramatic construction, which is both their greatest strength and potential weakness. In *Quai des Orfèvres* this thoroughness allowed him to manipulate his quite complicated plot to create uncertainty in true detective story fashion, but in this film the plot remains secondary to the examination of character and milieu. In *Le Salaire de la Peur* the balance of character and suspense is more equal: the four men's perilous journey serves both to spotlight their characters (by showing them at moments of extreme stress) and also to create an overwhelming feeling of tension among the audience. Since *Les Diaboliques*, however, Clouzot has shown a willingness to allow this suspense element to predominate, and character is distorted to accommodate the surprising twists of the narrative. This concentration on dramatic form, which at its lowest is the sacrificing of everything to the exigencies of the plot, has also been accompanied by an increasing lack of subtlety: the later Clouzot tends to hammer home his points more in the manner of André Cayatte, whereas previously he was content to suggest and hint. Clouzot remains, however, one of the more important of French directors. The vitality of his work is a reflection of Clouzot's own character. The four years he spent helpless in a sanatorium in the thirties have left him with an extreme pessimism about human life and an urge to dominate that drives him to bend every aspect of his films to his own will. While these two qualities give his best work its overwhelming force, they can also result in the air of contrivance and artificiality which mars some of his later work and puts him out of sympathy with many of the younger film-makers.

*   *   *

93

RENÉ CLÉMENT made his début as a feature director only after the war, having preferred to make short documentaries rather than features on which he would have been merely a technician. He came to the cinema with clear ideas about the need for documentary realism and the use of natural settings and his first film, **La Bataille du Rail** (released in 1946) was both a personal work and a uniquely powerful account of one aspect of the Resistance. Scripted with the aid of the novelist Colette Audry, this film belongs to the difficult genre of fictionalised documentary. It was based on actual events and Clément used mostly railwaymen, supported by a few professional actors, to tell his story. He succeeds admirably in capturing the atmosphere of the Resistance without falling into the trap of false heroics. The material is soberly handled and the various sequences excellently constructed, particularly impressive being the derailment and the scene where the engine-drivers sound their whistles in protest at the execution of the Resistance men. Such passages raise the film above mere factual reportage and indeed it constitutes a remarkable début, though its affirmation and glorification of heroism are not typical of the later Clément. *La Bataille du Rail* is a work of the stature of Roberto Rossellini's *Paisa*, but unlike the Italian film it did not herald the arrival of a new realist movement. Producers seemed wary of subjects treating the immediate past, and most of those films which do deal with war and resistance are best forgotten.

That same year René Clément worked on two other films to which, however, he made only a very small contribution. First he was "technical collaborator" for *La Belle et la Bête* (1946), which belongs entirely to its author, Jean Cocteau. Then Clément worked with the author-actor Noël-Noël on **Le Père Tranquille** (1946). Though he was nominally director of this film — a minor work inspired by the Resistance — he contributed no more than his technical knowledge and skill. Noël-Noël, who played the hero, a quiet little insurance man who is secretly head of a Resistance group, filled the film with his own charm, quiet humour and distaste for disagreeable realities.

Les Maudits (1947), Clément's second personal work, was a further war film, concerned this time with a submarine filled with leading Nazis and collaborators which sets out from Oslo shortly before the fall of

Berlin to continue the fight in South America. The mutual hatred and contempt which grows up among these men during their confinement are observed by a kidnapped French doctor. After the submarine has been unable to land in South America the tensions increase and the Nazis kill themselves or each other. The climax comes when the S.S. leader on board sinks a German tanker (which has provided them with fuel), in order to prevent it falling into Allied hands, although he knows that the war is over. At last only the doctor is left alive, alone on the drifting submarine. *Les Maudits*, which is the first of Clément's bi-lingual productions, shows the director's impressive technical command. To ensure authenticity he had an exact replica of the submarine built within the studio and set his director of photography, Henri Alekan, innumerable problems (resolved most triumphantly in the long back-tracking shot that accompanies the doctor's first entry into the submarine). But the script, by Clément and Jacques Rémy with dialogue by Henri Jeanson, is weak and rhetorical and the characterisation never rises above the conventional.

Au Delà des Grilles (1949) was the first of Clément's films to be made in Italy (where it was known as *Le Mure di Malapurga*) and aside from its intrinsic worth the film is interesting as an amalgam of two distinct modes of expression. The original script was written by Cesare Zavattini and Suso Cecchi d'Amico, two key members of the Neo-Realist movement, and the most successful elements in the film are those which result from this collaboration and develop the documentary qualities of *La Bataille du Rail*. But the film also reflects the artificiality of the French "film noir" tradition for the script was remodelled by the adaptors, Jean Aurenche and Pierre Bost, so that the film resembles in form the prewar films of Julien Duvivier and Marcel Carné. This similarity is accentuated by the appearance of Jean Gabin in the leading role of Pierre, a fugitive from justice, who enjoys a last few days of freedom in Genoa with a woman, Martha (Isa Miranda), and her young daughter, before the police net closes around him. The melodramatic elements of this plot (Pierre's past and Martha's marital problems) detract from the more interesting aspects of Pierre's impact on the woman and her daughter and undermine Clément's otherwise sensitive direction. This latter is shown best in the discreet use of symbolism (the bars keeping Pierre from the ships and freedom, the love scene of Pierre and Martha which seems to offer liberation and takes place in the open air overlooking the sea) and in the way Clément has taken his camera out into the streets of Genoa so that the tenements, trams and streets have absolute authenticity.

Le Château de Verre (1950), which followed, was yet another film handicapped from the start by an uninteresting plot, taken this time from a best seller by Vicki Baum. Clément attempted to compensate for this weakness with a brilliant visual style and by experimenting with the film's time sequence, so that the heroine's final death in a plane crash is anticipated earlier in the film. Such experiments, however, did not satisfy the critics and tended to upset the film's audience.

Clément returned to the subject of war and to his best form with **Jeux Interdits** (1952), made away from the studios and without star actors. The script, by Jean Aurenche and Pierre Bost from a novel by François Boyer, dealt with the war obliquely, seeing it through the eyes of two children. After a strikingly edited opening sequence showing the machine-gunning of a column of refugees, the film concentrates on a little Parisian girl, Paulette, whose parents are killed in the attack, and on Michel, the younger son of the peasant family which adopts her. The film draws us into their secret world, where, away from adult eyes but influenced by the carnage all about them, they build a cemetery for dead animals. They devote all their time and care to searching for dead animals and obtaining crosses for their graves, until the idyll is destroyed and Paulette handed over to the care of the Red Cross. The adult world is caricatured, as we see it through the eyes of two puzzled, uncomprehending children. Paulette and Michel, on the other hand, are observed with real sympathy and understanding as, despite their differences in background, they grow closer and closer together and retreat more and more into their fantasy world. Clément has drawn from his two young players Brigitte Fossey and Georges Poujouly performances of great naturalness. His mastery of technique has always been assured and here he recreates the children's world and their growing obsession with death strikingly through the images. He is helped too by a sensitive guitar accompaniment by Narciso Yepes.

Jeux Interdits remains Clément's most satisfying film but it did not

Above: the secret world of two small children: Brigitte Fossey and Georges Poujouly in René Clément's JEUX INTERDITS. Below, "The teeming world of late nineteenth century Paris": Maria Schell in Clément's GERVAISE.

achieve, initially at any rate, real commercial success in France and the director's next film was again made abroad. This time Clément, undeterred by his own inability to speak English, came to this country to make **Monsieur Ripois** (1954). The film was shot in two language versions, the English one being issued under the title *Knave of Hearts*, and apart from Gérard Philipe in the title role, the cast was predominantly English. *Monsieur Ripois* is a sophisticated comedy telling of the adventures of a young Frenchman who fills the emptiness of his life in London with a succession of amorous conquests. Gérard Philipe gives a marvellously delicate performance as André Ripois, making him a most charming and convincing seducer but revealing also the complexities lying beneath the surface of this young man incapable of not telling lies. He is genuinely moving in the scenes where André is reduced to begging for a meal from a friendly prostitute. The film's flashback technique, whereby André gives an account of his four principal loves in an attempt to convince a fifth young woman of his sincerity, is most effective and the film has the neatly ironic ending so necessary in this type of comedy. The humour is beautifully judged and the film, though cynical, is always entertaining. The film's greatest merit was perhaps its treatment of the background: all the exterior shots were of real places, photographed on the streets and amid the crowds. The authenticity is aided by the fact that this is always a lived-in, everyday London, with none of those tourist shots of easily identifiable famous places which serve as background to so many films. Oswald Morris's photography here achieved a degree of realism unequalled in the British cinema of the fifties, but this film, which could have served as an inspiration to British directors, remained without any immediate successors. The film is unique too in Clément's work, and when he made his next film in France, the director returned to the studio reproduction of reality.

Gervaise (1956) was from an adaptation by Aurenche and Bost of Emile Zola's novel "L'Assommoir". The scriptwriters have had to compress and to some extent simplify the original novel and the emphasis has been shifted, as the change of title suggests, from the problem of alcoholism to the fate of the individual characters. The film concentrates on the tragedy of Gervaise — her early love affair, her rivalry with

Virginie, her disastrous marriage to Coupeau, the destruction of all her hopes in Coupeau's wrecking of the shop and her final decline. To accentuate this tragedy, Clément shows us in the film's later scenes Gervaise's daughter Nana who observes her mother's degradation and seems doomed to follow her footsteps. This is Clément's only attempt at a period film and one of the things that attracted him to the story was its possible contemporary application: "*Gervaise* is not isolated to its period. I can take you to a Coupeau house in about ten different parts of Paris and you will find all the characters. This relevancy attracted me." His method of approach is absolute fidelity to detail in the reconstruction of the period settings, and the result is a completely convincing reproduction of Zola's world. This concern with detail does not, however, prevent the story from coming alive and the film has a succession of superbly vivid scenes, among which the visit to the Louvre, Gervaise's party and Coupeau's final destruction of the shop, the climax of the whole film, stand out. Nor does Clément show squeamishness in portraying the horror of his story: all the degradation is there, from women wrestling furiously to the drunken Coupeau lying in his own vomit. Clément has sought realism too in the conception of his characters and here François Périer's playing of the alcoholic Coupeau is outstanding. The one flaw is the miscasting of Maria Schell in the title role. She is altogether too light-weight an actress for the part of Gervaise and her mannered playing disturbs the tone of the film. The other characters are well drawn, Suzy Delair is excellent as the vengeful and unforgiving Virginie and the minor parts — Lantier, Gourget, the neighbours — are all admirably sketched in, while the child Nana is completely convincing.

Despite the quality and success of this film, it was six years before Clément worked in the French studios again. In the meantime he made three other films, one on location for Dino de Laurentiis and the other two in Italy itself. **Barrage contre le Pacifique** (1958) was an international co-production shot in Thailand with a mixed cast of Italians (Silvana Mangano and Alida Valli) and Americans (Anthony Perkins, Jo Van Fleet, Richard Conte). The script, adapted by Clément and Irwin Shaw from Marguerite Duras's novel, dealt superficially with a number of themes which really needed treatment at greater depth. The two principal threads of the plot: a woman's unceasing struggle against hostile natural forces, culminating in the typhoon which brings all her efforts to nought; and the impact of a corrupt society on two adolescents hitherto living isolated from the world in incestuous closeness, run parallel without ever achieving real unity.

In **Plein Soleil** (1959) René Clément appears to have attempted to come to terms with the new generation, using scriptwriter Paul Gégauff and director of photography Henri Decaë. The film is no more than a thriller, ingenious but unconvincing and lacking in real suspense. None of the characters come alive and the plot, based on envy, murder and impersonation, needs the zest and invention of a Hitchcock if it is to be made acceptable. The most promising clash of personality — that between the rich and arrogant Philip (Maurice Ronet) and Tom Ripley (Alain Delon) who intends to kill him and take his place — is not developed. Instead Clément offers only vast quantities of Mediterranean sunshine, elegant colour photography, some striking shots, mostly of irrelevant detail, and a fine surprise ending.

Quelle Joie de Vivre (1961) which followed, is again a story of pretended identity, set this time in Rome in 1922, a the time of rivalry and violence between fascists and anarchists. The hero, Ulysse, falls in love with the daughter of an anarchist and to win her pretends to be a celebrated bomb-thrower. The film traces the ensuing confusions and the hero's gradual progress to self-awareness. *Quelle Joie de Vivre*, a further attempt at comedy, is in the tradition of René Clair's *A Nous la Liberté*. It is handled with verve and technical brilliance and the period detail is skilfully caught, though it is doubtful whether Clément has sufficient real comic talent to control a plot that veers from burlesque to near tragedy.

In 1963 Clément returned to French studios and to the Occupation period that had given him two of his greatest successes with **Le Jour et l'Heure.** This is the story of Thérèse, a woman from a wealthy middle-class background, who becomes involved in Resistance activities when she agrees to hide an American airman. During the flight to the Pyrenees which the two are compelled to take together, a deeper relationship between the two of them is born. The script, on which Clément worked with Roger Vailland, again touched on the problems of choice and freedom which had been at the root of the previous two films and Clément took considerable care with the reconstruction of the wartime atmosphere. As in *Monsieur Ripois*, Clément had to cope with the problems of a bilingual film as Simone Signoret who played Thérèse and Stuart Whitman, the airman, converse largely in English. He also continued his experiments in fluid camera technique with Henri Decaë.

Les Félins (1963) was a further international co-production, made in a bilingual version and starring two American actresses, Jane Fonda and Lola Albright, alongside Alain Delon. The hero, as so often in Clément's later work, is a man on the run who seems to have struggled to safety, only to be defeated by a cruel and ironic twist of fate. The plot is highly complex but scarcely convincing, though it furnishes Clément with some genuinely strange décor (the house which is for Delon at first a refuge, and later a prison) and occasions some virtuoso camerawork (Decaë once more). The result is a further *tour de force* of stylistic fireworks which reveals the director's great talent but never comes near to being a wholly satisfying work.

The climax of Clément's internationalism is furnished by **Paris brûle-t-il?** (1966), his epic account of the Liberation of Paris by the Allied forces. At least in the cut (but still two and a quarter hour long) version shown in this country, the film is agreeable and even mildly exciting but its focus is too wide and the problems and identities of its characters are too sketchily drawn for it to have any great impact. The technical work is excellent and the production values are good—plenty of tanks, lorries, troops, explosions and so on—but the interesting notion of presenting little men making history against the inclinations and aims of powerful generals and leaders is negated by the policy of having every part, even the smallest, played by an internationally known star. Instead of becoming a study of wartime strategy or a depiction of the shifting balance of power between the Germans on the one hand and the Allies and the Resistance on the other, *Paris brûle-t-il?* remains a mere parlour game inciting the spectator to guess the maximum number of star identities in the shortest possible time. A few actors—Gert Froebe as the German commander for instance—manage to create a genuine part for themselves, but most are mere type-cast figureheads. The overall effect of the film is also weakened by the fact that its attempts at creating suspense—typified by the questioning title—are nullified by our certainty that, however much Hitler may rant and rave, Paris will not burn.

If one had to pick one single director whose work would best reflect the various complex and contradictory tendencies of the French cinema in the last twenty years one's choice would fall inevitably on **RENÉ CLÉMENT.** Immediately after the war it was he who gave the French cinema one of its rare, authentically realistic works (*La Bataille du Rail*) thereby laying the foundation for a realist school that in fact never came into being. In the late forties he contributed a typical work (*Au delà des Grilles*) to the "film noir" continuation of the thirties trends, with Gabin as yet another fugitive from justice enjoying a last few hours respite. Some of Clément's best work was done in the early fifties when he worked with scriptwriters Aurenche and Bost on literary adaptations that are in the mainstream of the French cinema of the first postwar decade (*Jeux Interdits* and *Gervaise*), but he has also worked with writers as diverse as Henri Jeanson (Christian-Jaque's habitual dialoguist) and Paul Gegauff (who has collaborated extensively with Claude Chabrol.) *Barrage contre le Pacifique* in 1958 was a big budget international co-production, filmed in Thailand for an Italian producer with a largely American cast, and is typical of a certain tendency of the French cinema in the years immediately preceding the "Nouvelle Vague". During the fifties Clément worked both within the studios (on *Gervaise*) and on location (for *Monsieur Ripois*), in the latter case being a good five years ahead of his time. Whereas in his early films he had used traditional methods of photography with the lighting in the care of such experienced craftsmen as Louis Page and Robert Juillard, after 1959 Clément has pursued with Henri Decaë his own experiments in camera flexibility in a manner that parallels the approach of many of the newer directors. There is thus hardly a trend, old or new, to which he has not made a notable contribution.

While Clément's work is from this angle the very essence of the French postwar cinema, it also illustrates better than any other the dangers and temptations of internationalism in the cinema. From the Franco-German *Les Maudits* in 1947 to the Franco-American *Les Félins* in 1963 the director has shown a predilection for the bilingual film. Much of his work has been done for Italian producers (to whom he turned after his quarrel with the French backers of *Gervaise*) but he has also filmed in England, making two versions, French and English, of *Monsieur Ripois*. Though this varied international work is of considerable interest, it remains true that Clément's three finest films were all made in France. *La Bataille du Rail*, *Jeux Interdits* and *Gervaise* are deeply rooted in French life and history, depicting respectively: the world of the Resistance, of men fighting to maintain France's national honour; the timeless world of the peasant, hostile to all the intrusions of a central government be it French or German; and the teeming world of late-nineteenth century Paris with its poverty, slums and broken lives. Each of these worlds is treated by Clément with complete realism, so that every word and gesture is convincing, indeed *Gervaise* is a miracle of painstaking reconstruction. Pressing down on the characters is the reality of death: the execution that awaits the Resistance workers on their capture in *La Bataille du Rail;* the slaughter that grows to obsess the children of *Jeux Interdits;* the madness and delirium preceding the death of an alcoholic in *Gervaise*. In this way the experience mirrored in these films is heightened to near-tragedy, while their dramatic force is created by the contrast of the vitality of the characters with the fate which weighs down upon them.

These three films have a satisfying unity which does not exist, however, in the remainder of Clément's work. True, it is possible to find certain recurrent themes, most notably a concern with the war (to which he returned in five features) and the figure of the fugitive (which emerges in some form or other in half-a-dozen of his films). Clément also reveals a consistent seriousness of mind so that even his comedies have sombre overtones: *Quelle Joie de Vivre*, for instance, is set in Italy in 1922, the year of Mussolini's march on Rome and *Monsieur Ripois* is both a diverting cynical comedy and the portrayal of a man's total moral collapse in a hostile city. Nevertheless Clément usually remains detached from the subject matter of his films and his scripts are quite often little more than the excuse for a stylistic exercise — in *Le Château de Verre*, *Plein Soleil* or *Les Félins* for example. It is more illuminating therefore to discuss stylistic features than thematic obsessions.

In all his best work Clément reveals the same obsession with the accuracy of every little detail as is shown by Clouzot and Becker. Of his approach to the nineteenth century settings of *Gervaise* he said: "Exactness must be a mania. One must not accept a hairstyle or a wallpaper that was not in existence at the time. The public does not always realise this, but knows subconsciously that it has not been cheated." The application of his approach to the characters is shown by Clément's account of how he fitted François Périer to his conception of the role of the alcoholic Coupeau in *Gervaise:* "I took François Périer to mental asylums and we saw many unfortunate creatures. We observed patients in delirious fits and took notes. Afterwards we asked: What do you feel? What do you remember? This might seem dreadful but it was necessary. It was only in that way that Périer could find his part: the way he made his eyelids droop, his way of speaking, of laughing, of being happy, of being irritable, of being casual." The same impulse to seek out the truth (which he has possessed since his days as a documentarist) has impelled Clément to make extensive use of real settings and locations. In *La Bataille du Rail* this was a basic requirement but even in the more artificial story of *Au delà des Grilles* the director managed to include some authentic shots of war-scarred Genoa. In *Monsieur Ripois* the picture of London as seen by a down-and-out is an integral part of the film, in a way quite revolutionary for its time. In *Les Maudits* (1947) Clément had to reproduce his submarine in the studio but for *Plein Soleil* (1959) he was able to use a real yacht and set his director of photography a whole host of problems by this desire for authenticity.

René Clément was trained as an architect and began his film career as a cameraman so it is not surprising that one of his principal concerns is with the film image. His visual sense never deserts him and occasionally indeed one feels that a shot was included less for telling dramatic quality than for its striking visual effect. Most of his works have sequences of striking imagery, never more apparent than when he is handling "thriller" material in a film like *Plein Soleil*. A constant preoccupation has been with the flexibility of his camera and he himself has said: "Every film I tell my director of photography that I want my camera to be weightless, whatever and wherever it may be, and I want it always to have as much suppleness as if it were constantly hand-held." This aspect is most clearly revealed in the four films which Clément has made since 1959 with Henri Decaë, but traces of it are to be found even in his earliest features. It is this fluency and movement that save Clément from the worst dangers of this concern with the image at the expense of the human being.

Clément's reputation as a "cold" director is not entirely unwarranted. His approach to character as typified by his handling of François Périer in *Gervaise*, tends to exclude the warmth which Becker, for instance, evinces, and in recent years he has shown an increasing willingness to use the plot as a mere prop for stylistic experiment. But his continued inventiveness and ability to create beautiful and memorable scenes keep him in the forefront of postwar French directors.

*   *   *

JACQUES BECKER was already an established director when the war ended. After eight years as assistant to Jean Renoir, Becker had directed three films during the Occupation: a conventional thriller in the American style *Dernier Atout* (1942), a peasant drama, *Goupi-Mains-Rouges* (1943) and *Falbalas* (directed in 1944 but not shown until after the Liberation) which was set in a Parisian fashion house. **Antoine et Antoinette** (1946) was ostensibly about a lost lottery ticket but in fact this served as little more than a pretext for Becker to give a sympathetic portrayal of the film's working class milieu and the young couple of the title, played by Roger Pigaut and Claire Mafféi. The misunderstandings, quarrels and reconciliations of this pair are treated with affectionate insight and a marked lack of sentimentality. The background of life in a Parisian suburb throbs with life and the various strands of the plot are admirably woven together, including a wedding party observed with a satiric eye worthy of René Clair himself. To capture this setting Becker has used a technique of accumulating a mass of tiny details (the film contains twice the normal number of individual shots). While the film makes its impact largely in visual terms there are occasional outstanding touches in the use of soundtrack too (the jangling chords produced by the piano tuner for instance as Antoine visits the lottery headquarters). *Antoine et Antoinette* has a limited scope — it ignores social questions and specifically postwar problems to concentrate entirely on the trivial and everyday — but it remains one of the director's most satisfying works.

Though Becker does not return to the working class setting of *Antoine et Antoinette*, the tone and manner of this film are carried forward into three other films in which the director explored Parisian characters and situations. In **Rendez-Vous de Juillet** (1949) Becker set out to examine postwar youth: "We are not concerned here with a sentimental film, a drama or an ordinary comedy. We are concerned rather with a real journey which will transport the spectator to an unknown setting and unknown characters. After the war which we have just undergone, *Rendez-Vous de Juillet* proposes to show the state of mind of the young people of today." The film deals with a group of young people, their friends, family backgrounds, ambitions and loves. At the centre of the film are five characters. Paul, Thérèse and Christiane all get their first acting chances; the first two succeed but the latter retains her part only by sleeping with the producer. Lucien and Roger, boy-friends of the two aspiring actresses, struggle to realise their ambitions by organising an expedition to the Congo, the one as ethnologist, the other as film cameraman. *Rendez-Vous de Juillet* is of necessity diffuse and loosely constructed, but it gives an honest and sympathetic view of youth. It does not put all the blame for their misdeeds on the young, indeed it includes some of Becker's most acid pictures of smugly successful bourgeois families. The characters are well differentiated and ably acted by a number of young actors, among them Daniel Gélin and Maurice Ronet. The tone is essentially lighthearted and Becker shows a positive enjoyment of the noisy exuberance of his youthful characters.

The third film of Becker's Parisian series, **Edouard et Caroline** (1951), is completely successful on its own level of light comedy. Scripted by Annette Wademant, the film is virtually plotless but Becker seems to delight in the challenge of making something memorable from such thin material. *Edouard et Caroline* combines a study of young married life with an amused and slightly ironic look at high society. The young people are beautifully played by Anne Vernon and Daniel Gélin. The handling of this relationship is full of neat, unemphatic touches and precise observation of the little differences which the tension of the forthcoming big occasion will raise into a full-scale quarrel. But the threat of divorce is never taken seriously by us or by Edouard and Caroline and the film ends fittingly with a deftly handled reconciliation in which the wealthy Texan Mr. Borsch acts as *deus ex machina*. The central portion of the film is given up to the reception organised by Caroline's rich uncle which they hope will help to launch Edouard on a successful career as a concert pianist. Edouard's awkwardness in this higher social setting is the source of some of the humour but never emerges as a problem; likewise the world of polite society is portrayed without caricature though the frivolity and emptiness of the lives of most of its members — with the exception of the redoubtable Mr. Borsch — are emphasised by the carefully composed images with which these scenes are shot. Insincerity, hypocrisy and lack of culture linger beneath the surface of these people — Uncle Beauchamp and his son, the Barvilles and their friends — but Becker is content to let us draw our own conclusions. The lightness of touch shown in the opening scenes is almost miraculously maintained throughout and we laugh at Edouard, Caroline and her uncle without ever ceasing to regard them as persons. There is little exaggeration and no farce: the comic situations arise spontaneously from the nature of the characters and their participation in the action. The whole film is bathed in the sympathetic warmth which Becker brought to his best films.

Two years later Jacques Becker and Annette Wademant attempted to repeat their success with **Rue de l'Estrapade** (1953) but with markedly inferior results. The script is equally thin and if anything weaker and more predictable than its predecessor, offering no fresh insight. That this film brought nothing new is aptly shown by Georges Sadoul's ironic summary: "A quarrel between Edouard and Caroline, Caroline going to live for her part in the Rue de l'Estrapade, Antoinette working in the world of *Falbalas* and meeting a boy from *Rendez-Vous de Juillet*".

Between these last two films Becker made what is undoubtedly his masterpiece, **Casque d'Or** (1952), a tragic love story set in Paris at the turn of the century. Becker has described the origins of his film as follows: "I have constructed my film round an historical fact (for Manda and Leca were the subject of the law reports of 1900). Manda who had been brought up in an orphanage had just begun his working life: I have shown him working for a small craftsman in Belleville. He is to marry his employer's daughter when he meets, in the company of an old friend who has taken to crime, the beautiful Casque d'Or. This is the lightning flash, and love leads Manda to a murder, then to the guillotine." Here Becker appears as a genuine creator, for the whole conception of the film, as well as most of the script and dialogue, is his. He called upon Jacques Companeez merely to help him bring the film to a satisfactory conclusion, the script-writer contributing notably the motivation for Manda's surrender to justice. In its final form the film is beautifully constructed, moving with ever-gathering momentum from the first splendid shots of the carefree group on the river, through scenes of love and murder to the final horror of execution. Becker shows all the hurried ugliness and squalor that surrounds the guillotine, so that we feel this execution to be an affront to humanity. Becker, despite his avowals to the contrary, has always been an optimist and he ends his film not on this tragic note, but with a final shot of Manda and Marie dancing together. Within the film the scenes are unfolded with a fine sense of rhythm and the action moves easily from the studio sets out into the open air and back again. The people in *Casque d'Or* seem at home in their costumes, the women with their long dresses, the men with their moustaches, and the Parisian background is sketched in with all its richness and variety. No attempt is made to romanticise the group of pimps and prostitutes who form the centre of the film's action. Leca, the leader of the group, played by Claude Dauphin, emerges as a complex and thoroughly unlikeable character (one of the few in Becker's work), and the brief shot of his face as he watches two men fight to the death at his feet is unforgettable. The playing of the two lovers is exceptional. Serge Reggiani brings to the part of Manda an inner strength, only partially concealed behind a frail exterior, that drives him twice to murder: first to obtain Marie and again to avenge the treachery of Leca. Simone Signoret as Marie, nicknamed Casque d'Or because of her flowing blond hair, reveals a full, ripe beauty and she moves convincingly from carefree enjoyment of her own power over men to tragic helplessness as she watches Manda's death. The idyllic love scenes in the

Above: "The tenderness shining through the everyday mishaps and misunderstandings of a married couple." Anne Vernon and Daniel Gélin in Jacques Becker's EDOUARD ET CAROLINE. Below, a high peak of happiness. Simone Signoret and Serge Reggiani in Becker's CASQUE D'OR.

countryside between these two have a truth and sensuous quality rare in the cinema. All Becker's usual attributes are present: a concern with love and friendship, exactitude in the handling of details of background, an ability to sustain transitions of mood and atmosphere; but here in *Casque d'Or* there is the added dimension of death, for the love is of a kind that drives a man to murder and the friendship of a degree that demands self-sacrifice.

Becker broke new ground with his next film **Touchez pas au Grisbi** (1954) which was adapted from a "série noire" novel by Albert Simonin. Together with Jules Dassin's *Du Rififi chez les Hommes*, another Simonin adaptation made the following year, this film started the vogue for gangster films which characterised the French cinema in the late fifties. The story is a conventional one about gang rivalries after a particularly successful gold robbery, and the film has a briskly handled climax of gang warfare on a lonely country road, complete with bombs and machine guns. But, inevitably, Becker's interest is elsewhere. He shows the hidden face of gangsterdom: the impeccably dressed and outwardly polite men whose business is violence, the methodical manner in which such men prepare for a gun battle, and the calmness with which they accept betrayals and setbacks. The background of elegant flats and gloomily expensive nightclubs is sketched in with convincing detail, but it is to the character of Max-le-Menteur that Becker brings all his sympathetic understanding. Through Max, who sacrifices a fortune out of loyalty to an old friend, the director gives a study of an ageing man of action, who as he approaches fifty is getting too old and tired for the excitements of his previous life. The figure of Max gave Jean Gabin one of his finest postwar roles and one which is characteristic of the postwar Gabin: a solid, successful man who hides his feelings behind an impassive, rock-like exterior. Despite the bursts of violence that punctuate the action, the film's rhythm is slow and thoughtful, benefiting from a haunting theme tune by Jean Wiener, and with many moments of insight into character that contribute nothing to the plot, as when the camera follows Max around his luxurious apartment or watches him sitting down to eat a pork-pie.

Becker's next three films were largely commercial efforts in which his talents were only intermittently apparent. **Ali Baba et les QuaranteVoleurs**

(1954) was a vehicle for Fernandel, on the script of which no less than eleven writers are said to have worked. Becker's style is submerged in the lavish décor and lush colour photography, and the story of the simple servant who outwits the thieves to win the love of a beautiful dancer is rather leadenly told, with only occasional flashes of real wit. **Les Aventures d'Arsène Lupin** (1956), also in colour, told of the adventures of a gentleman thief in Paris and Germany at the turn of the century. The film is extremely successful on its undemanding level of light entertainment, though the German episode is perhaps a little out of key. Robert Lamoureux was perfect as the smoothly resourceful hero, the settings were again elegant and there were plenty of beautiful women in the cast, but the film as a whole, though amiable, might have been directed by someone with a fraction of Becker's talent.

Montparnasse 19 (1957) had as its starting point the script on which Max Ophuls had been working with Henri Jeanson at the time of his death. Becker remodelled this scenario completely, thereby provoking a violent quarrel with Jeanson and earning the film wide pre-release notoriety. *Montparnasse 19* traces the last years of the life of the painter Modigliani as, unappreciated by critics, he succumbs to drink despite the efforts of a number of devoted women to save him. Gérard Philipe appeared as Modigliani, but Becker did not fully escape the clichés inherent in this sort of biographical film.

Jacques Becker's last film, **Le Trou** (1960), dealt with a prison escape and provides an interesting contrast to Robert Bresson's *Un Condamné à mort s'est échappé*, made three years earlier. Though unoriginal, the subject furnished Becker with excellent scope for the detailed observation of people in which he delighted. The plot is simple: into a cell containing four men who are planning an escape is sent a fifth prisoner, a young car salesman accused of the attempted murder of his rich wife. After some misgivings the four decide to include the newcomer in their plans and begin the arduous task of digging themselves out. The escape preparations are treated in an almost documentary manner. The tools and devices the men use have to be improvised — a hammer from the leg of a bed, a periscope from a toothbrush and fragment of mirror, a clock from two medicine bottles, dummies from cardboard boxes. In the course of the film we come to know almost every square foot of the men's cell, and gradually too the escape route is revealed to us as obstacle after obstacle is laboriously removed. From the beginning the humiliations of prison life are made clear and we can understand the men's need of freedom. Nothing is allowed to distract us from the action, the camera style is marvellously assured but unobtrusive, and there is no music, only natural sound used to create atmosphere. The tension and suspense are maintained throughout, up to the final scene of betrayal which, though surprising, is agonisingly true to life. The five main characters themselves, played by non-professionals, are not romanticised, nor are the moments of violence that flare up glossed over. But the co-operation and common need for freedom shared by these men bring out other qualities in them: persistence, ingenuity, courage and above all loyalty. By concentrating on these Becker is able to give the film a sense of affirmation which makes it a fitting conclusion to his work.

The death of **JACQUES BECKER** at the age of fifty-four was a real loss to the French cinema. He was one of the most talented and certainly the most versatile of his generation, for his unfeigned liking of people allowed him to be equally at home in domestic comedy and period tragedy, with peasants and with gangsters. Despite this diversity of subject matter virtually all Becker's work bears his distinctive signature. He was clearly more than just a craftsman or technician, yet equally he lacked the genuine creative impulse. He recognised the need for a film to be the work of one man but the terms in which he discussed authorship show clearly his limitations: "The author of a film only deserves this title if he is the complete author . . . I am of the opinion that the director, in particular, should do as many things by himself as he can. Whoever signs a film must have studied the script at length, gone deeply into the idea behind it, been in charge of the preparation and closely supervised the editing." It is significant that his best film is the one to whose script he contributed the most. Since he wrote as well as directed *Casque d'Or*, he was able to tell the story as far as possible through the images: "As I wrote visualising the scenes, I made the characters say the minimum of things necessary for the understanding of the situation." In most of his work, however, he was dependent on scenarios furnished by his scriptwriters, principally Maurice Griffe, Annette Wademant and Albert Simonin. His preference for thin plots was perhaps a way of ensuring the predominance of his own contribution, the visual element. But while he succeeded splendidly with *Antoine et Antoinette* and *Edouard et Caroline* in maintaining interest despite the lack of action, and managed to turn the absurdities of *Touchez pas au Grisbi* into an exercise in directorial expertise and sheer style, it is precisely the weakness of plot which mars *Rue de l'Estrapade* and his later minor works. This approach to the dramatic qualities of a film made enormous demands on Becker's skill as a director, and the remarkable thing about his work is the frequency with which he succeeded despite his script.

The centre of interest in any Becker film is humanity, observed not as a collection of isolated individuals but as a society linked together by ties of love, friendship, occupation and common interest. It was through his characters that Becker came to grips with his films: "My characters obsess me much more that the story itself. I want them to be true." He had the gift of sympathising with people of every conceivable sort and of treating their problems with respect. Though many of his characters are disreputable — for instance, Manda and Marie in *Casque d'Or*, Max-le-Menteur, Manu in *Le Trou* — unsympathetic types are rare, for almost all are treated with that warmth which is as characteristic of Becker's work as it is of Jean Renoir's. Despite his overwhelming fascination with his characters Becker never lost his ability to remain detached and see them in perspective, indeed he liked to describe himself as an entomologist. For this reason he never romanticises the figures in his films and one frequently finds hints of the less agreeable aspects of a person lying beneath the surface. Becker also liked to put the various people in his films firmly in their social setting: "I hate leaving people in a vacuum; in my view nothing is more false. I cannot conceive a character without worrying about the manner in which he lives, his social contacts, whatever class he may belong to." He studied milieu with a minuteness that became almost legendary. No detail was too small for his perfectionist eye: "When you have found a story to tell, you have to set it in a specific setting. The drawing of this setting, the search for the exact, sober detail drawn from life gives the vital depth to the character." But this approach

Above: Gérard Philipe and Anouk Aimée in MONTPAR-NASSE 19. Below, "Obstacle after obstacle is laboriously removed": Jean Keraudy in Jacques Becker's LE TROU.

never went beyond description and his affection for people means that social criticism is virtually non-existent in his work. The smart world of Uncle Beauchamp in *Edouard et Caroline* for example is viewed with great exactitude but there is little caricature or condemnation. Becker did not aspire to give a panorama of his age but each new film entailed the study of a new social group and his work will provide a mine of detailed information for future social historians: "And if, by carefully painting my characters, I give some people the illusion of having wanted to portray my epoch, so much the better, and it is very flattering; but we are faced here with an illusion, my pretensions do not go so far."

Jacques Becker's world was that of the ordinary and the commonplace. He was never attracted to the spectacular or the sensational: "I feel no real interest in what is exceptional. I have never been able to interest myself much in stories where the heroes are criminals; their case does not attract me." When he dealt with criminals it was precisely this concentration on the ordinary human qualities of those involved that gave the films their outstanding interest and it is for this reason that we find the gangsters of *Grisbi* and the convicts of *Le Trou* so fascinating. But Becker's lack of interest in wider problems, in political and social issues for instance, means that he runs the risk of lapsing into mere triviality when he deals with unexceptional people. This accounts for the reserves that most critics feel with regard to the films of Becker's Parisian series, unique though these films are in the contemporary French cinema. Since Becker was so interested in the ordinary, he sought naturalness above all from his actors: "In the studio, when you feel suddenly that a sentence comes badly from the lips of an actor, you have to arrange to remodel it so that it comes naturally." The director brought all his gifts of patience and warm sympathy to his relations with his actors, as the testimony of Simone Signoret makes clear: "Jacques Becker ... loved actors in a similar way to Renoir, who delights in the whole mystique of acting. Becker would say to a horrible actor "That was good", and have him start the scene again and again, perhaps fifteen times never getting what he wanted, but still complimenting and progressively leading the actor to the point that he wanted." Becker's genuine affection and infinite care allowed him to reach a special understanding with his players, and draw superlative performances from established actors like Simone Signoret, Serge Reggiani and Jean Gabin and the non-professionals of *Le Trou*.

The material of Jacques Becker's films was never personal and one could not have deduced what sort of a man he was simply from the stories he related in his films. Nevertheless he did put a great deal of himself into all his films and it is the truth with which he revealed his own insight into human relationships that gives his work its lasting interest. Two great themes run through all his major works. The first is love, which is seen both as the tenderness shining through the everyday mishaps and misunderstandings of a married couple in the comedies *Antoine et Antoinette* and *Edouard et Caroline*, and as the tragic passion suddenly unleashed in the lovers of *Casque d'Or*, where it drives Manda to murder. The second theme is friendship, which forms the core of the films dealing with the loyalties and rivalries of the masculine world. That the men concerned may be criminals does not lessen this tie: Max in *Grisbi* sacrifices his fortune, Manda in *Casque d'Or* his life to ransom a friend, and the treachery of Gaspard in *Le Trou* is a betrayal of friendship itself. It is the strength of these emotions that gives the execution in *Casque d'Or* (a film which it will be noticed unites these two themes) its shattering impact. Indeed it is the power which Jacques Becker, an avowed pessimist, attributed to love and friendship which caused his work to rise beyond a meticulous description of the mundane and become, ultimately, an affirmation of man.

* * *

CLAUDE AUTANT-LARA had already been active in the cinema for twenty years before he was given a chance to exercise his talents as a director freely during the Occupation. The three films he directed then, and his first postwar work **Sylvie et le Fantôme** (1945), all starred the young Odette Joyeux and were delicate escapist works, handled with remarkable elegance and lightness of touch. The latter film, for example, tells of a girl of sixteen who falls in love with a ghost. Soon the ancestral castle is full of people impersonating the ghost, and the heroine transfers her affection to the most deserving of these, much to the bitter disappointment of the real ghost whose attempts to communicate with her are all unsuccessful.

116

Autant-Lara's second postwar film and his first really personal film, **Le Diable au Corps** (1947) was altogether more substantial. Like most of the films scripted for the director by Jean Aurenche and Pierre Bost *Le Diable au Corps* is an adaptation of a novel, in this case by Raymond Radiguet. It is the tragic love story of an adolescent and a young married woman whose husband is away at the war. A series of flashbacks is used to convey this love which made the pair defy society, even to the extent of longing for the continuation of the war which alone makes their liaison possible. The film begins with the hero, François (Gérard Philipe), alone and despairing amid the armistice celebrations of 1918. Marthe (Micheline Presle) has died giving birth to his child but he is excluded from the family gathering at her funeral and utterly at odds with the rejoicing crowds around him. As he follows the church service from a distance François relives his now vanished happiness. The film is skilfully constructed (each flashback is heralded by an agonising slowing down of the sound track recording the church bells) and the first world war atmosphere admirably conveyed through Max Douy's sets. The script offers some penetrating insight into the characters of Marthe and François. Gérard Philipe in particular captures brilliantly the mental state of the schoolboy here, half man and half child, who is so confident and demanding in his relations with Marthe yet fails her at moments of crisis. With this film Autant-Lara gave the first expression to the themes which dominate all his postwar work and established his own international reputation as a director.

After trying unsuccessfully to make his anti-military film "L'Objecteur" (which was eventually made in 1960 under the title *Tu ne tueras point*) Autant-Lara directed a less ambitious work **Occupe-toi d'Amélie** (1949). Adapted from a farce by Feydeau, this film bears some resemblance to René Clair's classic *Un Chapeau de Paille d'Italie*. Accepting the artificiality of his subject, treating the pompous bourgeois characters as mere puppets and taking the whole plot at an incredibly fast pace, Autant-Lara has made the most of the play's ingenuity. The attractive personality of Danielle Darrieux in the central role keeps the film as gay as it is lightheartedly immoral. Autant-Lara's training as a designer is clearly shown in his handling of décor to comment wittily on the intricacies of a play within a play which is itself within a film. *Occupe-toi d'Amélie* is perfect of its kind but hardly a full expression of Autant-Lara's personality.

L'Auberge Rouge (1951) is also a comedy with a period setting but its success is on a quite different level, for here the elements of farce are inextricably bound up with a remarkably outspoken attack on Catholicism. To a lonely inn whose owners make a living by murdering all travellers who venture under their roof, come a monk, his handsome young novice and a coach-load of travellers. The pious inn-keeper's wife confesses her plans to the monk and he makes frantic efforts to save the travellers without breaking his vow of secrecy, only to see them plunge to their death. He is left with his faith shattered and only the two innocents — the inn-keeper's daughter and the novice — find happiness. Though the script of Aurenche and Bost is at times perhaps a little too explicit the film contains a wonderful collection of priestly and bourgeois foibles, at the centre of which is Fernandel's portrait of the monk who combines cowardice with cupidity, eloquence and low cunning. Throughout the film appearances are deceptive: the welcoming inn is a veritable slaughterhouse, the respectable travellers a collection of mean and callous gluttons, the friendly looking snowman a dead man's grave. Much of the humour is coarsely anti-clerical but the film is constantly hilarious, director and writers exploiting with the greatest relish the satirical possibilities of those scenes where Fernandel carries out his functions as a priest: hearing the confession of the innkeeper's wife through a toasting grid, or marrying the novice and the inn-keeper's daughter in a room decorated with candles and crucifixes plundered from a slaughtered salesman, in front of a congregation comprising the drugged and snoring travellers and a gun-holding inn-keeper.

After making the **Pride** episode in *Les Sept Péchés Capitaux* (1952) and a minor work **Le Bon Dieu sans Confession** (1953), on which for once he did not have the collaboration of Aurenche and Bost, Autant-Lara embarked on the filming of Colette's novel **Le Blé en Herbe** (1954). This film traced the relationship between a pair of sixteen-years-olds on holiday with their families by the sea. Gradually their feeling for one another is growing into love, but their realisation of this comes only after the boy has been seduced by a much older woman who occupies a neighbouring villa. The makers capture perfectly both the embarrassments and uncertainties of adolescence and the plight of the older woman who retreats when she finds her situation growing too impossible. The playing is uniformly good, especially the beautifully judged performance of Edwige Feuillère as the older woman, and the whole film is handled with great delicacy and insight, so that the theme, though disturbing, is never offensive.

Autant-Lara's next film was a version of Stendhal's **Le Rouge et le Noir** (1954). Aurenche and Bost have made an honourable attempt to transpose the complexities of the novel but even three hours screen time is insufficient to capture its full richness. (Autant-Lara would have preferred an eight hour version in several parts). The most successful scenes are those at the beginning of the film depicting Julien's love for Madame de Rênal, the tutor of whose children he has become. The acting is at its best here with Gérard Philipe and Danielle Darrieux incarnating to perfection the lovers separated, as so often in Autant-Lara's work, by both age and social position. The film's later development which traces Julien's career as he hesitates between the scarlet of a military uniform and the black of priesthood is less satisfying and Antonella Lualdi is not the best actress to portray the haughty and aristocratic Mathilde. Despite an attempt to order the material into a pattern of flashbacks and the employment of a first person narration by Gérard Philipe as Julien, the film fails to encompass adequately Stendhal's combination of analytic style and melodramatic plot development. Autant-Lara may have accomplished his stated ambition of sending his audience back to the novel, but despite a promising beginning he has not created a fully satisfying autonomous work of art.

After this over-ambitious film Autant-Lara's work shows a decline, slight at first but more marked as the rate of his output increases. **Marguerite de la Nuit** (1955), a version of the Faust legend set in the nineteen twenties, was an experiment that did not quite succeed. For once without his habitual scriptwriters, Autant-Lara concentrated all his attention on the visual effects, using deliberately stylised and unreal settings and changes of colour to indicate mood and atmosphere. The film is a reminder that Autant-Lara began his film career as designer on Marcel L'Herbier's expressionist films in the early twenties, but its final effect is cold and stilted.

La Traversée de Paris (1956), which was another semi-success, is set during the Occupation and tells of two men who carry four suitcases full of pork across Paris for a blackmarket butcher. The details of this journey, some taken from Marcel Aymé's short story on which the story is based, others invented by the adaptors Aurenche and Bost, are fascinating and often very funny. The contrast of the two men—Grandgil (Jean Gabin) a famous painter in search of adventure, and Martin (Bourvil) the down-trodden but conscientious blackmarketeer — is vividly drawn, satire and irony abound (as when Grandgil escapes arrest by quoting Heine) and Autant-Lara is not afraid to question cherished ideas and beliefs. Nonetheless the film is not a complete triumph, largely because the transition from farce to tragedy is made too abruptly with the sudden intrusion of reality in the grim shape of the S.S. **En Cas de Malheur** (1958), like H.-G. Clouzot's *La Vérité*, derived much of its impact from the clash of two worlds — that of the wealthy ageing lawyer and his wife, and that of the young prostitute and her student lover. Again it is with the older couple (played here by Jean Gabin and Edwige Feuillère) that the director seems most at home. The characters played by Brigitte Bardot and Franco Interlenghi are drawn and acted with noticeably less insight. The development and *dénouement* do not altogether convince and the film as a whole lacks the atmosphere and conviction with which Simenon was able to invest the situations in the original novel.

With **Le Joueur** (1958) Autant-Lara again tackled a period drama but here, despite the playing of Gérard Philipe in the title role, the director and his scriptwriters were unable to do full justice to Dostoievski's novel and produced a work that was uncertain and uneven in tone and acting. **Les Régates de San Francisco** (1959) returned to a theme which had given Autant-Lara some of his finest achievements: that of the emergence of young people from adolescence into their first experiences of love. The young lovers were played by Laurent Terzieff and Danièle Gaubert, and inevitably their love meets with fierce parental opposition and incomprehension. The film was one of Autant-Lara's most outspoken treatments of love and it was cut by its producer and by the censors. For **La Jument Verte** (1959) Autant-Lara again turned to Marcel Aymé for his material. The problem with this bucolic farce of rape, feud and revenge was to find a filmic equivalent of Aymé's deadpan prose style that made these sordid and vulgar happenings acceptable in the novel. Autant-Lara does not entirely succeed in this and shows a lack of genuine comic invention. The script too, by Aurenche and Bost, struggles valiantly to cover all the events of the novel but never integrates the various threads into a coherent whole. The direction is flat and often stodgy, lacking the necessary gusto and enthusiasm. The film is redeemed only by a few tiny incidents, such as the scene with the dying mayor or the postman's story of the lost umbrella. **Le Bois des Amants** (1960), another minor work, was not scripted by Autant-Lara's usual collaborators but does contain many of the themes already treated in the director's earlier work. It is an attack on the forces that destroy love — war, nationalism and bourgeois hypocrisy — here personified in the figure of the mother, vividly played by Françoise Rosay. The lovers are typical Autant-Lara figures: the young man (Laurent Terzieff) just emerging from adolescence, the woman (Erika Remberg) older, married and more experienced. But they are hopelessly divided in their allegiances — she is a German and wife of a submarine-base commander, he a resistance fighter parachuted into occupied France by the British — and their love ends in an apocalyptic climax of murder and devastation.

In Yugoslavia in the summer of 1960 Autant-Lara finally succeeded in making a film for which he had been seeking backing for over a dozen years. **Tu ne tueras point** (1961), scripted inevitably by Aurenche and Bost, attacks yet another aspect of war — the failure of French law to recognise conscientious objection and the provisions whereby those who refuse to bear arms can be imprisoned indefinitely. The film contrasts two cases which happen to be judged the same day in 1949 by the same military tribunal. A German priest, Adler, who shot a French civilian in 1944 on the orders of his superiors is acquitted; a young Frenchman, Cordier, who refuses to wear military uniform is sentenced. The film is neatly constructed and the ironic possibilities of the contrast are developed to the full but the film is more argument than work of art. The Cordier scenes are handled with sympathy and insight and contain the film's best acting from Laurent Terzieff as Cordier and Suzanne Flon as his mother. But in the scenes with Adler, shot in German, Autant-Lara has not been able to avoid the temptations of oversimplification and caricature. By making all the priests hypocritical the director weakens his case, and significantly none of the characterisation or acting here is particularly convincing. The film's principal weakness lies in the script. The structure is unadventurous and full of the typical devices of the conventional scriptwriter's cinema (for example the positioning of the flashback to Adler's crime). The only real originality lies in the use of songs by Charles Aznavour. Imposed on the opening shots of war-graves, the device is successful but the lyrics at the end are very weak indeed. Elsewhere the film relies almost entirely on dialogue for its effects and for all his evident passion and sincerity, Autant-Lara has not succeeded in making the film more than a somewhat ponderous if well-intentioned tract.

Tu ne tueras point was banned in Italy and France, and in completing it Autant-Lara got into considerable financial difficulties. His next two films were therefore purely commercial efforts: **Vive Henri Quatre, Vive l'Amour** (1961) and **Le Comte de Monte Cristo** (1961) were entertainment films, relying on colour, historical settings and well tried actors for their effects. They were followed by **Le Meurtrier** (1963), a thriller adapted from a novel by Patricia Highsmith, and **Le Magot de Joséfa** (1963), a rustic comedy starring Bourvil and Anna Magnani. The director's personality is more apparent in **Journal d'une Femme en Blanc** (1965) which tackled the questions of abortion and contraception. Beginning in characteristic Autant-Lara fashion with the climax (the young doctor's discovery that she is pregnant), the film goes back to trace her story and that of a patient who, though happily married, is driven by social conditions to have an abortion from the effects of which she eventually dies. The film is solid and workmanlike but the conventionality and lack of depth of the best-selling novel from which it is adapted remain constantly apparent. Much of the same qualities and defects are to be found in the sequel, **Une Femme en Blanc se révolte** (1966), made by Autant-Lara the following year. More recently the director has contributed the episode **Aujourd'hui** to the collective film *Le Plus Vieux Métier du Monde* (1967) and completed a new feature film, **Le Franciscain de Bourges** (1968), from an Aurenche and Bost adaptation of a prize-winning novel.

Though he established a secure claim to fame with *Le Diable au Corps* in 1947, **CLAUDE AUTANT-LARA** has not enjoyed the kind of constant critical support usually accorded to directors whose careers are a continual struggle against producers and censors. In a sense this is a tribute to Autant-Lara's talents as a polemicist, the way in which for the last twenty years he has consistently attacked the comfortable myths and assumptions of bourgeois life.

There is little in the director's early career that would have led one to anticipate the new tone set by his first personal work, *Le Diable au Corps*, made when he was already forty-four. He came from a theatrical family (his mother was an actress, his father an architect and stage director) and in his youth — from the age of sixteen in fact — he was Marcel L'Herbier's designer for a number of consciously "artistic" works. Subsequently he became assistant to René Clair but he failed to establish himself as a director and spent long years of servitude in the cinema, engaged on such thankless tasks as dubbing American films in Hollywood and directing, in France, a series of films whose authorship was claimed by his producer. These experiences have left their mark on his work. Occasionally he experiments with artificial décor in the manner of the twenties, but this is perhaps an unconscious attempt to disguise his limitations and tackle themes that are really beyond his reach, such as novels by Stendhal *(Le Rouge et le Noir)* and Dostoievski *(Le Joueur)* or the Faust legend, which formed the basis of *Marguerite de la Nuit*. In general, however, Autant-Lara's style is as bare and unemphatic as that of Luis Buñuel, totally lacking in technical flourish or visual exuberance.

Autant-Lara's craftsmanship is always evident and he still has the ability to turn out a slick and successful commercial work when the need arises. Film-making for him is very much a team effort and since 1947 his collaborators have seldom varied: the scriptwriters Jean Aurenche and Pierre Bost, the designer Max Douy, composer René Cloërec and editor Madeleine Gug. Jacques Natteau joined the group in 1949 as cameraman and became director of photography some six years later. Autant-Lara has never written his own scripts and has relied largely on Aurenche and Bost for his material. The adaptations with which these two capable writers have furnished him have a wide range of sources but as usual the merits of the resulting film have very little to do with the value of the original. That Autant-Lara has a forceful personality cannot be doubted by anyone who has read any of his contributions to the numerous controversies aroused by his films, but his work shows little originality of construction. Films as different in scope and intention as *Le Diable au Corps* (1947), *Le Rouge et le Noir* (1954) and *Journal d'une Femme en Blanc* (1965) all follow the same pattern, beginning with the climax (respectively: Marthe's death, Julien Sorel's trial and the young doctor's discovery of her pregnancy) and then recounting the events which lead up to this in chronological order and in three or four long sections. Even *Tu ne tueras point* for which Autant-Lara struggled so long and sacrificed so much is nonetheless conceived in scriptwriter's terms and derives much of its impact from dialogue.

The most interesting aspect of Autant-Lara's work is the consistency with which he expounds his idiosyncratic views. A militant atheist of extreme left-wing views, he rejects everything connected with the Church, the Army and the Bourgeoisie. The bitter farce of *L'Auberge Rouge* and the serious polemics of *Tu ne tueras point* both show a priest faced with the problem of killing and reveal by their outcome the belief that religion is a mere system of evasions which offers no real help or guidance to men. Several of Autant-Lara's films touch on the problem of war. *La Traversée de Paris* and *Le Bois des Amants* both attempt to deprive the Occupation period of its aura of maquis heroics and show the pettiness and degradation which the Nazis brought with them. *Tu ne tueras point* is Autant-Lara's most direct and forceful assault on the whole military mystique. In it he probes the hypocrisy of senior officers and generals and pours contempt on the military mind itself as it is revealed in its elaborate rituals. In a similar way bourgeois attitudes are attacked in almost all Autant-Lara's films, in the persons of the parents who try to separate the lovers and in such richly drawn characters as Grandgil in *La Traversée de Paris* and Maître Gobillot in *En Cas de Malheur*, both

124

Appearances are deceptive: the young innocents (Marie-Claire Olivia and Lud Germain) meet at the pedlar's grave in Claude Autant-Lara's L'AUBERGE ROUGE, (above).

A young priest's progress towards sainthood: Claude Laydu in Robert Bresson's JOURNAL D'UN CURÉ DE CAM-PAGNE (below).

played by Jean Gabin.

While these views are unlikely to endear Autant-Lara to the authorities or to Catholic and right-wing critics, they would not of themselves have led to the sort of scandal which his work has always provoked. Even *L'Auberge Rouge* which may claim to be the most anti-clerical film ever made was shown without cuts in France. The aspect of Autant-Lara's work which has struck home most is his outspoken vindication of sexual love. His analysis of the transition from adolescence to maturity and the first bitter-sweet experiences of love, in such films as *Le Diable au Corps* and *Le Blé en Herbe*, is tender, truthful and sensitive. It is difficult to find comparable insight elsewhere in the contemporary cinema. Autant-Lara does not hesitate to reveal disconcerting truths about love — that an adulterous union can be purer than many a married relationship, or that adolescents in their teens are fully capable of enjoying physical love, and a recurring theme is the relationship of a very young man with an older woman. Like Kenji Mizoguchi, the postwar cinema's other great chronicler of love, Autant-Lara demonstrates his belief that love and society are incompatible.

Claude Autant-Lara's reputation has declined since the early fifties and lately his serious works have been outweighed by a mass of purely commercial films. But since he was first given the freedom to make the type of film he wanted he has unflinchingly expressed the views he holds deeply. This, as he has reached an age when most men come to terms with life, and works in a national cinema in which concern with society is rare, is a considerable achievement.

4. Innovators and Independents

IN THE Postwar French Cinema there are a number of men who stand apart from the general trends, directors who, either by choice or because of commercial restrictions, have created only a small number of works. Among these we may distinguish two groups: on the one hand, Bresson and Tati, who both possess a certain severity of

126

mind which has led them to limit their output and by this means retain absolute control over it; on the other, Grémillon, Rouquier and Leenhardt who have rarely, if ever, been given this sort of freedom and have been driven to work largely outside the feature film.

Robert Bresson and Jacques Tati are the two most individualistic of the French directors of their generation and the mere juxtaposition of their names opens up fascinating perspectives. On the surface, few films could be further apart than *Mon Oncle* and *Pickpocket*, yet in fact the two directors do have many common attitudes. Each believes the cinema to be the supreme medium for the expression of his own particular ideas and both are utterly uncompromising in their relationship with film producers. As a result they have made only a handful of films but these are all completely their own. Each is totally absorbed in his own chosen field and returns continually to the same themes, though never simply repeating previous successes. Both are endlessly seeking to refine their work still further: as Bresson recoils from the theatrical, which he fears would destroy the purity of his work, so Tati avoids all those elements of farce and exaggeration that he associates with the circus. Both avoid stylistic flourish for its own sake but have the absolute command of the film medium that allows them to use it as a means of personal expression.

They take enormous care with every one of the various stages of film making and reveal their independence of mind throughout. Each new film begins with a long period of preparation so that what appears natural on the screen is in fact the result of many months of hard work. Chance and improvisation play no part in their films: the form of the whole work has been established in advance and each film given a definite pattern, though not a conventional one. When the time comes for the actual shooting of their films, both Tati and Bresson show, by their willingness to take their cameras out into the real world, that they are free from the limitations of the French studio tradition. They will both take endless trouble to register each word and gesture as they think it should be and their concern with the tiniest details of every scene is characteristic of all the great directors. When the shooting is completed they apply equal attention to the soundtrack and editing, by means of which the essential rhythm of the film is established.

The careers of Jean Grémillon, Georges Rouquier and Roger Leenhardt are less satisfying. In the Occupation years Grémillon had established a secure claim to greatness as a director but in the last fifteen years of his life he was allowed to make only three features, all of them marred by commercial requirements. Only in his short films, most notably *André Masson*, was he able to give full expression to his tastes and talents. Rouquier and Leenhardt each made one of the most interesting films of the forties (*Farrebique* and *Les Dernières Vacances* respectively), but then found great difficulty in continuing their careers as feature directors. Rouquier did make two further features in the fifties but Leenhardt waited until 1961 before filming a second fictional subject. Both turned, like Grémillon, to the documentary, where they too found greater freedom of expression.

* * *

ROBERT BRESSON had achieved mastery of his medium and a reputation as one of the leading French film directors with his first two films, both made during the Occupation years: *Les Anges du Péché* (1943) and *Les Dames du Bois de Boulogne* (1944-5). Even so it was not until 1951 that another film of his appeared, and then only after innumerable difficulties had been overcome. The original script for **Journal d'un Curé de Campagne** (1951) was written by the ubiquitous Aurenche and Bost but rejected as being too free an adaptation of Georges Bernanos's novel. Bresson set out to refashion the script himself, keeping as closely as possible to the original. It must be stated at the outset that Bresson has recreated the novel, not simply made an adaptation of it in the conventional manner. He has been concerned to seek out the central core of the book — the spiritual development of the young country priest — and prune all the side issues not directly related to this main theme (but which are nonetheless an essential part of the novel), thereby intensifying the story and giving it the purity of a Racinean tragedy.

The film traces the progress of its hero from his arrival as priest in the village of Ambricourt through his sufferings and struggles to his death of cancer. His temperament does not allow him to make contact with the peasants of the village but he does become involved in the domestic rivalries at the Château, where he reconciles the Countess to God shortly before her death. The whole world around him is an alien one, all his actions are misinterpreted and his neighbours despise him as a drunkard. Alone, he fights a solitary battle against illness, despair and finally death. Outwardly the Curé is a frail childlike figure but in the course of the film his impact on the characters around him makes clear to us his very real spiritual power. Bresson chose an inexperienced young actor, Claude Laydu, for this central role and under the director's guidance the part is lived rather than simply acted. The film is concerned with the struggle fought out in the soul of the hero, but contact with the outside world is maintained through the absolute authenticity of the village background and a most skilful use of a soundtrack recording the noises of everyday activity. Indeed the film derives a great deal from the village atmosphere and has a noticeably lessened impact when the characters move away from this setting.

Bresson has made every aspect of the film his own. Just as the script is his, so too the style of the film belongs entirely to him. He is not afraid to reject the conventions of the well-constructed dramatic film. In *Journal d'un Curé de Campagne* the various episodes are held together by shots of the Curé writing his diary and by his voice recounting calmly the sequence of events. These comments allow us to see into the very heart of the man and are thus essential to the film's impact. All the minor dramatic highlights are missing and we see only their emotional and spiritual aftermath, as in the handling of the suicide of the doctor who has lost his faith. Such an approach serves to emphasise the central incident in the film — the Curé's struggle to penetrate beneath the Countess's superficial arrogance. In a similar way the music, by Jean-Jacques Grunenwald, is reserved for the emotional climaxes. The quality of Léonce-Henry Burel's photography is excellent throughout but it never obtrudes to disturb the balance of the film. Skilful use is made of the possibilities of light and shade, as in the scene of the Curé's interview with the Countess's daughter, Chantal, and in the shots of the black-garbed priest making his way to the Château through woods bathed in light. The director's personality is to be felt too in the film's tone: all the emotions are muted and there is a lack of violence or passion. Bresson chose non-professionals for the minor parts and all the playing is restrained and stylised, reflecting the director's conception of the various roles, not the actor's own interpretations. This continual understating of the emotions, together with the hero's essentially passive submission to God's will, gives the film its particular rhythm and makes the death of the Curé a real climax. In his handling of this moment Bresson's approach is revealed most clearly: a letter recounting the Curé's death is read by his only real friend, the Curé de Torcy, and gradually the image of this man is replaced by that of the Cross which fills the screen as his voice records the Curé's last words: "Tout est Grâce" — "All is Grace"!

This first postwar film confirmed Bresson as one of the truly great film directors. The very difficulty of giving the apparently unfilmic subject matter of a man's spiritual development a filmic expression seems to have prompted him to create a work in which he not only developed a highly original and personal style but also attained a degree of depth and truth rarely equalled in the cinema. But despite the artistic success of *Journal d'un Curé de Campagne* Bresson had to wait a further five years before he was able to make another film. This time he chose as his subject a prison escape, basing his film on Commandant Devigny's account of his own wartime escape from the Nazi prison of Fort Montluc. **Un Condamné à Mort s'est échappé** (1956) may seem at first sight far removed from the previous film, but its subtitle, "Le Vent souffle où il veut", reveals both the significance for Bresson of the events related and the link with the previous work: the escape is seen as the working out of the Divine Will. In this respect the music employed in the film is significant. Mozart's C Minor Mass is used to accompany scenes of the prisoners going about their everyday tasks and serves to underline the hidden significance behind their actions and the supreme order behind even the carrying out of menial tasks. Again Bresson concentrates on his single theme, the prison escape planned and executed by the hero (here known as Lieutenant Fontaine), and all that is irrelevant to this is omitted. For this reason we learn nothing of the prisoner's antecedents or even the reasons why he is in prison; we can see what sort of a man he is from his actions and this suffices. Similarly the camera rarely leaves the prison; only the muffled sounds reaching Fontaine's cell remind us of the life going on outside.

Probing close-ups of Fontaine's face are used to give us insight into his personality, and again the hero's voice is heard linking the scenes, commenting on the action and revealing his own thoughts. In this film the physical details of Fontaine's escape are of very great importance and so the camera dwells on his hands as well as on his face, and on the objects in his cell which he utilises for his escape. Calmly and patiently Fontaine prepares to cheat his executioners, benefitting from another prisoner's unsuccessful attempt to escape. All seems ready, when unexpectedly a young lad, Jost, is put into his cell. Fontaine, torn by doubts, finally reveals his plan to the newcomer and persuades him of the effectiveness of his plan. Together they make the escape.

Bresson builds up tension and suspense during the escape but never by the obvious and more melodramatic methods of Clouzot. The ultimate outcome is never in doubt, but the method of escape is always totally absorbing. The photography is outstanding: greys and blacks are used to convey the claustrophobic prison atmosphere, so that one is made to feel the prisoners' need to escape. The players are all unknowns, none of them professional actors (though François Leterrier who plays Fontaine did later become a director), and even more than in *Journal d'un Curé de Campagne* the director's presence can be felt in the acting and even the manner of talking. Throughout the film there is a feeling of control, and an incident like Fontaine's hysterical laughter on being returned to his own cell after his death sentence has been confirmed is muffled and passes almost unnoticed. The whole film has an evenness of tone that marks it as the product of one man's personality. Fontaine has remarkable similarities with the Curé d'Ambricourt: he is intelligent, withdrawn, in control of himself even in moments of crisis and endowed with considerable force of character which allows him to impose his will on his fellow men and his physical surroundings. Confidently he awaits the success of his plan, and this calm passivity gives the film its rhythm and atmosphere.

Robert Bresson's next film came as something of a surprise. After it had been announced that he was about to begin a long cherished project, "Lancelot du Lac", his plans were suddenly changed and instead he directed **Pickpocket** (1959), a film which marks an interesting new departure in his work. For the first time Bresson composed an entirely original scenario instead of remodelling an existing work, though it is true that even here he has drawn some inspiration from Dostoievski's "Crime and Punishment". Michel, the Pickpocket, has the kind of face we have come to associate with the hero of a Bresson film: sensitive, alert and unemotional. Again he is a man isolated from the world around him, in this case the bustling Parisian crowds, but in contrast to the previous two heroes Michel is a man who has rejected God and is impelled by his arrogance to assert himself. To prove his superiority he turns his back on his mother and his friends and embarks on a life of petty crime, ignoring the advice of a friendly Police Inspector and eventually finding teachers and accomplices in the art of picking pockets. Ultimately, however, this very life of crime turns out to be no more than an immense detour on his path to salvation, which he achieves when he comes to realise and accept his love for the young girl Jeanne. The whole life of crime to which Michel's egotism has driven him is, in a sense, his prison, and paradoxically his soul finds freedom only when he is physically imprisoned in a police cell.

Pickpocket takes us more into the ordinary everyday world than before, among the crowds at race meetings, in underground trains and at railway stations. These settings, as always with Bresson, are absolutely authentic, with no trace of studio contrivance. But this is a world where God plays no part, where the hero's life is without spiritual meaning, and in this repect it is the antithesis of the prison world of Fort Montluc in the previous film. The hero's inner life is once more the core of the film and the real drama is the struggle that goes on behind Michel's emotionless face. Bresson has no interest in individual psychology except in so far as it illustrates the workings of the Divine Will and little motivation is offered for the Pickpocket's acts. Michel is narrator as well as central character, and his voice accompanies the action, but never does he attempt to explain or excuse his conduct. In order that the attention of the audience is concentrated on the conflict within him the secondary climaxes of Michel's life, such as the death of his mother, are played down. In this way his final arrest, which is the true climax of his spiritual development, and hence of the whole film, is made to stand out. This virtual surrender to justice is Michel's first act of submission and leads directly to

Above: "The love of Michel and Jeanne is muted with no effusion of emotion." Marika Green and Martin Lasalle in Robert Bresson's PICKPOCKET. Below, Nadine Nortier in the title role of Bresson's MOUCHETTE.

his salvation. His love for Jeanne, which is the means of this redemption, introduces a new element into the Bresson world. Jeanne is the opposite of Michel in that her attitude is one of passive acceptance of her fate. Her feelings are kept hidden and even the ill-treatment she receives from Michel's hypocritical friend Jacques arouses no bitterness in her. The love of Michel and Jeanne, though serving as the film's culmination, is muted, with no effusion of emotion shown, and it is typical of the film's treatment of love that their last embrace is through the bars imprisoning Michel.

None of the players in *Pickpocket* were well-known professionals (though Pierre Etaix, who plays one of Michel's accomplices, is the great hope of French comedy in the early sixties) and all the acting bears the imprint of the director's mind. The actors have all been drilled by Bresson to interpret each role entirely as he conceives it putting nothing of themselves into their parts. The film is slow and measured; pauses and stares are almost as important as words, and Michel's voice in his commentary on the action is intentionally flat. The film's technique shows Bresson's complete mastery of his medium. The scenes of the pickpockets at work have a ballet-like air, and the theme of hands, here more expressive than the faces of their owners, is one of the things which link this film to *Un Condamné*. The camera, when focussed on Michel, is remarkably static, dwelling on the settings of his life with intense scrutiny. For example, to show the hero entering a room, Bresson focusses on the doorway, allows Michel to pass through, and then holds the shot for a few seconds after he has gone. The cumulative effect of this method is not, however, one of boredom but of a calm and compelling rhythm.

If Michel in *Pickpocket* was a surprising addition to Bresson's gallery of heroes, Joan of Arc on the contrary is a character to whom we would expect him to be drawn. As its title suggests, **Procès de Jeanne d'Arc** (1962) concentrates upon the imprisonment and trial of Joan and it culminates in her condemnation and burning. Here Bresson is faced with a new challenge: in his previous films he had taken life in all its vigour and diversity, and distilled from it a single thread of action; in this film he attempts to breathe life into the historical documents which record the minutes of Joan's trial. For Bresson, with his eternal quest for authen-

134

ticity, these are the only possible sources for his film and he allows himself to invent nothing. He does, however, stylise the décor and even includes a few anachronistic details, in order to avoid anything picturesque that might disturb the spectator's concentration on the central conflict. Bresson's fidelity to recorded fact means that he has to do without one element that had been an essential part of the earlier films: the voice of a narrator. Words are as important in *Procès de Jeanne d'Arc* as in the preceding works but their function is different. Whereas previously they had shown an inner struggle and conflict, here they record an outward clash: Joan's verbal duel with Bishop Cauchon. This is perhaps a key to the peculiar coldness of the film. *Journal d'un Curé de Campagne* was near to tragedy in its chronicling of the doubts and hesitations of a terribly vulnerable young priest, but Joan of Arc, as Bresson sees her, has virtually no doubts or regrets at leaving this world; she is content, such is the strength of her faith, to submit herself totally to God's will. The resolute march of a saint to martyrdom may fill us with awe, but we do not feel any personal involvement with her.

Stylistically the film shows Bresson at his most austere. Only at the beginning and the end of the film are the full resources of the cinema used. The opening sequence of feet advancing ominously beneath flowing black robes is remarkable, but the conclusion of the film is even more so. Following the pattern of *Journal d'un Curé de Campagne* which had ended with a single long-held shot of the cross, *Procès de Jeanne d'Arc* concludes with a static image of the stake, here made even more overwhelming by the sinister crackling of the flames. The prison atmosphere is established, as in *Un Condamné à mort s'est échappé*, by meticulous observation of the objects in the cell, but the attempts to frighten Joan with the instruments of torture or humiliate her by testing her virginity are not built up into emotional scenes. The whole concentration is on the cross-examination and the path to martyrdom. The interrogation of Joan by her judges is filmed almost entirely in medium length shots, cross-cutting from Joan to her interrogators and back again, but always from the same camera angles. Bresson's intention is to create a sense of the monotony of prolonged imprisonment and interrogation and to include nothing in the visuals of his film which might draw the attention away from the words themselves. This technique gives the film a weight quite out of proportion to its length (a mere sixty five minutes), but does not allow the director to penetrate deeply into the character of Joan. Bresson shows us the saint that Joan becomes, but not the peasant girl she must have been.

With *Procès de Jeanne d'Arc* Bresson appeared to have reached the *ne plus ultra* of his stylistic development and it was difficult to foresee in which ways he could profitably proceed. But after a four year interval he returned with a film which marked a quite new level of mastery. **Au Hasard, Balthazar** (1966) not only forged a fresh stylistic approach, it also covered a new range of material with an inclusiveness that the earlier works had lacked. It takes in jazz and teenage dancing, violence and nudity, cruelty and leather-clad motor-cyclists while still preserving a Bressonian atmosphere. The director contrives to distance this material by means of a film structure that achieves an effect of de-dramatisation by breaking the action into a succession of tiny eliptical ·scenes connected in ways that are not immediately apparent. The film has the richness of plot of a Dos-toievskian story and an added element of strangeness in that its eponymous hero is a donkey. Balthazar begins life as a children's pet. He is cossetted and formally christened, a witness to the innocence of childhood and himself virtually worshipped like a pagan idol by the young Marie who adorns him with flowers. Then brutally the world of work intrudes: he is broken in, beaten and tormented, accompanies a half-crazed murderer on his wanderings in the mountains and works in a circus. Bought by a miser he is worked almost to death grading corn; rescued, he walks in a church procession and is hailed as a saint, only to be stolen by smugglers and shot by the customs men, to die on the mountain-side amid a flock of sheep.

Balthazar's story is itself impregnated with Christian overtones and linked to that of another victim, the girl Marie. He is present at most of the crises of her life: her rejection of the love offered her by the kind but uncomprehending Jacques in favour of the fascina-tion of the evil Gérard, who seduces her and submits her totally to his will. Her attempts to free herself from the oppressive atmosphere of her family lead her virtually to prostitute herself and offer herself for the humiliation which she duly receives from Gérard. While Balthazar dies in the hills, she is abandoned, naked and alone, by Gérard and his jeering companions. If Marie is the embodiment of submission, Gérard is the very incarnation of evil and all his appearances have a destructive element in them: he is thief, seducer, bully and hooligan combined. The film's distinctive mixture of obscure meaning (the donkey) and quite blatant symbolism (Gérard's leather jacket and motor bike) is held together by Bresson's extraordinary stylistic control. Characteristic Bresson touches such as the use of Schubert's music and the uniform style of gesture and enunciation—this is a film in which dialogue is rare and the silences are most meaningful—are combined in *Au Hasard, Balthazar* with moments of a quite unique unreality: the donkey in a deserted house or amid traffic, amid the sheep on the mountain-side or confronted with the animals in the zoo. The vision which emerges is that of a world of Dostoievskian corruption where evil flourishes and secret vices eat at the hearts of men. In following the course of Balthazar's life we encounter obliquely a whole wealth of worldly experience—the death of a child, pride and the quarrel of friends, pure destructiveness, lust, *amour fou*, avarice, humiliation, crime and death—and Bresson presents us with a world where simple love and laughter vanish with childhood but grace is never absent.

Mouchette (1967), adapted from the novel "Nouvelle Histoire de Mouchette" by Georges Bernanos (who had also furnished the subject for *Journal d'un Curé de Campagne*) is similarly a story of humiliation and defeat. It too is set in a world made to seem unreal by the juxtaposition of traditional life and modernity: in *Au Hasard, Balthazar* the donkey is set against Gérard's motor bikes and transistor radios, here in *Mouchette* the heroine wears clogs and a smock but also rides in a dodgem-car at the fair to the sound of jazzy modern music. Bresson's quest for authenticity has never made him shun anacronism (there are several examples in *Procès de Jeanne d'Arc*) and in adapting Bernano's novel he has only half modernised it. The film *Mouchette*, like the previous work, traces the experience of a whole life-time but obliquely in a succession of fragmentary shots and scenes welded in an almost musical rhythm. The fourteen-year-old heroine does not have to seek humiliation, it comes her way spontaneously. At home she is treated like a drudge, forced to nurse the baby and care for her dying, alcoholic mother. At school her sullen attitude cuts her off from teachers and pupils alike, and a tiny fragment of human contact at the fair (a smile exchanged with a boy of her own age) is rewarded with a brutal slap by her father. She befriends the poacher Arsène and nurses him when he has an epileptic fit (there is a marvellous scene where she cradles his head and sings to him with an almost maternal tenderness). But Arsène's response is to rape her brutally and when she runs off home, she arrives just in time to witness her mother's death. The failure of love and denial of all her tentative attempts at contact combined with her realisation of her natural instincts throw her into utter confusion. She rejects the morbid curiosity and smug superiority of the neighbours, but her pitiful revolt can be only negative and self-destructive.

The film's ending is characteristic of Bresson's refusal to dramatise or falsify. Out in the countryside Mouchette plays at rolling down a slope. The first time she stops to hail a passing tractor, the second she becomes entangled in some bushes and only at the third attempt does she succeed in rolling into the stream and so go gently to her death. The opening and closing minutes of the film are accompanied by portions of Monteverdi's *Magnificat* but elsewhere the director relies almost entirely on natural sounds and fragmentary snatches of dialogue. As in all his mature work, Bresson's personality is imprinted on every foot of *Mouchette*. This domination was achieved at the expense of his actors, as the painter Jean Vimenet (who played the gamekeeper) has pointed out: "None of us was ever aware of what was going on. He would not allow us to look at the script or see the photos taken in the course of shooting . . . He uses people like objects. He leaves absolutely nothing to their imagination: every detail, every gesture, every millimetre of movement of a finger or nose, your nose is in this position, you look in this direction, every indication is given down to the smallest detail by Bresson himself. You have nothing to contribute; you are a robot, you are put in a certain position and you remain like that. At a certain moment you have to turn your head . . ." Vimenet's words make clear how the distinctive acting style of Bresson's work is achieved but do little to illuminate the more mysterious aspects of his art: the ability to remain faithful

138

to a literary source and yet produce a work that is wholly his own, to shoot with non-professional actors on location and yet give his film an air of the supernatural, to insist on total realism at every stage and yet achieve a result that is a marvel of stylisation.

ROBERT BRESSON has made only eight films in twenty-five years as a director, but these have been sufficient to reveal him as one of the great masters of the cinema. It is a tribute to the French film industry that it has allowed this most austere of directors so large a measure of independence. He has had to endure long years of inactivity, but in the films he has made since the war he has not been compelled to make a single concession to commerce and has been able to bring together a team of gifted collaborators, of which the key members have been the veteran photographer Léonce-Henry Burel (who, in the twenties, worked with Abel Gance and Jacques Feyder) and the painter and designer Pierre Charbonnier. Bresson is above all a stylist, perhaps the most rigorous in the history of the European cinema. For him, a style—or in his own phrase 'une écriture'—is the first essential of a film: "The film is the very type of work which demands a style" and again: "A film is not a spectacle, it is in the first place a style." On all his work he imposes his own vision, but this does not mean that he finds the need to distort the material of his sources. His adaption of Bernanos's novel *Journal d'un Curé de Campagne* is a model of fidelity, and he has kept completely to the records of Joan of Arc's trial, inventing nothing, in *Procès de Jeanne d'Arc*. His method is to recreate the essence of his material in cinematographic terms, rejecting all that is extraneous and continually refining the work, until it is as bare and intense as a classical French tragedy.

As far as construction is concerned all of Bresson's postwar films follow the same pattern. He is suspicious of plot in the conventional sense: "I try more and more in my films to suppress what people call plot. Plot is a novelist's trick." Just as one isolated character is the core of every Bresson film, so a single theme runs through each one, and all that is not strictly relevant to this is ruthlessly sacrificed. All the minor dramatic highlights in the action are played down and the director shows a marked liking for ellipsis, moving smoothly from the beginning of one scene to the end of another, or omitting the central portion of a scene.

Bresson is interested only in the spiritual and emotional aftermath of violent and startling events, with the result that these latter invariably occur 'off-stage.' Everything in the film leads up to the single climax that presages the ending. In *Journal d'un Curé de Campagne* the death of the Countess marks the turning point in the Curé's relationship with the people around him and foreshadows his own death; in *Un Condamné à Mort s'est Échappé* the sudden entry of Jost into Fontaine's cell which seems to threaten his escape in fact ensures its success; in *Pickpocket* Michel's meeting with Jeanne after his years abroad leads directly to his submission and salvation; and in *Procès de Jeanne d'Arc*, Joan's withdrawal of her recantation makes martyrdom inevitable. In *Au Hasard, Balthazar* two fates run side by side to a twin climax: the donkey hailed as a saint dies on the mountainside, while Marie runs away from home and ends up naked and humiliated; but in *Mouchette* the pattern is simpler, the girl's rape driving her inevitably to death. In his handling of the final sequences of the films that end in death Bresson shows most forcefully his originality and independence. In the *Journal* the final image which is the culmination of all that has gone before is a long-held shot of the Cross, while in the *Procès* it is the stake, half concealed by smoke at the beginning, clear and empty at the end. The triple attempt at suicide in *Mouchette* with the mood changing imperceptibly from playfulness to determination is perhaps even more audacious.

Bresson's fidelity to his sources is paralleled by his faithfulness to reality in the settings of his films. The places and objects he films are completely authentic and subjected to an intense scrutiny. He films where possible on location — at Fort Montluc for *Un Condamné* or at the Gare de Lyon for *Pickpocket* — and when it was necessary to reconstruct Fontaine's cell in the studios, Bresson insisted on the use of real materials. But mere realism in the sense of adherence to external details is not sufficient for him, as he has said: "I want to and, indeed, do make myself as much of a realist as possible, using only raw material taken from real life. But I end up with a final realism that is not simply 'realism'." He wanted the prison in *Un Condamné* to be as authentic as possible, with all dullness and brutality, monotony and menial actions; but he aimed also at showing the order beneath the surface, what he has called "those extraordinary currents, the presence of something or someone, call it what you wish, which confirms that there is a hand guiding everything." The filming of *Procès de Jeanne d'Arc* set new difficulties for him and since he rejects totally the normal spectacle style of historical films he avoided all the crowd scenes which he thought would destroy the atmosphere he was seeking. His approach to history matches exactly his attitude towards a literary work that he is adapting. He has set out to reveal the universal significance of Joan of Arc's life and to free her from the conventional piety that surrounds a historical figure. He has tried to make Joan as far as possible a contemporary figure: "I wanted Joan of Arc to be a character of today. I wanted to make her up to date; and the inclusion of the few anachronistic details, such as her boots and her bed, was intended to further this impression of contemporaneity."

For Bresson, film and theatre are two completely distinct entities and in his view it is impossible for the film to borrow from the theatre without losing its independence: "As soon as one tries to express oneself through mimicry, through gestures, through vocal effects, what one gets ceases to be cinema and becomes photographed theatre." He has turned almost entirely to using young and inexperienced actors and complete non-professionals, for in his eyes a professional actor is a barrier to the portrayal of truth on the screen: "An actor, even (and above all) a talented actor gives us too simple an image of a human being, and therefore a false image." His main concern with his players is to ensure that they do not try to interpret their parts. He himself establishes the exact tone of each piece of dialogue and then rehearses his actors again and again until they can copy it perfectly. Roland Monod, who played the pastor in *Un Condamné*, has given a fine account of Bresson's attitude to his players. Bresson "would sit there before each new set-up, holding his head in his hands and repeating the lines over to himself, trying to arrive at the quality of directness and simplicity that he would then impose on us." Bresson's advice on how to speak the dialogue of his films was: "Forget about tone and meaning. Don't think about what you are saying; just speak the words automatically. When someone talks, he isn't thinking about the words he uses, or even what he wants to say. Only concerned with what he is saying, he just lets the words come out, simply and directly . . . The film actor should content himself with *saying* his lines. He should not allow himself to show that he already understands them. Play nothing, explain nothing." The result of this approach is the remarkable evenness of tone which characterises all Bresson's films: there is scarcely a single scene containing a real burst of anger or unstifled laughter in the whole of his work.

Bresson disclaims all interest in psychology and refuses to explain his characters: "I dislike psychology and try not to use it." To explain a character in words would be to deny the film as an art and use the methods of the theatre or the novel. In the cinema it must be the camera which reveals the personality: "Plastically, one must sculpt the idea into a face by means of light and shade." It becomes clear what Bresson means by this when we consider his explanation of the purpose of the interrogation scenes in *Procès de Jeanne d'Arc*: "The interrogations serve not so much to give information about the events — past or present — as to provoke on Joan's face her profound impressions, to imprint on the film the movements of her soul." It is what goes on in the minds of his characters that is important to him: "It is the interior that commands. I know that it may seem paradoxical in an art where everything is exterior. Only the knots which tie and untie inside the characters give the film its movement, its true movement." The real subject of each of his films is the inner life of the main character: the young priest's progress towards death and near sainthood; Fontaine's intense preparation for his escape and his complete submission to God's will; the struggle within Michel between love and vice; Joan's maintenance of purity and unshakeable steadfastness; Balthazar's passive submission and Marie's wilful search for humiliation; Mouchette's unhappy failure to achieve love.

Bresson originally studied painting and from the very first it was the visual effect that was the basis of his film style: "What I am seeking is not so much expression by means of gesture, speech, mimicry, but expression by means of the rhythm and combination of images, by position, relation and number." Bresson never considers any single image in isolation: the film's effect depends on the combinations and inter-relationships of the images. As Bresson has said, the cinema "must express itself not through images but through the relationships of images, which is not at all the same thing." The images must make contact with each other, create a sequence that is more than just the sum of the individual shots, or else the the film is not a work of art: "There must, at a certain moment, be a transformation; if not, there is no art." For images to relate fruitfully to one another there are, in Bresson's view, certain basic requirements. The first is that the images themselves are 'flat' and seemingly inexpressive: "I have noticed that the flatter an image is, the less it expresses, the more easily it is transformed in contact with other images." This means that the visual style must never have anything, even beauty, that is not strictly functional: "Painting taught me to make not beautiful images but necessary ones." A second requirement is that there must be nothing to destroy the flow from one image to another; the images must share some unity of tone if the flow and transformation is to be maintained. It is for this reason that all the players in a Bresson film are made to adopt a single style of performance: "It is necessary for the images to have something in common, to participate in a sort of union. For this reason I seek to give my characters a relationship and ask my actors (all my actors) to speak in a certain manner and to behave in a certain manner, which is furthermore always the same."

Whenever Bresson discusses his work it is always in terms of visual effect, but he does nevertheless lavish great care on the soundtrack. Carefully selected natural sounds are used with enormous effect: the creaking cartwheels in *Journal d'un Curé de Campagne;* the sound of the train at the end of *Un Condamné à Mort s'est échappé;* the Parisian street noises in *Pickpocket;* the crackling flames at the end of *Procès de Jeanne d'Arc;* the braying of the ass in *Au Hasard, Balthazar;* the beating wings of the trapped pheasant in *Mouchette.* In the Joan of Arc film the hostile crowds demanding Joan's death are never seen: we only hear their menacing shouts. Music is used sparingly in these films to reinforce the rhythm and to hint at the underlying significance of apparently mundane activity. It is to this end that Bresson employs classical music—the work of Mozart and Lulli—to accompany scenes from *Un Condamné* and *Pickpocket,* while the music of Schu-

143

bert and Monteverdi adds a new dimension to *Au Hasard, Balthazar* and *Mouchette*. Naturally great care is taken too with the film's dialogue. Robert Bresson has always been his own script-writer, but during the Occupation he employed Jean Giraudoux and Jean Cocteau respectively to write the dialogues for *Les Anges du Péché* and *Les Dames du Bois de Boulogne*. Since the war he has written his own dialogue for all his films and has said that he takes care to ensure that it is always subordinate to the images: "A film dialogue is neither a theatrical dialogue, nor the dialogue of a novel. The words must be extremely compressed so that the image that accompanies them does not become redundant." The first three postwar films are built around a balance of image and narrator; while the narrator's words make a major contribution to the creation of the films' rhythm, the images remain the decisive element. In *Procès de Jeanne d'Arc*, however, it is arguable that the dominant aspect is the dialogue of Joan's cross-examination and that the images are in fact subordinate to this, an impression which is strengthened by the increased severity of the visual style.

In his first four postwar films Bresson created a remarkable gallery of heroes. They share the same lean, intellectual and alert appearance and are isolated individuals, set apart from their fellows either by some physical barrier (the prisons of Fontaine and Joan) or by temperament (the Curé, Michel). The richness of their life comes therefore from within and though in outward appearance they may seem weak or timid, their spiritual power is real and is revealed somewhere within the course of the film when we see them in contact with another character: the Curé d'Ambricourt with the Countess, Fontaine with Jost, Michel with Jeanne, Joan of Arc with her judges. As persons they may lack many of the characteristics for which we are accustomed to look, particularly psychological complexity, but they compensate for this by a force and depth which are virtually unique in the cinema, and together they express one man's profoundly felt creative vision of the order underlying the apparent chaos of human life. In his more recent films Bresson has used a wider range of mood and colour to begin an equally impressive gallery of victims. Only the ass can achieve the perfect acceptance akin to sainthood, whereas

144

Marie and Mouchette, led astray by their carnal natures and a stubborn self-assertion, are slowly but remorselessly broken and destroyed by life. Taken as a whole, Bresson's characters show a unique coherence and constitute a profound investigation into the workings of divine grace in a life lived under the shadow of death.

* * *

JACQUES TATI, who had begun his career in the music hall, played in a number of short comic films in the thirties, beginning with *Oscar, Champion de Tennis* in 1932. But he regards his real career in the cinema as beginning with *L'Ecole des Facteurs* (1947), the first film for which he was his own director as well as leading player. This short film so impressed his producer that it was decided to turn the material into a feature length comedy. After considerable financial difficulties **Jour de Fête** (1949) was finally completed, though not in colour as Tati had planned it. The film is set in a French village on the day of its annual fair and the arrival and departure of a lorry loaded with wooden horses for the roundabouts for a fair form the action of the film. The authenticity of this background is ensured by Tati's method of shooting on location in Sainte-Sévère-sur-Inde and using villagers for the minor roles in the film. The regular life of the village, already upset by the fairground folk, is further disrupted by François, the Postman (played by Jacques Tati himself), who organises the erection of the flagpole before completing his round. The programme shown at the fair's mobile cinema includes a documentary on the most advanced methods used by the American Postal Services for the delivery of mail. François, mocked at by the villagers for his own old fashioned methods, decides to outdo the Americans. His efforts to accomplish this provide the film with its comic highlights. He acquires the knack of leaping on and off his bicycle, riding straight through a bonfire, using the tailboard of a speeding lorry as his sorting desk and continually finding more and more ingenious places to leave his letters, in the absence of a real letter-box. But this burst of frantic activity lasts only a single day and when the fair leaves the village again, all has returned to normal and François is back in his old way of life.

145

Jour de Fête mixes comedy of all kinds — gentle rustic humour, pure slapstick and satire on the modern craze for speed. Jacques Tati was a mime before becoming a film-maker and this film recalls silent screen comedy in its reliance on visual humour. Tati shows a predilection for long shots where the whole of the action is enclosed in a single frame, and close-ups are rare. His gangling postman acts with his whole body and the humour comes less from his facial expressions than from his antics with the ancient bicycle to which he is inseparably attached. François, like the villagers themselves, is a sympathetically drawn character but his predicament never arouses pathos. Though the film's dialogue is unimportant and at times unintelligible, the sound track does play a vital role, as for example in the gag where François is troubled by a wasp: we never see this creature but its presence is unmistakable from the harsh buzzing it makes as it flies in to attack. The music of Jean Yatove helps too to maintain the film's atmosphere. *Jour de Fête* is a film that lacks technical polish — its lighting and recording are often fairly primitive — but Tati's music hall training has enabled him to master the essential of all screen comedy: the art of timing his gags. This work is an isolated one in the French production of the forties. It heralded no new school of comedy and four years passed before another film of Tati's appeared, but *Jour de Fête* was sufficient to mark out its director and star as one of the most original talents in the history of the French cinema.

In **Les Vacances de Monsieur Hulot** (1953) Tati appeared as a new comic character, Hulot, who was less farcical than his predecessor François but equally an outsider and disrupter of everyday life. In repose, Hulot is a normal enough type, pipe-smoking and solidly middle-class, with a battered old car that is the counterpart of François's bicycle, but his gait marks him out as an oddity and sets him off from those around him. *Les Vacances* follows the same pattern of construction as the previous film. The action is enclosed between shots of the arrival of Monsieur Hulot and the other guests at their holiday hotel and their departure a week or so later. The early scenes build up the atmosphere of the hotel and the sleepy seaside resort which the presence of Hulot is to disturb. Among the guests is a pretty girl, Martine, who attracts Hulot's attention, but nothing comes of their relationship despite a few clumsy and tentative advances on his part. Most of the other guests and the staff are alienated by Hulot's behaviour but he does win the support and affection of the children and of the solitary little man who spends his entire holiday walking just a few paces behind his domineering wife.

The principal gags in *Les Vacances* are to be found in the second half of the film and constitute a succession of classic comic sequences. There is Hulot sitting painting a canoe at the water's edge, the paint-pot floating to and fro on the waves but always miraculously there to receive his brush. Then follows Hulot's second, and much less successful, encounter with a canoe which folds up beneath him (appearing in long shot like a giant fish closing its jaws) and soaking him to the skin. On his return to the hotel the fantastic trail of wet footprints he leaves serves to sow still further confusion there. A trip in his car ends with a breakdown in a cemetery where his spare tyre, to which wet leaves have stuck, is accepted as a wreath by the funeral mourners, whom he helps to restore to good spirits. Beaten at tennis he learns a remarkable service which pulverises his hapless opponents and recalls Tati's early sporting mimes. As a climax to his holiday and to the film, Hulot contrives to set fire to a hut full of fireworks.

In none of these situations does Hulot actually take the initiative and invent his gags and Tati has used this fact to differentiate his own work from that of Chaplin: "Take, for instance, the scene in the cemetery, the wreath with the dead leaves. Hulot just wanted to take out his car tyre, and without his doing anything about it, the leaves stick to it and it makes a wreath. If this had happened to Chaplin he would have deliberately put the leaves on the tyre, in order to transform it into a wreath and thus be able to leave the cemetery decently. Hulot does not get out, he stays until the end, shakes hands with everybody." *Les Vacances de Monsieur Hulot* is also totally lacking in the sentimentality that colours so much of Chaplin's later work. As in *Jour de Fête* virtually all the humour is visual. Words again play only a minor part: the early scene at the railway station with the loud-speakers blaring out gibberish sets the pattern for the whole film. The music, a catchy tune by Alain Romans, serves chiefly to help capture the holiday mood.

A further five years passed before Tati's next film appeared, this time in colour. **Mon Oncle** (1958) again featured Monsieur Hulot but tackled wider issues than the previous two films and is indicative of Jacques Tati's increasingly serious attitude to comedy. The film attacks the soullessness of modern life in the manner of René Clair's *A Nous la Liberté* or *Tout l'Or du Monde* and rests on a contrast of the worlds of Hulot and his brother-in-law Arpel. The latter lives in an ultra-modern house with a bare, functional open-plan interior and a completely symmetrical garden of cement paths and coloured pebble beds, with the occasional ornamental tree rigidly trained and clipped. Indeed so tidy and geometrical is this garden that even a single leaf on the path is a cause of surprise. Within the house, the kitchen is as hygienic and antiseptic as an operating theatre, full of fearfully complicated devices, so that even to boil an egg is a major feat of engineering. The regimentation of Arpel's life comes out well in the opening sequence depicting him driving to work and its emptiness in the scene of the Arpels' evening out. Hulot by contrast lives, as one might expect, in the dilapidated old quarter of the town where life is more leisurely and human. The rambling maze of passages and stairways he has to pass through to reach his attic room is the complete opposite of the Arpels' bare and functional dwelling. In the old quarter too there is time for talk, affection and real neighbourliness. Between these two districts lies a strip of wasteland, the haunt of dogs and small boys who play there, grubby but happy. It is here that Arpel's young son Gérard feels at home, not in his parents' inhospitable house.

The contrast of Hulot and Arpel is also expressed in other ways. The colour photography of Jean Bourgoin brings out the essential difference by its tonal qualities: the colours of Arpel's house are cold, acid and violent, and they stand out against the softer, muted tones of the old quarter. That there are here two distinct ways of life is made clear also by the soundtrack. In the Arpel's house the mechanical rattling and whirring of the innumerable gadgets — the sweeper, the kitchen equipment, the fountain and door buzzers — succeed in drowning all human conversation, whereas the square overlooked by Hulot's house is full of people laughing, talking and arguing together, and his own room filled with the song of a canary. The separateness of these two worlds makes Hulot's excursions into the Arpel territory all the more striking. Arpel is already plagued by his gadgets going wrong: he and his wife get locked in their new 'magic-eye' operated garage and his ornamental fountain breaks down on the very day of his wife's party. Hulot's visits serve to wreak fresh havoc: tempted by the bounceable cooking bowls in Madame Arpel's kitchen he experiments fatally with the glassware. Visiting Arpel's factory he leaves his bicycle in the space reserved for Arpel's car and when given a job he brings chaos to the factory. When he is interviewed elsewhere on Arpel's recommendation he contrives to cover the office with white foot-prints. Hulot comes off best in all his encounters with his brother-in-law mainly because of his own complete imperturbability but his world is in fact a dying one. The pneumatic drills and building operations that accompany the film's credit titles have a symbolic significance: the old quarter is doomed. At the end of the film Hulot is packed off into the country, but perhaps his influence has been decisive; certainly it is a very human Arpel who hides guiltily with his son at the end of the film.

The gags in *Mon Oncle* have been meticulously worked out. The tone of the film is leisurely and Tati aims at provoking smiles rather than guffaws. To hold the film together he employs a number of running jokes, such as Hulot's pruning of the ornamental tree after young Gérard has broken off one branch, and the boy's lamp-post game. It is noticeable that Gérard and the other boys accept Hulot as an ally and do not see him as a representative of the adult world. The construction of the film is neat and carefully thought out, and the usual framework is provided by a group of dogs running to and from the new quarter. As in the previous films the music serves to give unity and maintain the mood. Again the dialogue is unimportant — typically we do not hear the joke Hulot tells at Madame Arpel's party, we only see its effects on the two people who hear it: the laughter of the first woman and the horrified shock of Madame Arpel's neighbour. Occasionally too there are touches of almost surrealist humour — for instance the scene where the two Arpels appear at their windows so that the house appears to be rolling its eyes — and sometimes the film raises the ordinary rhythm of life to an almost formal ballet, as in the garden party scene.

Jacques Tati's fourth feature film, **Playtime** (1967), was, like *Mon*

Above: François and the wasp: Jacques Tati in his own JOUR DE FETE. Below, Tati strikes back in LES VACANCES DE MONSIEUR HULOT.

Oncle, the product of a great deal of thought and many years of preparation but it differs from all the director's previous work in the scope of the technical means employed. Tati spent three years and a reputed one million pounds to shoot the film and had at his disposal the full resources of colour, 70mm and stereophonic sound. The resulting work originally ran for some two and a half hours (pruned by thirty minutes in the English version) but rests on no more than the slenderest pattern of plot. A group of American women tourists arrive at Orly for a lightning tour of Paris but instead of the monuments and old quarters of the city they see only the ultra-modern steel and glass Paris of tomorrow, an architecturally and aesthetically pleasing environment but a cold and impersonal one at the same time. All is not lost, however, for in the course of their evening at the newly opened Royal Garden Hotel something of the real Parisian atmosphere emerges as the would-be efficiency of the staff and the pretentious luxury of the surroundings disintegrate into a more human chaos under the benevolent eye of Monsieur Hulot, whose wanderings around this part of Paris have several times brought him into contact with the tourists.

Nearly ten years before the completion of this film, Tati had stated his ambition "to make a film without the character of Hulot, with nothing but the people whom I see, whom I observe, whom I pass in the street, and to prove to them that, in spite of everything, every week or month something happens to them and that the comic effect belongs to everyone." With *Playtime* he has come near to this ideal, for Hulot is reduced to an episodic character on the same level as the rest of the people in the film and not presented as a privileged figure inventing a multitude of gags. The comic effects come not from exaggeration or a contrived sequence of farcical incidents but from the observation of life reproduced with as great a fidelity as possible. The costly sets of *Playtime* were not built to give a stylised or distorted image of the Paris of tomorrow, but to allow the director the maximum control in the creation of a realistic effect. From this approach comes the notion, already apparent to some degree in *Les Vacances de Monsieur Hulot* and absolutely fundamental to *Playtime,* of the film as a window opening out onto the world and permitting people to see their own and others' foibles and to laugh at life as it is. In this connection it is interesting to note that many of the most beautiful visual sequences and some of the best gags in *Playtime* derive from the use of glass and windows.

Playtime was received with considerable reticence by critics, perhaps because of the uncompromising demands that it makes on its audience. In a conventional comedy spectators are provoked and stimulated by a welter of incident and heavily emphasised effects, but here they are required to remain alert and observant all the time as the crucial happening in a scene may well be taking place unobtrusively in a remote corner of the large screen image. Tati was approaching the age of sixty when he completed the film and perhaps for this reason *Playtime* has a calm, reflective rhythm which allows deliberate *longueurs* and an affectionate repetition of little scenes or incidents. While clearly a major film and a fitting climax to a lifetime's concern with comedy, it is hardly a work for the mass audience. As few directors before him have contrived to do, Tati has taken the technical resources of film spectacle and used them to make a tender, delicate and totally personal statement about life as he sees it.

JACQUES TATI has made only four films as actor and director in some twenty years and if we examine the reasons for this we shall obtain some insight into the qualities of the films themselves. None of Tati's first three feature films was expensive, and all have been successful, but Tati has never found it easy to obtain backing. For one thing he has never agreed to exploit his past successes. He refused to make a sequel to *Jour de Fête* showing François married, or to co-operate, after *Les Vacances de M. Hulot*, on a proposed co-production with an Italian company entitled "Toto et Tati", or for that matter to follow *Mon Oncle* with an American version "M. Hulot goes West." The project Fellini once had for making a film of "Don Quixote" with Tati in the title role was one that appealed to the Frenchman, and he has said that he would enjoy working with Bresson, but otherwise Tati is concerned to make his own films in his own way, and the smallness of his output allows him his freedom. In any case, even under the most favourable conditions he would not make a large number of films, as he takes up to three years to prepare and film a single work, so thorough is his method of working. *Playtime,* though made with an enormously larger budget, was shaped in much the same way and Tati contrived to maintain his absolute independence.

Tati's point of departure in all four of his films is his characters: "First of all I work on my characters. I create them. Then I make them evolve in their setting. I get to know them better." It is only after this that the comic situations are developed: "It is when the character has once been created that I find him his gags." At this stage Tati makes use of script writers, such as Henri Marquet for *Jour de Fête* and *Les Vacances de Monsieur Hulot*, and Jacques Lagrange for *Playtime* and *Mon Oncle*. In collaboration with these helpers Tati begins to shape his story, slowly and always in accordance with the characters that have been fixed in advance. Equal care is given to the choice and adaption of settings, for the décor of Tati's films is extremely important. Even the tiniest part is cast only after enormous thought; for example, Tati saw some sixty people before deciding on the actress to play the part of Madame Arpel in *Mon Oncle*. When the shooting begins, the film has been planned in every detail: "I shoot without a script. I know my film by heart and I shoot it by heart . . . On the set I know exactly what I am going to ask of my actors, what I am going to do." Despite appearances to the contrary, improvisation plays no part in Tati's films: "I do not improvise, I know everything in advance," and "I do without a script, not because I do not attach any importance to it, but because I know my story by heart, shot by shot, word by word, gesture by gesture." Inevitably the timing of the film is also fixed in advance, so that Tati edits the film "by heart" too. When the shooting itself has been completed, Tati turns his attention to the soundtrack: "It remains for me to 're-shoot' each scene, this time not for the images but for the sound. I take very great care with this aspect. Indeed I consider the sound to be of capital importance." The soundtrack is one of the most memorable aspects of a Tati film: the buzzing of the invisible wasp that attacks François in *Jour de Fête;* the holiday sounds of waves, children and casual conversations that contribute so much to the atmosphere of *Les Vacances de M. Hulot;* the inhuman clatter of Mme. Arpel's household gadgets in *Mon Oncle;* and the stereophonic sound effects in *Playtime*.

Tati approaches his films with the attitude of a craftsman: "I defend craftsmanship with all my might. I am a craftsman." But he has never felt any great interest in technique except as a means of accomplishing certain very definite aims: "One has to know what one must not do. Apart from that it is not so much a question of technique. One must follow reality and one's own inspiration." For this reason it is never the technical aspects of Tati's films that arouse the interest and he never indulges in technical display for its own sake. Tati originally came to the cinema as an actor and he conceives his films in terms of characters: "It is necessary for my characters to evolve, not for my camera to move." As an actor and mime Tati makes remarkable little use of facial expressions, acting instead with his whole body. For this reason close-ups are rare in his work: "I like long shots. It is up to the spectator to discover what there is to see. The close-up underlines, emphasises: "Look, this is funny!" By contrast, in a long shot you show several elements, characters and objects. Why isolate their relationships and what may be typical or comic in them?" Tati is one of the great advocates of colour films, and colour is a vital aspect of the kind of films he makes: "To tell the truth, even when I shot my films in black-and-white, I always thought them in colour." In this respect *Mon Oncle* represented a considerable advance, while *Playtime,* with its elaborate technical resources, satisfied one of his greatest ambitions.

Tati began his career as an entertainer with a series of mimes that reflected his interest in and skill at sport. It was from these mimes that he developed the music hall act with which he began his stage career in 1933 and they still featured in the spectacle "Jour de Fête à L'Olympia" which he staged in 1961. Tati is obviously generalising from his own particular experience when he states: "What is demanded above all of a comic actor is a training in sport." These early experiences in sporting mime have influenced Tati's art in two ways. Firstly they have caused him to act with his whole body and, secondly, to conceive his films in visual terms, virtually without dialogue: "The story is told better with images, sound and music. *Mon Oncle* is almost a silent film." Tati's music hall experience is the basis of all his later work: "All film comedians worthy of the name were formed first of all in the music hall or circus. It is impossible to make a comic film without having learned one's job on the boards, in contact with the public. Otherwise one just makes literary comedy." His sense of timing is one of his greatest assets and it is this rather than inventiveness or handling of colour that makes *Mon Oncle* so infinitely preferable to, say, Louis Malle's *Zazie dans le Métro*. His years on the stage have also given Tati a respect for his audience: "I believe that the spectator needs to relax, but I absolutely refuse to make him laugh by means of low or vulgar methods. One should not despise the public. It has taste and good sense, infinitely more than certain people who affirm the contrary."

In his first three films Tati created two outstanding and unforgettable characters. François, the postman in *Jour de Fête*, is a fully rounded figure and the more obviously comic of the two. He is, at one and the same time, unthinkable outside this particular village setting, and at a distance from the other characters, a brilliant mime's comic act amid a carefully observed and realistic setting. He is a marvellous creation, but incapable of further development. Tati put much more of himself into his second *personnage*, Hulot, Hulot is a realistic character and fits more closely into the life around him. In appearance he is quite ordinary: "Hulot . . . has the physique of a solid sort of chap; he behaves like anyone else living in Paris or the provinces." Tati takes care that Hulot never becomes exaggerated, that he always exists on exactly the same level as the other characters. For this reason we smile rather than laugh outright at his actions. Hulot is as we have seen the very opposite of Chaplin in that he never invents his gags or shows himself aware that his actions might seem funny to other people. In *Playtime* this process is taken a stage further with the central figure virtually omitted in favour of a mass of realistically observed vignettes. This is obviously a much more sophisticated form of comedy than that practised by most comedians and it is a measure of Tati's skill that he creates so much humour despite these self-imposed limitations.

The basis of Tati's music hall act and hence of all his art is observation. He always has a notebook with him in which he can jot down his observations of human foibles and quirks of behaviour: "I watch people live, I walk, go to football matches . . . I stay for hours on the motorway watching the vehicles stream past. I listen to conversations, observe the mannerisms, the details, the modes of life which reveal the personality of every individual." One of Tati's aims in his films is to reveal to others what he has seen and noted: "The possibility of opening a terrace on to life and making known all its riches, seems to me one of the many uses of the cinema." There is, of course, no cold classification of people; Tati is full of affection for the people he meets: "I like people, all people, all sorts of people." As a result of this sympathetic observation, the backgrounds of Tati's films are always full of life and interest. One finds in his work an attempt to chronicle certain aspects of French life: the village community of *Jour de Fête,* the sleepy little seaside town of *Les Vacances de M. Hulot,* the old quarter of Saint Maur in *Mon Oncle,* and, by contrast, the rather bleak and coldly beautiful futuristic Paris of *Playtime.* The early films were shot on location, and in *Jour de Fête* and *Mon Oncle* the local inhabitants are included among the players. To all his settings Tati has devoted as much care as to the working out of François's or Hulot's gags. Indeed he has said explicitly of *Les Vacances de M. Hulot*: "I wanted to show a slice of holiday life," and of a planned film: "In short I shall show, by means of a succession of individual stories, the life of a town. Besides the film could be entitled 'The Town.' "

Tati's constant preoccupation with realism has caused some critics to evoke comparisons with the Italian Neo-Realists, but there is a fundamental difference that cannot be overlooked. The Italian cinema is critical of society but believes in the possibility and desirability of progress; its most characteristic directors are Marxist in outlook. Tati, on the other hand, is resolutely non-political. He views old Saint-Maur with nostalgic affection; the decaying houses are picturesque remains that deserve to be defended against the advocates of progress, not distressing slums that tell of social injustice. Similarly Tati's attack on modernity in the persons of the Arpels is exactly in line with that of a reactionary like Clair: "I do not look for a message, I simply interest myself in people, families, children, services rendered, all sorts of little problems that exist in a world more and more planned and mechanised." Tati aims at revealing the truth in his films, but affectionately, not in a critical fashion.

Two stills from Jacques Tati's PLAYTIME. Above: Monsieur Hulot strolling round the exhibition. Below, chaos in the Royal Garden restaurant.

In *Jour de Fête* there is an unresolved gap between the villagers and François. The authenticity of the former is disturbed by the obvious artificiality of the latter, who is an almost completely farcical character. This is one reason for Tati's refusal to make other films with this character, and Hulot is an attempt to create a character who will fit in better with his surroundings, whatever they may be. This integration is the inevitable outcome of Tati's attempt to make comedy more realistic: "What I have tried to do since the beginning is to give more truth to the comic character." Whereas François was a man apart, Hulot participates much more in the life around him; it is possible for him to belong to a family, to be a real, if marvellously entertaining, uncle to his young nephew: "I could have given Hulot a few 'numbers' during the film; instead I try to put him on exactly the same level as, shall we say M. Arpel, to take the case of *Mon Oncle*." This is in line with the experience Tati once had in London after an unsuccessful audition, when the essence of comedy seemed revealed to him. Observing the people he met he felt that his aim should be not to mime other people, but to show them directly: "How could I be so ambitious as to want to make people laugh, when they themselves were marvellous mimics, when the least passer-by knew more than I?" Tati's stated desire to avoid vulgar means of provoking laughter is linked with this tendency away from exaggeration. Its logical conclusion is, of course, a film without Hulot or any other extraordinary character, and this ambition is what he triumphantly achieves in *Playtime*.

* * *

JEAN GRÉMILLON is ranked by many French critics among the half-dozen greatest of all French directors. The full scale revaluation which his work merits lies outside the scope of this volume for his career extended over some thirty-five years. He came to the cinema about 1923 with a series of short documentaries and made his first feature in 1927. The failure of his first sound film led to work on a number of purely commercial films and made him seek work abroad, first in Spain and then at the Ufa studios in Berlin. It was only during the Occupation that he was able to achieve real success with *Lumière d'Été* (1943) and *Le Ciel est à Vous* (1944). Unhappily the postwar years followed the pattern of the

158

thirties and Grémillon was unable (in the feature film at least) to give full expression to his considerable talents as director, writer and musician.

His first postwar work was a documentary which had as its subject the Normandy landings and was entitled **Le Six Juin à l'Aube** (1945). The mutilation this film suffered at the hands of its distributors was a foretaste for Grémillon of the difficulties that were in store for him. Despite the film's subtitle 'Notes cinématographiques sur le Débarquement Anglo-Americain', the actual landings are dealt with summarily — in the distributed version at least — and the director's interest would appear to lie elsewhere. The film begins with a pastorale of rural life in Normandy which is followed by an account of the various battles told largely through maps. The greater part of the film consists of an elegaic meditation on the tragic aftermath of war: the cemeteries and the ruins amid which men are striving to re-establish themselves. Grémillon's own wonderfully expressive music and the beautifully composed images of his four cameramen make this a very moving if sombre work.

Subsequently much of Jean Grémillon's energy was spent on administrative work — he was president of the Syndicat des Techniciens and of the Cinémathèque — for none of his plans in the years 1945 to 1948 were realised. A list of the projects on which he worked gives some idea of the scope of his ambitions: "La Commune", a film on the popular risings of 1871; "Le Massacre des Innocents", written with Charles Spaak, which was to have been a trilogy focussed on three moments of history: 1936 and the Spanish Civil War, 1938 and Munich, 1944 and the Resistance; "La Commedia dell' Arte", showing the involvement of a band of Italian actors in the Saint Bartholomew massacre of 1572; and "Le Printemps de la Liberté". This latter, designed to commemorate the 1848 Revolution, was finally dropped by its sponsors, the Ministry of Education, after fourteen months of preparation. It was to have been a real "film d'auteur" for Grémillon wrote the script, dialogue and music as well as preparing the direction. The work was broadcast in 1948 and the script published the same year but the shooting of the film itself was never begun.

Jean Grémillon returned therefore to the harsh realities of commercial film production and made three features, none of which was successful enough for him to be given the chance to work in real freedom. **Pattes**

Blanches (1949) was made from a script which Jean Anouilh had written in collaboration with Jean Bernard Luc and had intended to direct himself. It is typical of the dramatist in his blacker mood and tells of the obsessive rivalry of the Comte de Keriadec's two sons (Paul Bernard and Michel Bouquet) for the love of an innkeeper's pretty but vicious mistress (Suzy Delair). The plot is violent and contorted, full of strange scenes and confrontations, but never very convincing. Grémillon's handling of it, however, is masterly. The Breton backgrounds are lovingly recreated, the acting of the whole cast is of a very high standard and several sequences are outstanding, most notably that of the inn-keeper's wedding where music, settings and movement combine to wonderful effect. **L'Étrange Madame X** (1951) was a further story of impossible passion, with the lovers played this time by Michèle Morgan and Henri Vidal. The latter plays a young cabinet-maker who falls in love with a woman who he thinks is a chamber-maid but who is in fact the wife of a wealthy man. Grémillon depicted the contrasting social backgrounds with a sure touch and kept rigorously to his allotted budget and schedule but again commercial success eluded him. In 1954 came **L'Amour d'une Femme**, made from a script by Grémillon himself but unbalanced as a result of international co-production requirements. The film contained many characteristic elements — a tragic love story (here of a woman doctor torn between her profession and her love for a young engineer), a setting of Grémillon's native Britanny and some carefully composed photography by the director's habitual lighting cameraman, Louis Page — but it did not turn out to be the success that Grémillon needed, and proved indeed to be his last chance at feature film making. Jean Grémillon's qualities as a director, his careful methods of preparation and direction, his taste for great tragic themes and his view of the film as a medium of artistic expression, combined to prevent him from making the simple money-making film he needed to destroy the legend of box-office failure that had grown up around his name.

With remarkable resolution Grémillon turned his back on this sad sequence of features and found a new centre of interest in the documentary. In collaboration with his former assistant Pierre Kast he co-directed **Les Charmes de l'Existence** (1950) which gave a portrait of society in the

A film full of strange scenes and confrontations: Arlette Thomas and Paul Bernard in Jean Grémillon's PATTES BLANCHES.

fifty years preceding the outbreak of war in 1914 through the painting of the period. The following year Grémillon provided the commentary and music for Kast's own *Les Désastres de la Guerre* (1951), which showed the Napoleonic wars as depicted in the works of Goya, and then contributed two films, **Alchimie** and **Astrologie** to the short-lived *Encyclopédie Filmée* series. **Au Coeur de l'Ile de France** (1954), his next short, traced the architecture and painting of the Ile de France from Gothic to Impressionism, showing realism and love of nature to be constant features of eight centuries of art. Grémillon's last three films are his major achievements in the art film. In them the director used colour for the first time (the camera being in the able hands of Louis Page) to explore contemporary art. **La Maison aux Images** (1956) showed one aspect of the activities of Montmartre that lie behind the tourist-orientated façade. It revealed the work of artists and craftsmen who create or reproduce works of art by means of the processes of etching and engraving. **Haute Lisse** (1957) was an equally sympathetic look at another form of contemporary craftsmanship which likewise has its roots in the past: the weaving of tapestries at the Manufacture des Gobelins. It showed both the history of tapestry making and the modern refinements in such matters as the making of dyes, but its most lasting impression is the image of the craftsmen's gestures as they work at their tapestries, a single one of which may need up to two years' work. **André Masson et les Quatre Éléments** (1958) is Grémillon's finest achievement in the documentary. It took him a year to complete and was shot in and around the home and studio of the tachiste painter at Aix-en-Provence. It traces with penetrating insight the intimate connections between Masson's abstract paintings and collages and the Provençal landscape. The film is both a meditation on the mysteries of artistic creation and also itself a totally realised work of art in which vision (landscapes, paintings and gestures of Masson) and sound (Grémillon's voice and music) fuse perfectly. This proved to be Jean Grémillon's last work for he died in November 1959. It is fitting that this director who was so rarely able to give full expression to his personality should have concluded his career with a film which, though brief in length, is one of his most satisfying and successful works.

* * *

GEORGES ROUQUIER, whose first contact with the cinema had been an amateur documentary, *Vendanges*, shot in 1929, returned to the film world during the war years to direct a number of shorts, including two on rural crafts: *Le Tonnelier* (1942) and *Le Charron* (1943). The work which is generally regarded as his masterpiece is the feature-length documentary **Farrebique** (1946). This film took a year to shoot and traces life on a farm in the Massif Central from autumn to autumn. Inevitably it is a fragmentary work, but its very unevenness adds to its air of absolute authenticity. The film's double title, *Farrebique ou les Quatre Saisons*, indicates its double focus: the farm itself and the pattern of Nature. The manner in which the everyday activity of the family is observed — the bread-making, ploughing and harvesting, evening prayers and trips to church and bistrot — recalls Rouquier's earlier short films. The major events that take place within the family in the course of the year — the Grandfather's account of the family history, his death and the birth of a baby, the younger son's injury and engagement — are all underplayed and the slight clumsiness with which they are handled is in perfect keeping with the film's tone. Parallel to the life within the farm is the pageant of the seasons which Rouquier's camera reveals to us. The director views Nature with all the intensity of a true poet and stresses always its dynamic aspect, particularly in the long lyrical passage celebrating the coming of spring. Rouquier once described *Farrebique* as a diary of childhood memories and this defines very well the film's special quality. The director does not attempt to integrate rural life into the framework of society as Luchino Visconti was to do with the life of the fishermen in *La Terra Trema*, made two years later. In *Farrebique* virtually the only contact with the outside world is the installation of electricity and even this is treated as a minor incident. The simple life led by those on the farm is seen as satisfying and is observed with a warm and good-natured attitude utterly lacking in condescension. Rouquier's view is always optimistic and affirmative and it is significant in this respect that he breaks with chronology and ends his film not with the Grandfather's death but with the son's engagement and the promise of spring.

Rouquier wanted to follow this film with normal features using actors and fictional stories, but seven years passed before he was given the

*The old grandfather views his lands for the last time in Georges Rouquier's
FARREBIQUE.*

chance. **Sang et Lumières** (1953), adapted from a novel by Joseph Peyré, was probably doomed in advance, being a bi-lingual Franco-Spanish production, dialogued by Michel Audiard and starring Daniel Gélin and Zsa Zsa Gabor as toreador and *femme fatale*. Another four years passed before Rouquier could follow it with a second fiction film. **S.O.S. Noronha** (1957) starred Jean Marais and dealt with a group of Frenchmen who run a South American radio station despite the difficulties caused by revolutionary upheavals. The film achieved only a limited success and no further chance came Rouquier's way.

Because of this inability to work within the commercial framework of the feature film most of Rouquier's work since *Farrebique* consists of short and medium-length documentaries. His first two postwar shorts were solid but unadventurous works. In 1947 he collaborated with Jean Painlevé (himself a noted documentarist) on **L'Oeuvre Scientifique de Pasteur** which reconstructed the great French scientist's struggle to get his ideas on germs accepted and showed the application of his remarkable achievements to the preservation of liquids and the combatting of disease by vaccination. **Le Chaudronnier** (1949) traced the work of the coppersmith from the middle ages to the present and with its study of the craftsmanship involved in beating copper recalls Rouquier's earlier studies of rural crafts. But here the scope is wider for since the invention of soft steel the techniques of the coppersmith have found far wider application in the manufacture of cars, planes and ships. In **Le Sel de la Terre** (1950) Rouquier's talent as a director and his ability to give epic stature to the most humdrum of human activities are again as fully apparent as in *Farrebique* and his debt to the Russian cinema of the twenties is clear. Again the setting is a rural one, this time the Camargue, and the film begins by following the ride to two 'gardiens' through the unspoiled natural marshland, the haunt of foxes and flamingoes. The photography of Marcel Fradetal in this opening section is exceptionally beautiful and serene. But from the beginning there are signs of encroaching modern life and the film's second half deals with this aspect: the methods of land reclamation which have turned large areas of salt-poisoned wasteland into the finest rice-growing land in France. By a combination of Guy Bernard's music and montage effects in the manner of Eisenstein, Rouquier builds up a uniquely powerful effect, an exaltation of man's triumphant battle against adversity. With its lyricism and beautiful photography, its vigour and concentration on the world of men, *Le Sel de la Terre* is a perfect example of Rouquier's poetic personality.

Equally successful is the shorter documentary **Malgovert** (1952) which deals with the building of a hydro-electric station in the mountains of Savoie. It begins with the sad fate of the villagers of Tignes who are forced to leave their homes and land to make way for the new reservoir, and then proceeds to the actual construction work itself. As *Le Sel de la Terre* showed man's triumph over the seas, so *Malgovert* celebrates the conquest of a mountain, though at a cost of sixty lives. Again the director's sympathy for the workers and his ability to capture and record the gestures of everyday life are apparent, and Guy Bernard's music and Rouquier's own editing methods make an enthralling crescendo of the digging of the tunnel which will take water from the dam to the generators. In a very different mood was **Arthur Honegger** (1955) which traced the career of the great composer by means of a filmed interview and excerpts from his works. Probably the finest of Rouquier's works after *Farrebique* was the one he directed just before this film on Honegger: **Lourdes et ses Miracles** (1954). It is a three-part examination of the Lourdes phenomenon from an admirably detached and impersonal standpoint. The director's views are never stated explicitly and it is left to each member of the audience to make up his mind for himself. The recognised miracles are examined, one sees those who have been cured and those who have recovered since the film was begun. The question remains as to whether faith is strengthened by the miraculous (or at least inexplicable) cure of the few, or whether one is horrified by the disappointed hopes of the commercially exploited majority.

* * *

ROGER LEENHARDT was already an influential film critic and experienced director of short films when he made **Les Dernières Vacances** in 1947. This film, which has become something of a minor classic, has all the personal style and scope of an autobiographical novel. It studies with sensitivity and intelligence the first awakenings of adult emotions in

"*The first awakenings of adult emotions.*" *Odile Versois and Michel François in Roger Leenhardt's LES DERNIÈRES VACANCES.*

two young people who have grown up together, setting their problems against those of their elders who have assembled to debate the necessity for selling the family estate. The background of holiday life in a country house during the nineteen twenties is beautifully evoked and though the amorous intrigues of the adults are perhaps given excessive weight, the truth with which the adolescents are observed more than compensates for Leenhardt's occasional awkwardness in handling his material. Many years passed before Leenhardt was offered a similar opportunity to make a film in absolute freedom and he preferred to withdraw from the feature film world rather than be compelled to make commercial concessions. He preserved the ambition of one day filming Garcia Lorca's "La Maison de Bernarda" but devoted most of his energy to the production and direction of short films, deriving from these an artistic satisfaction he felt he could never have got from the commercial cinema.

Since the war Leenhardt has directed some thirty short films which reveal his wide interests in art and literature. Among the more interesting of these are a study of the prehistory of the cinema: **Naissance du Cinéma** (1946); an investigation of the coming of new methods of agriculture to Morocco, seen through the eyes of a young Arab and the French teacher who befriends him: **La Fugue de Mahmoud** (1950); and a whole series of biographical studies of great men: **Victor Hugo** (1951); **François Mauriac** (1954); **Jean-Jacques** (1958) on Rousseau; **Paul Valéry** (1960) and **L'Homme à la Pipe** (1962) on the painter Gustave Courbet.

In 1961 Leenhardt did make a second feature, **Le Rendez-Vous de Minuit** (1962) but unlike *Les Dernières Vacances* this was an impersonal film, representing the working out of an interesting aesthetic idea (that of a film within a film) rather than the expression of any deeply-held feelings or emotions. It concerns a woman, Eva, who identifies herself with the heroine of a film and the journalist who tries to save her from the heroine's fate of a suicide leap from a Paris bridge. The 'film' story and the 'real' story run side by side and Leenhardt handles their stylistic clash adroitly, maintaining intellectual interest, but failing to involve us deeply, despite a subtly shaded pair of performances by Lili Palmer.

5. Filmographies

THE following filmographies of the principal directors treated in this volume are as complete as I have been able to make them, but inevitably a number of gaps and queries remain. I am deeply indebted to all my predecessors who have worked to establish full and accurate filmographies and take this opportunity of offering my thanks to them. The dates given are normally those of the first public showing of a film and the various abbreviations are, I think, self explanatory. Each filmography is followed by a select bibliography, comprising (a) monographs and pamphlets on and principal interviews given by the director concerned, and (b) published scripts. Normally these sources are in French, but those in English are marked with an asterisk (*) and those in German with a dagger (†). For reasons of space it has been impossible to list all magazine references, but it is self-evident that a work of this kind would have been impossible without the information and stimulus offered by the various specialised magazines, both French and English.

Apart from chapters in the general histories of the cinema by Georges Sadoul, Paul Rotha, Charles Ford and René Jeanne etc., there are a number of other studies that offer valuable insight into the French cinema of the postwar years and before. The best survey is undoubtedly Georges Sadoul's *Histoire du Cinéma Français* (Club des Editeurs, Paris, 1962) which covers the whole period from 1890 to 1962 and includes a dictionary of 200 cinéastes and chronological tables of all films produced between 1892 and 1960. Sadoul is also the author of the best English account: *French Film* (Falcon Press, London, 1953). Pierre Leprohon has given a useful survey: *Cinquante Ans de Cinéma Français* (1895-1945) (Ed. du Cerf, Paris, 1954), which is supplemented by *Sept Ans de Cinéma Français* (1945-1952), published by the same firm and written by seven critics led by Henri Agel. The first three volumes of André Bazin's *Qu'est-ce que le Cinéma?* (Ed. du Cerf, Paris, 1958-1962—partially translated by Hugh Gray for the University of California Press, 1967) though fragmentary in form, offer many pieces of precise analysis. Two other works contain chapters on the directors dealt with in this book: Henri Agel's *Les Grands Cinéastes* (Ed. Universitaires, Paris, 1960) has studies of fourteen French directors, while Pierre Leprohon's enormously informative *Presénces Contemporaines Cinéma* (Nouvelles Editions Debresse, Paris, 1951) surveys the work of twenty-five directors (but not Leenhardt or Rouquier).

CLAUDE AUTANT-LARA

b. 5 Aug. 1903 at Luzarches. Active in the cinema from the age of sixteen. Designed décor and costumes for films of Marcel L'Herbier — *Le Carnaval des Vérités* (1919), *L'Homme du Large* (1920), *Villa Destin* (1921), *Don Juan et Faust* (1922), *L'Inhumaine* (1923), *Le Diable au Coeur* (1927); Jacque Catelain — *Le Marchand de Plaisir* (1923); and Jean Renoir — *Nana* (1926). Also assistant to René Clair for *Paris qui Dort* (1923) and *Le Voyage Imaginaire* (1925).

In 1923 he directed an avant-garde short *Fait Divers*, followed by a documentary *Vittel* (1926) and *Construire un feu* (1927-8), an early wide screen experiment. From 1930 to 1932 he was in Hollywood, directing French versions of American films [*Buster se Marie* (1930), *La Perte*, *Pur Sang*, *Le Plombier Amoureux* (1931), *L'Athlète Incomplet* (1932)] In 1932 on his return to France he directed a number of shorts: *Le Gendarme est sans pitié, Un Client Sérieux, Monsieur le Duc, La Peur des Coups, Invite Monsieur à Dîner*.

Feature Films:

CIBOULETTE (1933)
prod: Cipar Films. *dir:* Claude Autant-Lara. *sc:* (from the operetta by Reynaldo Hahn). *adapt:* Autant-Lara & Jacques Prévert. *dial:* Prévert. *ph:* Curt Courant. *des:* Lazare Meerson. *mus:* Reynaldo Hahn. *ed:* Henri Taverna.
players: Simone Berriau, Dranem, Thérèse Dorny, Robert Burnier, Pomiès, Urban.
MY PARTNER MASTER DAVIS (1936 in G.B.)
prod: Oxford. *dir:* Claude Autant-Lara. *sc:* (from the novel by Jeraro Prieto). *adapt. & dial:* Jacques Prévert.
players: Alastair Sim, Henry Kendall, Kathleen Kelly, Guy Middleton. (Also known as *The Mysterious Mr. Davis*).
L'AFFAIRE DU COURRIER DE LYON (1937)
prod: Maurice Lehmann. *dir:* Claude Autant-Lara. *sc:* (from the play by Moreau, Siraudin & Delacour). *adapt:* Jean Aurenche. *dial:* Jacques Prévert. *ph:* Michel Kelber. *des:* Jacques Krauss. *mus:* Louis Beydts. *ed:* Yvonne Baugé.
players: Pierre Blanchar, Dita Parlo, Jacques Copeau, Charles Dullin, Dorville.
LE RUISSEAU (1938)
prod: Maurice Lehmann. *dir:* Claude Autant-Lara. *sc:* (from the play by Pierre Wolff), *adapt:*

Jean Aurenche. *dial:* Michel Duran. *ph:* Michel Kelber. *des:* Jacques Krauss. *mus:* Tiarko Richepin. *players:* Françoise Rosay, Paul Cambo, Michel Simon, Gaby Silvia.
FRIC-FRAC (1939)
prod: Maurice Lehmann. *dir:* Claude Autant-Lara. *sc:* (from the play by Edouard Bourdet). *adapt. & dial:* Michel Duran. *ph:* Armand Thirard. *des:* René Renoux. *mus:* Casimir Oberfeld. *ed:* Elizabeth Harris.
players: Fernandel, Michel Simon, Arletty, Helène Robert, Marcel Vallée.
LE MARIAGE DE CHIFFON (1942)
prod: L'Industrie Cinématographique. *dir:* Claude Autant-Lara. *sc:* (from the novel by Gyp). *adapt:* Jean Aurenche & Maurice Blondeau. *dial:* Aurenche. *ph:* Jean Isnard & Philippe Agostini. *des:* Jacques Krauss. *mus:* Jean Wiener.
players: Odette Joyeux, André Luguet, Jacques Dumesnil, Suzanne Dantès, Louis Seigner.
LETTRES D'AMOUR (1942)
prod: Synops. *dir:* Claude Autant-Lara. *sc:* Jean Aurenche. *adapt:* Aurenche & Maurice Blondeau. *dial:* Aurenche. *ph:* Philippe Agostini. *des:* Dumesnil (from sketches by Jacques Krauss.) *mus:* Maurice Yvain.
players: Odette Joyeux, François Périer, Simone Renant, Alerme, Carette, Parédès.
DOUCE (1943)
prod: L'Industrie Cinématographique. *dir:* Claude Autant-Lara. *sc:* (from the novel by Michel Davet). *adapt. & dial:* Jean Aurenche & Pierre Bost. *ph:* Philippe Agostini. *des:* Jacques Krauss. *mus:* René Cloërec. *ed:* Madeleine Gug.
players: Odette Joyeux, Madeleine Robinson, Marguerite Moreno, Jean Debucourt, Roger Pigaut.
SYLVIE ET LE FANTÔME (1945)
prod: André Paulvé/Ecran Français. *dir:* Claude Autant-Lara. *sc:* (from the play by Alfred Adam). *adapt. & dial:* Jean Aurenche. *ph:* Philippe Agostini. *des:* Lucien Carré (from sketches by Jacques Krauss). *mus:* René Cloërec. *ed:* Madeleine Gug.
players: Odette Joyeux, François Périer, Louis Salou, Julien Carette, Pierre Larquey, Jean Desailly.
LE DIABLE AU CORPS (1947)
prod: Transcontinental Films. *dir:* Claude Autant-Lara. *sc:* (from the novel by Raymond Radiguet). *adapt. & dial:* Jean Aurenche & Pierre Bost. *ph:* Michel Kelber. *des:* Max Douy. *mus:* René Cloërec. *ed:* Madeleine Gug.
players: Micheline Presle, Gérard Philipe, Denise Grey, Jean Debucourt.
OCCUPE-TOI D'AMÉLIE (1949)
prod: Lux Films. *dir:* Claude Autant-Lara. *sc:* (from the play by Georges Feydeau). *adapt. & dial:* Jean Aurenche & Pierre Bost. *ph:* André Bac. *des:* Max Douy. *mus:* René Cloërec. *ed:* Madeleine Gug.
players: Danielle Darrieux, Jean Desailly, Louise Conte, Bervil, Armontel, Carette.
L'AUBERGE ROUGE (1951)
prod: Memnon Films. *dir:* Claude Autant-Lara. *sc:* Jean Aurenche. *adapt. & dial:* Aurenche, Pierre Bost & Autant-Lara. *ph:* André Bac. *des:* Max Douy. *mus:* René Cloërec. *ed:* Madeleine Gug.
players: Fernandel, Françoise Rosay, Carette, Marie-Claude Olivia, Grégoire Aslan.
episode L'ORGUEIL in LES SEPT PÉCHÉS CAPITAUX (1952)
prod: Franco-London Films (Paris)/Film Costellazione (Rome). *dir:* Claude Autant-Lara. *sc. adapt. & dial:* Jean Aurenche, Pierre Bost & Autant-Lara. *ph:* Jacques Natteau. *des:* Max Douy. *mus:* René Cloërec. *ed:* Madeleine Gug.
players: Michèle Morgan, Françoise Rosay, Louis Seigner, Jean Debucourt.
LE BON DIEU SANS CONFESSION (1953)
prod: Films Gibé. *dir:* Claude Autant-Lara. *sc:* (from the novel "M. Dupont est Mort" by Paul Vialar). *adapt:* Autant-Lara, Ghislaine Auboin & Roland Laudenbach. *dial:* Auboin. *ph:* André Bac. *des:* Max Douy. *mus:* René Cloërec. *ed:* Madeleine Gug.
players: Danielle Darrieux, Henri Vilbert, Mino Burney, Claude Laydu, Grégoire Aslan.
LE BLÉ EN HERBE (1954)
prod: Franco-London Films. *dir:* Claude Autant-Lara. *sc:* (from the novel by Colette). *adapt. & dial:* Jean Aurenche, Pierre Bost & Autant-Lara. *ph:* Robert Le Febvre. *des:* Max Douy. *mus:* René Cloërec. *ed:* Madeleine Gug.

players: Edwige Feuillère, Pierre-Michel Beck, Nicole Berger, Renée Devillers, Charles Deschamps.

LE ROUGE ET LE NOIR (1954)
prod: Franco-London Films/Documento Film. *dir:* Claude Autant-Lara. *sc:* (from the novel by Stendhal). *adapt.* & *dial:* Jean Aurenche & Pierre Bost. *ph:* Michel Kelber. *des:* Max Douy. *mus:* René Cloërec. *ed:* Madeleine Gug & Boris Lewin.
players: Gérard Philipe, Danielle Darrieux, Jean Martinelli, Antonella Lualdi, Antoine Balpêtré.

MARGUERITE DE LA NUIT (1955)
prod: S. N. E. Gaumont/Del Duca Films (Cino Del Duca). *dir:* Claude Autant-Lara. *sc:* (from the novel by Pierre MacOrlan). *adapt.* & *dial:* Ghislaine Autant-Lara & Gabriel Arout. *ph:* Jacques Natteau. *des:* Max Douy. *mus:* René Cloërec. *ed:* Madeleine Gug.
players: Michèle Morgan, Yves Montand, Jean-François Calvé, Palau, Massimo Girotti.

LA TRAVERSÉE DE PARIS (1956)
prod: Franco-London Films/Continentale Produzione. *dir:* Claude Autant-Lara. *sc:* (from the story by Marcel Aymé). *adapt.* & *dial:* Jean Aurenche & Pierre Bost. *ph:* Jacques Natteau. *des:* Max Douy. *mus:* René Cloërec. *ed:* Madeleine Gug.
players: Jean Gabin, Bourvil, Louis de Funès, Jeanette Batti, Bernard Lajarrige.

EN CAS DE MALHEUR (1958)
prod: Iéna (Raoul Lévy). *dir:* Claude Autant-Lara. *sc:* (from the novel by Georges Simenon). *adapt.* & *dial:* Jean Aurenche & Pierre Bost. *ph:* Jacques Natteau. *des:* Max Douy. *mus:* René Cloërec. *ed:* Madeleine Gug.
players: Jean Gabin, Brigitte Bardot, Edwige Feuillère, Franco Interlenghi.

LE JOUEUR (1958)
prod: Franco London Films (Paris)/Zebra Films (Rome). *dir:* Claude Autant-Lara. *sc:* (from the novel by Dostoievski). *adapt:* Jean Aurenche & François Boyer. *dial:* Aurenche, Boyer & Pierre Bost. *ph:* Jacques Natteau. *des:* Max Douy. *mus:* René Cloërec. *ed:* Madeleine Gug.
players: Gérard Philipe, Liselotte Pulver, Bernard Blier, Nadine Alari, Françoise Rosay, Carette.

LES RÉGATES DE SAN FRANCISCO (1959)
prod: Iéna Productions (Raoul Lévy). *dir:* Claude Autant-Lara. *sc:* (from the novel by Quarantotti Gambini). *adapt.* & *dial:* Jean Aurenche & Pierre Bost. *ph:* Armand Thirard. *des:* Max Douy. *mus:* René Cloërec. *ed:* Madeleine Gug.
players: Suzy Delair, Folco Lulli, Laurent Terzieff, Nelly Benedetti, Danièle Gaubert, François Nocher.

LA JUMENT VERTE (1959)
prod: S. N. E. Gaumont/Sopac Films (Paris)/Zebra Film (Rome). *dir:* Claude Autant-Lara. *sc:* (from the novel by Marcel Aymé). *adapt.* & *dial:* Jean Aurenche & Pierre Bost. *ph:* Jacques Natteau. *des:* Max Douy. *mus:* René Cloërec. *ed:* Madeleine Gug.
players: Bourvil, Sandra Milo, Françis Blanche, Yves Robert, Valerie Lagrange, Mireille Perrey.

LE BOIS DES AMANTS (1960)
prod: Hoche Productions (Ray Ventura) (Paris)/Dama Cinematografica (Rome). *dir:* Claude Autant-Lara. *sc:* (from the play "Terre Inhumaine" by François de Curel). *adapt:* Jacques Rémy & René Hardy. *dial:* Albert Husson. *ph:* Jacques Natteau. *des:* Max Douy. *mus:* René Cloërec. *ed:* Madeleine Gug.
players: Erika Remberg, Françoise Rosay, Laurent Terzieff, Horst Franck, Gert Froebe.

TU NE TUERAS POINT (NON UCCIDERE) (1961 in Yugoslavia)
prod: Loven Film (Belgrade)/Gold Film Anstalt (Vaduz) (Morris Ergas). *dir:* Claude Autant-Lara. *sc.* Jean Aurenche. *adapt.* & *dial:* Aurenche, Pierre Bost & Autant-Lara. *ph:* Jacques Natteau. *des:* Max Douy. *mus:* Charles Aznavour. *ed:* Madeleine Gug.
players: Laurent Terzieff, Horst Frank, Suzanne Flon, Mica Orlovic, Marjan Lorric, Ivo Jaksic, Vladeta Dragutinovic.

VIVE HENRI IV, VIVE L'AMOUR (1961)
prod: Hoche Productions/Dama Cinematografica. *dir:* Claude Autant-Lara. *sc.* & *adapt:* Henri Jeanson & Jean Aurenche. *dial:* Jeanson. *ph:* Jacques Natteau. *des:* Max Douy. *mus:* René Cloërec. *ed:* Madeleine Gug.
players: Francis Claude, Jean Sorel, Bernard Blier, Danièle Gaubert, Melina Mercuri, Pierre Brasseur.

LE COMTE DE MONTE CRISTO (1961)
prod: J. J. Vital/Films René Modiano/S.N.E. Gaumont (Paris)/Cineriz/Royal Film (Rome).
dir: Claude Autant-Lara. *sc:* (from the novel by Alexandre Dumas). *adapt.* & *dial:* Jean Halain.
ph: Jacques Natteau & Jean Isnard. *des:* Max Douy. *mus:* René Cloërec. *ed:* Madeleine Gug.
players: Louis Jourdan, Yvonne Furneaux, Pierre Mondy, Bernard Dhéran, Franco Silva.
LE MEURTRIER (1963)
prod: International Prod./Marceau-Cocinor (Paris)/Corona Film (Munich)/Centro Film (Rome).
dir: Claude Autant-Lara. *sc:* (from the novel by Patricia Highsmith) *adapt.* & *dial:* Jean Aurenche
& Pierre Bost. *ph:* Jacques Natteau. *des:* Max Douy. *mus:* René Cloerec. *ed:*
Madeleine Gug.
players: Maurice Ronet, Marina Vlady, Robert Hossein, Gert Frobe, Jacques Monod.
LE MAGOT DE JOSÉFA (1963)
prod: S.O.F.A.C./Raimbourg/Star Press/Arco Film. *dir:* Claude Autant-Lara. *sc:* (from the novel
by Catherine Claude). *adapt:* Jean Aurenche & Pierre Bost & Autant-Lara. *dial:* Bernard Dimay.
ph: Jacques Natteau. *des:* Max Douy. *mus:* René Cloërec. *ed:* Madeleine Gug.
players: Anna Magnani, Pierre Brasseur, Bourvil, Ramon Iglesias, Henri Virlojeux.
JOURNAL D'UNE FEMME EN BLANC (1965)
prod: S.O.P.A.C./S.N.E. Gaumont (Paris)/Arco Film (Rome). *dir:* Claude Autant-Lara. *sc:*
(from the novel by André Soubiran). *adapt.* & *dial:* Jean Aurenche & René Wheeler. *ph:* Michel
Kelber. *des:* Max Douy. *mus:* Michel Magne. *ed:* Madeleine Gug.
players: Marie-José Nat, Jean Valmont, Claude Gensac, Robert Benoît, Paloma Matta, Jean-
Pierre Dorat.
UNE FEMME EN BLANC SE REVOLTE (1966)
prod: S.O.P.A.C./S.N.E. Gaumont. *dir:* Claude Autant-Lara. *sc:* (from the novel
by André Soubiran). *adapt:* Jean Aurenche. *ph:* Michel Kelber. *des:* Max Douy.
mus: Michel Magne. *ed:* Madeleine Gug.
players: Danielle Volle, Bernard Dhéran, Michel Ruhl, Josée Steiner, Claude Titre,
Sophie Leclair, Hélène Tossy.
episode **AUJOURD'HUI** in **LE PLUS VIEUX METIER DU MONDE** (1967)
prod: Les Films Gibé/Francoriz (Paris)/Rialto (Berlin)/Rizzoli (Rome). *dir:*
Claude Autant-Lara. *sc:* Jean Aurenche. *des:* Max Douy.
players: France Anglade, Nadia Gray, Francis Blanche, Jacques Duby, Dalio.
LE FRANCISCAIN DE BOURGES (1968)
prod: S.O.P.A.C./S.N.E. Gaumont. *dir:* Claude Autant-Lara. *sc:* (from the novel by
Marc Tolédano). *adapt:* Jean Aurenche & Pierre Bost. *ph:* Michel Keller. *des:* Max
Douy. *ed:* Madeleine Gug.
players: Hardy Kruger, Jean-Pierre Dorat, Jean Desailly, Suzanne Flon, Christian
Barbier.

Bibliography:

(a) There is no full study of Autant-Lara's work. Best articles are:
*Raymond Durgnat: "The Rebel with Kid Gloves" *(Films & Filming.*
Oct. & Nov. 1960).
Raymond Borde: "Un Emigré de l'Intérieur" *(Positif 41.* Sept. 1961).
Interviews in *Cinéma 61* No. 61. and *Cahiers du Cinéma* No. 188.
(b) "La Traversée de Paris" (*Avant-Scène 66.* Jan. 1967).

JACQUES BECKER

b. 15 Sept. 1906 in Paris. d. 20 Feb. 1960 in Paris. Interest in the cinema stimulated by meetings with Jean Renoir and King Vidor. Worked as assistant to Renoir from 1932 to 1939. In 1934 collaborated with Pierre Prévert on a short film *LE COMMISSAIRE EST BON ENFANT*, adapted from Courteline, ph: Michel Kelber, players: Palau, Marcel Duhamel, Etienne Decroux. In 1939 began a feature film *L'OR DU CRISTOBAL*, which he was not allowed to complete. His real career as a director dates from his return from captivity in Germany in 1942.

Films:

DERNIER ATOUT (1942)
prod: Essor Cinématographique Français. *dir:* Jacques Becker. *sc:* Maurice Aubergé. *adapt:* Aubergé, Louis Chavance, Maurice Griffe & Becker. *dial:* Pierre Bost. *ph:* Nicolas Hayer. *des* Max Douy. *mus:* Jean Alfaro. *ed:* Marguerite Renoir.
players: Raymond Rouleau, Georges Rollin, Pierre Renoir, Noël Roquevert, Jean Debucourt

GOUPI-MAINS-ROUGES (1943)
prod: Minerva. dir: Jacques Becker. *sc:* (from the novel by Pierre Véry). *adapt:* Véry & Becker. *dial:* Véry. *ph:* Jean Bourgoin & Pierre Montazel. *des:* Pierre Marquet. *mus:* Jean Alfaro. *ed:* Marguerite Renoir.
players: Fernand Ledoux, Georges Rollin, Robert le Vigan, Arthur Devère, Maurice Schutz, René Génin.

FALBALAS (1944-5)
prod: Essor Cinématographique Français *dir:* Jacques Becker. *sc.* & *adapt:* Maurice Aubergé, Maurice Griffe & Becker. *dial:* Aubergé. *ph:* Nicolas Hayer. *des:* Max Douy. *mus:* Jean-Jacques Grunenwald. *ed:* Marguerite Renoir.
players: Raymond Rouleau, Micheline Presle, Jean Chrevrier, Françoise Lugagne.

ANTOINE ET ANTOINETTE (1946)
prod: S.N.E. Gaumont. *dir:* Jacques Becker. *sc.* & *dial:* Maurice Griffe, Françoise Giroud & Becker. *ph:* Pierre Montazel. *des:* Robert Jules Garnier. *mus:* Jean-Jacques Grunenwald. *ed:* Marguerite Renoir.
players: Roger Pigaut, Claire Mafféi, Noël Roquevert, Pierre Trabaud, Gérard Oury, Annette Poivre, Gaston Modot.

RENDEZ-VOUS DE JUILLET (1949)
prod: U.G.C./S.N.E. Gaumont. *dir:* Jacques Becker. *sc:* Becker & Maurice Griffe. *adapt* & *dial:* Becker. *ph:* Claude Renoir. *des:* Robert Jules Garnier. *mus:* Jean Wiener & Mezz Mezzrow. *ed:* Marguerite Renoir.
players: Daniel Gélin, Bernard Lajarrige, Maurice Ronet, Pierre Trabaud, Nicole Courcel, Brigitte Auber, Louis Seigner.

EDOUARD ET CAROLINE (1951)
prod: U.G.C. *dir:* Jacques Becker. *sc:* Annette Wademant & Becker. *dial:* Wademant. *ph:* Robert le Febvre. *des:* Jacques Colombier. *mus:* Jean-Jacques Grunenwald. *ed:* Marguerite Renoir.
players: Anne Vernon, Daniel Gélin, Jacques François, Jean Galland, Elisa Labourdette.

CASQUE D'OR (1952)
prod: Speva Films/Paris Films. *dir:* Jacques Becker. *sc:* Becker & Jacques Companeez. *dial:* Becker. *ph:* Robert le Febvre. *des:* Jean d'Eaubonne. *mus:* Georges Van Parys. *ed:* Marguerite Renoir.
players: Serge Reggiani, Simone Signoret, Claude Dauphin, Raymond Bussières, Paul Azaïs.

RUE DE L'ESTRAPADE (1953)
prod: Cinéphonic/S.G.G.C. *dir:* Jacques Becker. *sc.* & *dial:* Annette Wademant. *ph:* Marcel Grignon. *des:* Jean d'Eaubonne. *mus:* Marguerite Monod & Georges Van Parys. *ed:* Marguerite Renoir.
players: Daniel Gélin, Louis Jourdan, Anne Vernon, Jean Servais, Micheline Dax, Michel Flamme, Jacques Morel, Marcelle Praince.

TOUCHEZ PAS AU GRISBI (1954)
prod: Del Duca Films/Silver Films (Paris)/Antarès Films (Rome). *dir:* Jacques Becker. *sc:* (from the novel by Albert Simonin). *adapt:* Becker, Maurice Griffe & Simonin, *dial:* Simonin. *ph:* Pierre Montazel. *des:* Jean d'Eaubonne. *mus:* Jean Wiener. *ed:* Marguerite Renoir.
players: Jean Gabin, René Dary, Paul Frankeur, Lino Ventura, Jeanne Moreau, Dora Doll, Delia Scala.
ALI BABA ET LES QUARANTE VOLEURS (1954)
prod: Films du Cyclope. *dir:* Jacques Becker. *sc. & adapt:* Becker, Marc Maurette, Cesare Zavattini, Jean Manse. *dial:* André Tabet. *ph:* Robert le Febvre. *des:* Georges Wakhevitch.
players: Fernandel, Dieter Borsche, Henri Vilbert, Delmont, Samia Gamal.
LES AVENTURES D'ARSÈNE LUPIN (1956)
prod: S.N.E. Gaumont/Lambor Films/Films Constellazione. *dir:* Jacques Becker. *sc:* Becker & Albert Simonin (from works of Maurice Leblanc). *dial:* Simonin. *ph:* Edmond Séchan. *des:* Rino Mondellini. *mus:* Jean-Jacques Grunenwald. *ed:* Geneviève Vaury.
players: Robert Lamoureux, O. E. Hasse, Liselotte Pulver, Huguette Hue, Georges Chamarat.
MONTPARNASSE 19 (1957)
prod: Franco London Films/Astra Cinematografica. *dir:* Jacques Becker. *sc:* (from the novel "Les Montparnos" by Michel Georges-Michel): *orig. adapt:* Henri Jeanson, *rewritten* Becker. *ph:* Christian Matras. *des:* Jean d'Eaubonne. *mus:* Paul Misraki. *ed:* Marguerite Renoir.
players: Gérard Philipe, Gérard Séty, Lino Ventura, Anouk Aimée, Lilli Palmer, Lea Padovani.
LE TROU (1960)
prod: Play Art/Filmsonor (Paris)/Titanus (Rome). *dir:* Jacques Becker. *sc:* (from José Giovanni's novel) *adapt:* Becker, Giovanni & Jean Aurel. *dial:* Becker & Giovanni. *ph:* Ghislain Cloquet. *des:* Rino Mondellini. *mus:* none. *ed:* Marguerite Renoir.
players: Michel Constantin, Jean Keraudy, Philippe Leroy, Raymond Meunier, Marc Michel.

Bibliography:

(a) Raymond Queneau & Jean Queval: "Rendez-Vous de Juillet" (Chavane, Paris, 1949).

Jean Queval: "Jacques Becker" (Seghers, Paris, 1962).

René Gilson: "Becker" (*Anthologie du Cinéma 14*, April 1966). Interview in *Cahiers du Cinéma*, No. 32.

(b) "Casque d'Or" *(Avant-Scène 43*. Dec. 1964).

"Le Trou" *(Avant-Scène 13*. Mar. 1962).

ROBERT BRESSON

b. 27 Sept. 1907 at Bromont-Lamothe. Early interest in painting. Early activity in the cinema includes (a) work on a number of scripts: *C'était un Musicien* (Frédéric Zelnick, 1933), *Les Jumeaux de Brighton* (Claude Heymann, 1936) & *Courier Sud* (Pierre Billon, 1937) and (b) a medium length comedy *LES AFFAIRES PUBLIQUES* (1934) — *dir. & sc:* Robert Bresson. *mus:* Jean Wiener. *ed:* Bresson & Pierre Charbonnier. *players:* Béby, Dalio, Gilles Margaritis, Andrée Servilanges. Bresson also worked briefly as René Clair's assistant on the unfinished *Air Pur* in 1939. He regards his real career as beginning with his first feature film.

Feature films:

LES ANGES DU PÉCHÉ (1943)
prod: Synops/Roland Tual. *dir:* Robert Bresson. *sc:* Bresson & Father Bruckberger. *dial:* Jean Giraudoux. *ph:* Philippe Agostini. *des:* René Renoux. *mus:* Jean-Jacques Grunenwald. *ed:* Yvonne Martin.
players: Renée Faure, Jany Holt, Sylvie, Marie-Hélène Dasté, Paula Dehelly, Silvia Montfort, Mila Parély, Yolande Laffon, Louis Seigner.

LES DAMES DU BOIS DE BOULOGNE (1944-5)
prod: Raoul Ploquin. *dir. & sc:* Robert Bresson (from an episode in the novel "Jacques le Fataliste" by Diderot). *dial:* Jean Cocteau. *ph:* Philippe Agostini. *des:* Max Douy. *mus:* Jean-Jacques Grunenwald. *ed:* Jean Feyte.
players: Maria Casarès, Elina Labourdette, Lucienne Bogaert, Paul Bernard, Jean Marchat.

LE JOURNAL D'UN CURÉ DE CAMPAGNE (1951)
prod: U.G.C. *dir. sc. & dial:* Robert Bresson (from the novel by Georges Bernanos). *ph:* Léonce-Henry Burel. *des:* Pierre Charbonnier. *mus:* Jean-Jacques Grunenwald. *ed:* Paulette Robert.
players: Claude Laydu, Armand Guibert, Marie-Monique Arkell, Nicole Ladmiral, Jean Riveyre, Nicole Maurey, Jean Danet, Antoine Balpêtré, Martine Lemaire.

UN CONDAMNÉ À MORT S'EST ÉCHAPPÉ (1956)
prod: S.N.E. Gaumont/N.E.F. *dir. sc. & dial:* Robert Bresson (from André Devigny's account of his escape). *ph:* Léonce-Henry Burel. *des:* Pierre Charbonnier. *mus:* Mozart (C Minor Mass). *ed:* Raymond Lamy.
players: François Leterrier, Charles le Clainche, Maurice Beerblock, Roland Monod, Jacques Ertaud, Roger Tréherne.

PICKPOCKET (1959)
prod: Agnès Delahaie. *dir. sc. & dial:* Robert Bresson. *ph:* Léonce-Henry Burel. *des:* Pierre Charbonnier. *mus:* Lulli. *ed:* Raymond Lamy.
players: Martin Lasalle, Pierre Leymarie, Jean Pelegri, Marika Green, Kassagi, Pierre Etaix, Dolly Seal.

PROCÈS DE JEANNE D'ARC (1962)
prod: Agnès Delahaie. *dir. sc. & dial:* Robert Bresson (from the records of Joan of Arc's trial.) *ph:* Léonce-Henry Burel. *des:* Pierre Charbonnier. *mus:* Francis Seyrig. *ed:* Germaine Artus.
players: Florence Carrez, Jean-Claude Fourneau, Roger Honorat, Marc Jacquier, Michel Herubel, Richard Pratt, André Brunet, Philippe Dreux, Gérard Zing.

AU HASARD, BALTHAZAR (1966)
prod: Parc Film/Athos Films/Argos (Paris)/ Svensk Filmindustri/Svenski Filminstitutet (Stockholm). *dir. sc. & dial:* Robert Bresson. *ph:* Ghislain Cloquet. *des:* Pierre Charbonnier. *mus:* Schubert & Jean Wiener. *ed:* Raymond Lamy.
players: Anne Wiazemsky, François Lafarge, Philippe Asselin, Nathalie Joyaut, Walter Green, Jean-Claude Guilbert, François Sullerot, M. C. Frémont, Pierre Klossowsky.

MOUCHETTE (1967)
prod: Parc Film/Argos Films. *dir. sc. & dial:* Robert Bresson (from the novel "Nouvelle Histoire de Mouchette" by Georges Bernanos). *ph:* Ghislain Cloquet. *des:* Pierre Guffroy. *mus:* Monteverdi & Jean Wiener. *ed:* Raymond Lamy.
players: Nadine Nortier, Jean-Claude Guilbert, Marie Cardinal, Paul Hebert, Jean Vimenet, Marie Susini, Raymonde Chabrun, Suzanne Huguenin, Marine Trichet.

UNE FEMME DOUCE (1969)
prod: Parc Film/Marianne Productions. *dir. sc. & dial:* Robert Bresson (from a story by Dostoievsky). *ph:* Ghislain Cloquet. *des:* Pierre Charbonnier. *ed:* Raymond Lamy.
players: Dominique Sanda, Guy Frangin, Jane Lobre.

Bibliography:
(a) René Briot: "Robert Bresson" (Ed. du Cerf, Paris, 1957).
Jean Sémolué: "Bresson". (Ed. Universitaires, Paris, 1959).
Michel Estève: "Robert Bresson" (Seghers, Paris, 1962).
* Chapter in John Russell Taylor: "Cinema Eye Cinema Ear" (Methuen, London, 1964).
Interviews in *Cahiers du Cinéma* Nos. 75 & 104.
Robert Droguet: "Robert Bresson" (*Premier Plan 42,* Lyon, 1966).
(b) dialogue of "Les Dames du Bois de Boulogne" *(Cahiers du Cinéma* Nos. 75, 76, 77, 1957).
script of "Procès de Jeanne d'Arc" (Julliard, Paris, 1962).
"Mouchette" (*Avant-Scène 80,* April 1968)

MARCEL CARNÉ

b. 18 Aug. 1909 in Paris. Assistant cameraman to Georges Périnal for *Les Nouveaux Messieurs* (1928, Feyder), Jules Kruger for *Cagliostro* (1929, Oswald). Film journalist on various magazines. With Jean Aurenche (writer) and Paul Grimault (designer) made a number of very short advertising films in thirties. Directed short film: *NOGENT ELDORADO DU DIMANCHE* (1930) with Michel Sanvoisin. Assistant to Clair (*Sous les Toits de Paris* (1929), and Feyder *(Le Grand Jeu* (1933), *Pension Mimosas* (1934), *La Kermesse Héroique* (1935)).

Films:
JENNY (1936)
prod: R.A.C. *dir:* Marcel Carné. *sc:* (from the novel by Pierre Rocher). *adapt:* Jacques Prévert & Jacques Constant. *dial:* Prévert. *ph:* Roger Hubert. *des:* Jean d'Eaubonne. *mus:* Joseph Kosma & Lionel Cazeau. *ed:* Ernest Hajos.
players: Françoise Rosay, Lisette Lanvin, Margo Lion, Albert Préjean, Charles Vanel.
DRÔLE DE DRAME (1937)
prod: Corniglion-Molinier. *dir:* Marcel Carné. *sc:* (from the novel by Storer-Clouston "His first Offence"). *adapt.* & *dial:* Jacques Prévert. *ph:* Eugen Schufftan. *des:* Alexandre Trauner. *mus:* Maurice Jaubert. *ed:* Marthe Poncin.
players: Michel Simon, Françoise Rosay, Louis Jouvet, Annie Cariel, Jean-Louis Barrault.
QUAI DES BRUMES (1938)
prod: Rabinovich. *dir:* Marcel Carné. *sc:* (from the novel by Pierre MacOrlan). *adapt.* & *dial:* Jacques Prévert. *ph:* Eugen Schufftan. *des:* Alexandre Trauner. *mus:* Maurice Jaubert. *ed:* René le Hénaff.
players: Jean Gabin, Michel Simon, Michèle Morgan, Aimos, René Génin, Pierre Brasseur.
HÔTEL DU NORD (1938)
prod: Sedif. *dir:* Marcel Carné. *sc:* (from the novel by Eugène Dabit) *adapt:* Henri Jeanson,

Jean Aurenche. *dial:* Jeanson. *ph:* Armand Thirard. *des:* Alexandre Trauner. *mus:* Maurice Jaubert.

players: Annabella, Jean-Pierre Aumont, Arletty, Louis Jouvet, André Brunot, Jane Marken.

LE JOUR SE LÈVE (1939)

prod: Vog/Sigma. *dir:* Marcel Carné. *sc:* Jacques Viot. *adapt.* & *dial:* Jacques Prévert. *ph:* Curt Courant. *des:* Alexandre Trauner. *mus:* Maurice Jaubert. *ed:* René le Hénaff.

players: Jean Gabin, Arletty, Jacqueline Laurent, Jules Berry, Mady Berry, Jacques Baumer.

LES VISITEURS DU SOIR (1942)

prod: André Paulvé. *dir:* Marcel Carné. *sc.* & *dial:* Jacques Prévert & Pierre Laroche. *ph:* Roger Hubert. *des:* Georges Wakhévitch & Alexandre Trauner. *mus:* Maurice Thiriet & Joseph Kosma. *ed:* Henri Rust.

players: Arletty, Marie Déa, Jules Berry, Fernand Ledoux, Alain Cuny, Marcel Herrand

LES ENFANTS DU PARADIS (1944-5)

prod: Pathé-Cinéma. *dir:* Marcel Carné. *sc:* Jacques Prévert & Carné. *dial:* Prévert. *ph:* Roger Hubert. *des:* Léon Barsacq, Raymond Gabutti & Alexandre Trauner. *mus:* Maurice Thiriet & Joseph Kosma. *ed:* Henri Rust.

players: Arletty, Jean-Louis Barrault, Maria Casarès, Pierre Brasseur, Marcel Herrand, Louis Salou, Pierre Renoir, Paul Frankeur, Jane Marken.

LES PORTES DE LA NUIT (1946)

prod: Pathé-Cinéma. *dir:* Marcel Carné. *sc:* (from Prévert's ballet "Le Rendez-Vous") *adapt:* Jacques Prévert & Carné. *dial:* Prévert. *ph:* Philippe Agostini. *des:* Alexandre Trauner. *mus:* Joseph Kosma. *ed:* Jean Feyté.

players: Pierre Brasseur, Yves Montand, Nathalie Nattier, Jean Vilar, Serge Reggiani.

LA MARIE DU PORT (1950)

prod: Sacha Gordine. *dir:* Marcel Carné. *sc:* (from the novel by Georges Simenon). *adapt:* Louis Chavance & Carné. *dial:* Georges Ribemont-Dessaignes. *ph:* Henri Alekan. *des:* Alexandre Trauner. *mus:* Joseph Kosma. *ed:* Léonide Azar.

players: Jean Gabin, Nicole Courcel, Blanchette Brunoy, Julien Carette, Claude Romain.

JULIETTE OU LA CLEF DES SONGES (1951)

prod: Sacha Gordine. *dir:* Marcel Carné. *sc:* (from the play by Georges Neveux) *adapt:* Carné & Jacques Viot. *dial:* Georges Neveux. *ph:* Henri Alekan. *des:* Alexandre Trauner. *mus:* Joseph Kosma. *ed:* Léonide Azar.

players: Gérard Philipe, Suzanne Cloutier, Jean-Roger Caussimon, René Génin, Yves Robert.

THÉRÈSE RAQUIN (1953)

prod: Paris Film/Lux. *dir:* Marcel Carné. *sc:* (from the novel by Zola). *adapt:* Carné & Charles Spaak. *dial:* Spaak. *ph:* Roger Hubert. *des:* Paul Bertrand. *mus:* Maurice Thiriet. *ed:* Henri Rust.

players: Simone Signoret, Raf Vallone, Roland Lesaffre, Sylvie, Jacques Duby.

L'AIR DE PARIS (1954)

prod: Del Duca film (Paris)/Galatea (Rome). *dir:* Marcel Carné. *sc:* Carné & Jacques Sigurd. *dial:* Sigurd. *ph:* Roger Hubert. *des:* Paul Bertrand. *mus:* Maurice Thiriet (songs: Francis Lemarque & Bob Costella). *ed:* Henri Rust.

players: Jean Gabin, Roland Lesaffre, Arletty, Marie Daems, Jean Parédès, Simone Paris.

LE PAYS D'OÙ JE VIENS (1956)

prod: Clément Duhour. *dir:* Marcel Carné. *sc:* Jacques Emmanuel. *adapt:* Carné, Marcel Achard, Emmanuel. *dial:* Achard. *ph:* Philippe Agostini. *des:* Jean Douarinou. *mus:* Gilbert Bécaud. *ed:* Paulette Robert.

players: Gilbert Bécaud, Françoise Arnoul, Madeleine Lebeau, Gabriello, Claude Brasseur.

LES TRICHEURS (1958)

prod: Silver Films (Robert Dorfmann)/Cinétel. *dir:* Marcel Carné. *sc:* Carné & Charles Spaak. *adapt.* & *dial:* Jacques Sigurd. *ph:* Claude Renoir. *des:* Paul Bertrann *mus:* Recorded Jazz. *ed:* Albert Jurgenson.

players: Pascal Petit, Andréa Parisy, Jacques Charrier, Laurent Terzieff, Roland Lesaffre.

TERRAIN VAGUE (1960)

prod: Gray Film/Films Rive Gauche/Jolly Films. *dir:* Marcel Carné. *sc:* (from the novel "Tomboy" by Hal Ellson). *adapt.* & *dial:* Carné & Henri François-Rey. *ph:* Claude Renoir. *des:* Paul Bertrand. *mus:* Michel Legrand & Francis Lemarque. *ed:* Henri Rust & Marguerite Renoir.

players: Roland Lesaffre, Danièle Gaubert, Jean-Louis Bras, Maurice Caffarelli.
DU MOURON POUR LES PETITS OISEAUX (1963)
prod: Champs-Elysées prod. (Jules Borkon)/Films Borderie (Paris)/Variety Film (Rome). *dir.* Marcel Carné. *sc.* (from the novel by Albert Simonin). *adapt:* Carné & Jacques Sigurd. *dial:* Sigurd. *ph:* Jacques Natteau. *des:* Jacques Saulnier. *mus:* Georges Garvarentz. *ed:* Albert Jurgenson.
players: Paul Meurisse, Dany Saval, Jean Richard, Suzy Delair, Franco Citti, Suzanne Gabriello, Roland Lesaffre.
TROIS CHAMBRES À MANHATTAN (1965)
prod: Les Productions Montaigne. *dir:* Marcel Carné. *sc:* (from the novel by Georges Simenon). *adapt:* Jacques Sigurd & Carné. *dial:* Sigurd. *ph:* Eugen Schufftan. *des:* Léon Barsacq. *mus:* Mal Waldron. *ed:* Henri Rust.
players: Annie Girardot, Maurice Ronet. O. E. Hasse, Roland Lesaffre, Gabrielle Ferzetti. Geneviève Page, Robert Hoffman.
LES JEUNES LOUPS (1968)
prod: S.N.C. (Paris)/West Films (Rome). *dir:* Marcel Carné. *sc:* Claude Accursi & Carné. *dial:* Accursi. *ph:* Jacques Robin. *des:* Rino Mondolini. *mus:* Jack Arel. *ed:* René Gillet.
players: Haydée Politoff, Christian Hay, Roland Lesaffre, Yves Beneyton, Maurice Garrel, Bernard Dhéran, Elina Labourdette.

Bibliography:

(a) Marcel Lapierre: "Aux Portes de la Nuit" (Nouvelle Edition, Paris, 1946).

Jean Queval: "Marcel Carné" (Ed. du Cerf, Paris, 1952).

Bernard Chardère (ed): "Jacques Prévert" *(Premier Plan* 14. Lyon. 1960).

Robert Chazal: "Marcel Carné" (Seghers, Paris, 1965).

Gérard Guillot: "Les Prévert" (Seghers, Paris, 1966).

(b) "Les Visiteurs du Soir" *(Avant-Scène* 12. Feb. 1962).

"Le Jour se lève" *(Avant-Scène* 53, Oct. 1965).

"Les Enfants du Paradis" *(Avant-Scène 72-3,* July 1967).

"Nogent, Eldorado Du Dimanche" and "Les Jeunes Loups" *(Avant-Scène 81,* May 1968)

RENÉ CLAIR

b. 11 Nov. 1898; real name René Chomette. Served briefly in ambulance corps in 1917, invalided out. Wrote poetry: "La Fête de l'Homme" (1917), "Terre" (1918-19). In 1919 began work as journalist on "L'Intransigeant". First connection with the cinema was as an actor in Loïe Fuller's *Le Lys de la Vie* (1920), followed by Protozanov's *Le Sens de la Mort* (1921) and two serials directed by Louis Feuillade: *L'Orpheline* (1921) and *Parisette* (1921). Assistant to Jacques de Baron-celli for *Carillon de Minuit* (1922) and *La Légende de soeur Béatrix* (1922). Other works of Clair include a novel "Adams" (1926), two stories

"De Fil en Aiguille" and "La Princesse de Chine" (1952) and a book of film criticism "Réflexion Faite" (1951). He also produced a radio version of Gautier's "Une Larme de Diable" (1951) and translated Garson Kanin's "Born Yesterday" as "Voyage à Washington."

Films:

PARIS QUI DORT (1923)
prod: Films Diamant (Henri Diamant-Berger). *dir. & sc:* René Clair. *ph:* Maurice Desfassiaux & Paul Guichard. *des:* André Foy.
players: Henri Rolland. Madeleine Rodrigue, Albert Préjean, Martinelli, Marcel Vallée, Pré fils, Stacquet, Myla Seller.

ENTR'ACTE (1924)
prod: Ballets Suédois (Rolf de Maré). *dir:* René Clair. *sc. & des:* Francis Picabia. *ph:* Jimmy Berliet. *mus:* Erik Satie.
players: Jean Borlin, Inge Fries, Francis Picabia, Man Ray, Marcel Duchamp, Erik Satie, Georges Auric.

LE FANTÔME DU MOULIN ROUGE (1924)
prod: Films René Fernand. *dir. & sc:* René Clair. *ph:* Jimmy Berliet & Louis Chaix. *des:* Robert Gys.
players: Albert Préjean, Sandra Milovanoff, Georges Vaultier, José Davert, Maurice Schutz, Paul Olivier, Madeleine Rodrigue.

LE VOYAGE IMAGINAIRE (1925)
prod: Rolf de Maré. *dir. & sc:* René Clair. *ph:* Jimmy Berliet & Amédée Morin. *des:* Robert Gys.
players: Dolly Davis, Jean Borlin, Albert Préjean, Jim Gérald, Maurice Schutz, Paul Olivier, Marguerite Madys, Yvonne Legeay.

LA PROIE DU VENT (1926)
prod: Films Albatros (Alexandre Kamenka). *dir. & sc.* René Clair (from the novel by Armand Mercier "L'Aventure amoureuse de Pierre Vignal"). *ph:* Robert Batton, Nicolas Roudakoff, Emile Gondois. *des:* Lazare Meerson & Bruni.
players: Charles Vanel, Lilian Hall Davis, Sandra Milovanoff, Jean Murat, Jim Gérald.

UN CHAPEAU DE PAILLE D'ITALIE (1927)
prod: Films Albatros (Alexandre Kamenka). *dir. & sc:* René Clair (from the play by Eugène Labiche & Marc Michel). *ph:* Maurice Desfassiaux & Nicolas Roudakoff. *des:* Lazare Meerson.
players: Albert Préjean, Olga Tchekova, Marise Maïa, Yvonneck, Alice Tissot, Alexis Bondireff, Pré fils, Alex Alin, Vital Geymond, Paul Olivier, Jim Gérald, Volbert.

LA TOUR (1928) short documentary on the Eiffel Tower.
prod: Films Albatros. *dir. & sc:* René Clair. *ph:* Georges Périnal & Nicolas Roudakoff.

LES DEUX TIMIDES (1928)
prod: Films Albatros/Sequana. *dir. & sc:* René Clair (from the play by Eugene Labiche & Marc Michel). *ph:* Robert Batton & Nicolas Roudakoff. *des:* Lazare Meerson.
players: Maurice de Féraudy, Vera Flory, Pierre Batcheff, Jim Gérald, Françoise Rosay, Yvette Andreyor, Madeleine Guitty, Paul Olivier, Pré fils, Stacquet.

SOUS LES TOITS DE PARIS (1930)
prod: Films Sonores Tobis. *dir. sc. & dial:* René Clair. *ph:* Georges Périnal. *des:* Lazare Meerson.
songs: Raoul Moretti & R. Nazelles (arranged Armand Bernard). *ed:* René Le Hénaff.
players: Albert Préjean, Pola Illery, Gaston Modot, Edmond Gréville, Paul Olivier, Bill Bocket, Aimos, Jane Pierson.

LE MILLION (1931)
prod: Films Sonores Tobis. *dir. sc. & dial:* René Clair (from the play by Georges Berr & Guillemand) *ph:* Georges Périnal. *des:* Lazare Meerson. *mus:* Armand Bernard, Philippe Parès & Georges Van Parys. *ed:* René Le Hénaff.
players: Annabella, René Lefèvre, Vanda Gréville, Paul Olivier, Louis Alliberi, Constantin Stroesco, Odette Talazac, Pitouto, Jane Pierson, André Michaud, Raymond Cordy.

À NOUS LA LIBERTÉ (1931)
prod: Film Sonores Tobis. *dir. sc.* & *dial:* René Clair. *ph:* Georges Périnal. *des:* Lazare Meerson.
mus: Georges Auric, *ed:* René Le Hénaff.
players: Raymond Cordy, Henri Marchand, Rolla France, Germaine Aussey, Paul Olivier,
Jacques Shelley, André Michaud, Alexandre d'Arcy, Léon Lorin, Vincent Hyspa, William
Burke.
QUATORZE JUILLET (1932)
prod: Films Sonores Tobis. *dir. sc.* & *dial:* René Clair. *ph:* Georges Périnal. *des:* Lazare Meerson.
mus: Maurice Jaubert. *ed:* René le Hénaff.
players: Annabella, Georges Rigaud, Pola Illery, Raymond Cordy, Paul Olivier, Raymond Aimos.
Thomy Bourdelle, Pré fils.
LE DERNIER MILLIARDAIRE (1934)
prod: Pathé Nathan. *dir. sc.* & *dial:* René Clair. *ph:* Rudolph Maté. *des:* Lucien Aguettand &
Lucien Carré. *mus:* Maurice Jaubert. *ed:* Jean Pouzet.
players: Max Dearly, Renée Saint-Cyr, Marthe Mellot, Raymond Cordy, José Noguéro, Aimos,
Sinoël, Paul Olivier, Marcel Carpentier, Charles Redgie, Jean Aymé, Christiane Ribes.
THE GHOST GOES WEST (1935, in G.B.)
prod: London Films (Alexander Korda). *dir:* René Clair. *sc.* (from the story by Eric Keown
"Sir Tristram Goes West"). *adapt.* & *dial:* Robert Sherwood & Geoffrey Kerr. *ph:* Harold
Rosson. *des:* Vincent Korda. *mus:* Misha Spoliansky. *ed:* Harold Earle-Fishback.
players: Robert Donat, Jean Parker, Eugene Pallette, Elsa Lanchester, Everly Gregg, Hay Petrie,
Morton Selten.
BREAK THE NEWS (1937 in G.B.)
prod: Jack Buchanan Productions/René Clair. *dir:* René Clair. *sc:* Geoffrey Kerr & Clair (from
the novel by Loic le Gouriadec "La Mort en Fuite"). *dial:* Kerr. *ph:* Philip Tannura. *des:* Lazare
Meerson. *mus:* Theo Mackeben.
players: Jack Buchanan, Maurice Chevalier, June Knight, Martha Labarr, Gertrude Musgrove,
Charles Lefeaux, Garry Marsh, Wallace Douglas, Felix Aylmer.
AIR PUR (1939, interrupted by the war & never completed)
prod: Corniglion-Molinier (Nice). *dir.* & *sc:* René Clair. *dial:* Pierre Bost & Clair. *ph:* Michel
Kelber. *des:* Georges Lourié. *mus:* Maurice Jaubert.
players: Elina Labourdette, Jean Mercanton & children.
THE FLAME OF NEW ORLEANS (1940 in U.S.A.)
prod: Universal (Joe Pasternak). *dir:* René Clair. *sc:* Norman Krasna. *ph:* Rudolph Maté. *des:*
Jack Otterson. *mus:* Frank Skinner & Charles Previn. *ed:* Frank Gross.
players: Marlene Dietrich, Bruce Cabot, Roland Young, Mischa Auer, Laura Hope Crews.
FOREVER AND A DAY (1942 in U.S.A.)
Clair directed one episode of this collective film, replacing Hitchcock at the last moment
(film had 7 directors, 21 writers & a speaking cast of 70).
I MARRIED A WITCH (1942 in U.S.A.)
prod: Paramount. *dir:* René Clair. *sc:* (from a novel by Thorne Smith & Norman Matson)
adapt. & *dial:* Robert Pirosh & Marc Connelly. *ph:* Ted Tetzlaff. *des:* Hans Dreier & Ernst Fegte.
mus: Roy Webb. *ed:* Eda Warren.
players: Veronica Lake, Fredric March, Susan Hayward, Cecil Kellaway, Robert Benchley.
IT HAPPENED TOMORROW (1943 in U.S.A.)
prod: United Artists (Arnold Pressburger). *dir:* René Clair. *sc:* Dudley Nichols & Clair (from
stories by Lord Dunsany, Hugh Wedlock & Howard Snyder & an idea by Lewis R. Foster)
add. dial: Helene Fraenkel. *ph:* Archie Stout. *des:* Erno Metzer. *mus:* Robert Stolz. *ed:* Fred
Pressburger.
players: Dick Powell, Linda Darnell, Jack Oakie, Edgar Kennedy, John Philliber.
AND THEN THERE WERE NONE (1945 in U.S.A.)
prod: Popular Pictures Corporation for 20th Century-Fox. *dir:* René Clair. *sc:* (from the novel
by Agatha Christie" Ten little Niggers") *adapt.* & *dial:* Dudley Nichols. *ph:* Lucien Andriot.
des: Ernst Fegte. *mus:* Charles Previn. *ed:* Harvey Manger.
players: Barry Fitzgerald, Walter Huston, Louis Hayward, Roland Young, June Duprez,
Sir C. Aubrey Smith, Judith Anderson, Mischa Auer

LE SILENCE EST D'OR (1947)

prod: Pathé/R.K.O. *dir. & sc:* René Clair. *ph:* Armand Thirard. *des:* Léon Barsacq. *mus:* Georges Van Parys. *ed:* Louisette Hautecoeur.

players: Maurice Chevalier, François Périer, Marcelle Derrien, Dany Robin, Robert Pizani, Raymond Cordy, Paul Olivier, Roland Armontel, Gaston Modot, Bernard la Jarrige.

LA BEAUTÉ DU DIABLE (1949 in Italy)

prod: Universalia/Production E.N.I.E./Franco London Film (Salvo d'Angelo). *dir:* René Clair. *sc. & dial:* Clair & Armand Salacrou. *ph:* Michel Kelber. *des:* Léon Barsacq. *mus:* Roman Vlad. *ed:* James Cuenet.

players: Michel Simon, Gérard Philipe, Nicole Besnard, Simone Valère, Carlo Ninchi, Paolo Stoppa, Raymond Cordy, Tullio Carminati, Gaston Modot.

LES BELLES—DE—NUIT (1952)

prod: Franco London Film (Paris)/Rizzoli Films (Rome). *dir. sc. & dial:* René Clair. *ph:* Armand Thirard & Robert Juillard. *des:* Léon Barsacq. *mus:* Georges Van Parys. *ed:* Louisette Hautecoeur.

players: Gérard Philipe, Martine Carol, Gina Lollobrigida, Magali Vendeuil, Marylin Bufferd, Paolo Stoppa, Raymond Bussières, Bernard la Jarrige, Jean Paradès, Raymond Cordy.

LES GRANDES MANOEUVRES (1955)

prod: Filmsonor (Paris)/Rizzoli Films (Rome). *dir:* René Clair. *sc. & dial:* Clair *with collab. of* Jérôme Géronimi & Jean Marson (from a story by Courteline). *ph:* Robert le Febvre & Robert Juillard. *des:* Léon Barsacq. *mus:* Georges Van Parys. *ed:* Louisette Hautecoeur.

players: Michèle Morgan, Gérard Philipe, Brigitte Bardot, Yves Robert, Jean Desailly, Pierre Dux, Jacques François, Lise Delamare, Jacqueline Maillan, Magali Noël.

PORTE DES LILAS (1957)

prod: Filmsonor/Cinetel/Seca (Paris)/Rizzoli Films (Rome). *dir:* René Clair. *sc:* Clair *with collab. of* Jean Aurel (from René Fallet's novel "La Grande Ceinture"). *ph:* Robert le Febvre. *des:* Léon Barsacq. *mus:* Georges Brassens. *ed:* Louisette Hautecoeur.

players: Pierre Brasseur, Georges Brassens, Henri Vidal, Dany Carrel, Raymond Bussières, Amedée, Alain Bouvette, Bugette, Gérard Buhr, Annette Poivre.

sketch **LE MARIAGE** in **LA FRANÇAISE ET L'AMOUR** (1960)

prod: Les Films Metzger & Woog/Paris Elysée Film/Unidex. *dir. & sc:* René Clair. *ph:* Robert le Febvre. *des:* Lucien Aguettand. *mus:* Jacques Metchen. *ed:* Louisette Hautecoeur.

players: Marie-José Nat, Claude Rich, Yves Robert, Liliane Patrick, Jacques Fabri.

TOUT L'OR DU MONDE (1961)

prod: S.E.C.A./Filmsonor (Paris)/Cineriz/Royal Film (Rome). *dir:* René Clair. *sc:* Clair *with collab. of* Jacques Rémy & Jean Marsan. *ph:* Pierre Petit. *des:* Léon Barsacq. *mus:* Georges Van Parys. *ed:* Arlette Lalande & Louisette Hautecoeur.

players: Bourvil, Philippe Noiret, Claude Rich, Alfred Adam, Annie Fratellini, Colette Castel, Nicole Chollet, Françoise Dorléac, Albert Michel, Michel Modo, Claude Véga.

sketch **LES DEUX PIGEONS** in **LES QUATRE VÉRITÉS** (1962)

prod: Madeleine/Franco London Film (Paris)/Ajace Cinematografica (Rome)/Hispamer (Madrid) (Gilbert de Goldschmidt). *dir. & sc:* René Clair (from one of La Fontaine's fables). *ph:* Armand Thirard. *des:* Léon Barsacq. *mus:* Georges Garvarentz & Charles Aznavour. *ed:* Denise Natot.

players: Leslie Caron, Charles Aznavour.

LES FÊTES GALANTES (1965)

prod: Gaumont International (Paris)/Studioul Bucaresti (Bucarest). *dir. sc. & dial:* René Clair. *ph:* Christian Matras. *des:* Georges Wakhévitch. *mus:* George Van Parys. *ed:* Louisette Hautecoeur. *players:* Jean-Pierre Cassel, Philippe Avron, Marie Dubois, Geneviève Casile.

Bibliography:

(a) Jacques Bourgeois: "René Clair" (Roulet, Geneva/Paris, 1949).

Georges Charensol & Roger Régent: "Un Maître du Cinéma: René Clair" (Table Ronde, Paris, 1952).

Georges Charensol: "René Clair et les Belles de Nuit" (Ed. du Cerf, Paris, 1953).

* Catherine de la Roche: "René Clair: an Index" (B.F.I., London 1958).

Jean Mitry: "René Clair" (Ed. Universitaires, Paris, 1960).

Barthélemy Amengual: "René Clair" (Seghers, Paris, 1963).

René Clair: "Réflexion Faite" (Gallimard, Paris, 1951).

* Translated as "Reflections on the Cinema" (William Kimber, London, 1953).

* Interview in *Films & Filming* (June 1957).

(b) "Le Silence est d'Or", "La Beauté du Diable", "Les Belles-de-Nuit", "Les Grandes Manoeuvres" & "Porte des Lilas" in "Comédies et Commentaires" (Gallimard, Paris, 1959).

"Tout l'Or du Monde" (Gallimard, Paris, 1962).

"Entr'acte" and "A Nous la Liberté" (*Avant-Scène 86,* Nov. 1968)

RENÉ CLÉMENT

b. 18 March 1913 at Bordeaux. Studied to become an architect. Interest in the cinema from about 1934 when he began work as cameraman and assistant director.

1937-1944 directed a number of short films including: *SOIGNE TON GAUCHE* (1937, an early Tati film), *LA GRANDE CHARTREUSE* (1937) *ARABIE INTERDITE* (1938, a series of three shorts on Arabia), *LA BIÈVRE* (1939), *LE TIRAGE, CEUX DU RAIL* (1942), *TOULOUSE, LA GRANDE PASTORALE, CHEFS DE DEMAIN, MOUNTAIN* (1934-4).

After making his feature début he also worked as technical collaborator on Jean Cocteau's *La Belle et la Bête* (1946).

Films:
LA BATAILLE DU RAIL (1946)
prod: Coopérative Générale du Cinéma Français. *dir:* René Clément. *sc:* Clément, *in collab.* with Colette Audry & Jean Daurand. *ph:* Henri Alekan. *des:* none. *mus:* Yves Baudrier. *ed:* Jacques Désagneaux.
players: Jean Daurand, Clarieux, Désagneaux, Laurent & railway workers.
LE PÈRE TRANQUILLE (1946)
prod: B.C.M. *dir:* René Clément. *sc. & dial:* Noël-Noël. *ph:* Claude Renoir. *des:* Lucien Carré. *mus:* René Cloërec. *ed:* Mme. Wurtzer.
players: Noël-Noël, Jean Varas, Nadine Alari, José Arthur.

LES MAUDITS (1947)

prod: André Paulvé. *dir:* René Clément. *sc. & adapt:* Clément & Jacques Rémy (from an idea by Jacques Companeez & Victor Alexandroff). *dial:* Henri Jeanson. *ph:* Henri Alekan. *des:* Paul Bertrand. *mus:* Yves Baudrier. *ed:* Roger Dwyre.

players: Henri Vidal, Michel Auclair, Dalio, Paul Bernard, Florence Marly, Jo Dest, Karl Munch, Fosco Giachetti, Anne Campion.

AU DELÀ DES GRILLES (1949, in Italy: LE MURE DI MALAPURGA)

prod: Guarini/Francinex. *dir:* René Clément. *sc:* Cesare Zavattini & Suso Cecchi d'Amico. *adapt. & dial:* Jean Aurenche & Pierre Bost. *ph:* Louis Page. *des:* Piero Filippone. *mus:* Roman Vlad. *ed:* Mario Serandrei.

players: Isa Miranda, Jean Gabin, Andréa Cecchi, Vera Talchi, Robert Dalban.

LE CHATEAU DE VERRE (1950)

prod: Franco-London/Fortezza. *dir:* René Clément. *sc:* (from the novel by Vicky Baum "Sait-on Jamais") *adapt:* Clément & Pierre Bost. *dial:* Bost. *ph:* Robert le Febvre. *des:* Léon Barsacq. *mus:* Yves Baudrier. *ed:* Roger Dwyre.

players: Michèle Morgan, Jean Marais, Jean Servais, Elina Labourdette, Elsa Cegani, Alain Durthal, Anne-Marie Cazalis.

JEUX INTERDITS (1952)

prod: Robert Dorfman/Silver Films. *dir:* René Clément. *sc:* François Boyer (from his own story) *adapt. & dial:* Clément, Jean Aurenche & Pierre Bost. *ph:* Robert Juillard. *des:* Paul Bertrand. *mus:* Narcisco Yepes. *ed:* Roger Dwyre.

players: Brigitte Fossey, Georges Poujouly, Lucien Hubert, Suzanne Courtal, Jacques Marin, Laurence Badie, André Wasley, Ademée.

MONSIEUR RIPOIS (1954, in Great Britain: KNAVE OF HEARTS)

prod: Transcontinental (Paul Graetz). *dir:* René Clément. *sc:* (from the novel "M. Ripois et la Némésis" by Louis Hémon). *adapt:* Clément & Hugh Mills, *dial:* Hugh Mills *(Eng. version)* & Raymond Queneau *(Fr. version)* . *ph:* Oswald Morris. *des:* Ralph Brinton. *mus:* Roman Vlad. *ed:* Françoise Javet.

players: Gérard Philipe, Natasha Parry, Valerie Hobson, Joan Greenwood, Margaret Johnston, Germaine Montero.

GERVAISE (1956)

prod: Agnès Delahaie Productions/Silver Films. *dir:* René Clément. *sc:* (from Zola's novel "L'Assommoir") *adapt. & dial:* Jean Aurenche & Pierre Bost. *ph:* Robert Juillard. *des:* Paul Bertrand. *mus:* Georges Auric. *ed:* Henri Rust.

players: Maria Schell, François Périer, Suzy Delair, Mathilde Casadessus, Armand Mestral, Jacques Harden.

BARRAGE CONTRE LE PACIFIQUE (1958, in Italy: LA DIGA SUL PACIFICO)

prod: Dino de Laurentiis. *dir:* René Clément. *sc:* (from the novel by Marguerite Duras) *adapt. & dial:* Clément & Irwin Shaw. *ph:* Otello Martelli. *des:* Mario Chiari. *mus:* Nino Rota. *ed:* Leo Catozzo.

players: Silvana Mangano, Anthony Perkins, Jo Van Fleet, Richard Conte, Yvonne Sanson, Alida Valli, Nehemiah Persoff.

PLEIN SOLEIL (1959, in Italy)

prod: Paris Film Prod./Panitalia (Robert & Raymond Hakim). *dir:* René Clément. *sc:* (from the novel "The Talented Mr. Ripley" by Patricia Highsmith). *adapt. & dial:* Clément & Paul Gégauff. *ph:* Henri Decae. *des:* Paul Bertrand. *mus:* Nino Rota. *ed:* Françoise Javet.

players: Alain Delon, Marie Laforêt, Maurice Ronet, Elvire Popesco, Erno Crista, Ave Ninchi.

QUELLE JOIE DE VIVRE! (1961, in Italy: CHE JOIA VIVERE)

prod: Cinematografica Rire — Tempo (Rome)/Francinex (Paris) *dir:* René Clément. *sc. & adapt:* Clément, Léo Benvenuti & Piero de Bernardi (from an idea by Gualtiero Jacopetti). *dial:* Pierre Bost. *ph:* Henri Decae. *des:* Piero Zuffi. *mus:* Francesco Lavagnino.

players: Alain Delon, Barbara Lass, Gino Cervi, Rina Morelli, Carlo Pisacane.

LE JOUR ET L'HEURE (1963)

prod: Cipra — Terra Films (Paris)/C.C.M. — Monica Films (Rome). *dir:* René Clément. *sc:* André Barret. *adapt:* Clément & Roger Vailland. *dial:* Vailland. *ph:* Henri Decae. *des:* Bernard Evein. *mus:* Claude Bolling. *ed:* Fedora Zincone.

players: Simone Signoret, Stuart Whitman, Geneviève Page, Michel Piccoli Billy Kearns, Pierre Dux.

LES FÉLINS/THE LOVE CAGE (1963)
prod: CIPRA (Jacques Bar.) *dir:* René Clément. *sc:* (from the novel "Vive le Marié" (Joy House) by Day Keene). *adapt:* Clément, Pascal Jardin, Charles Williams. *dial:* Pascal Jardin (Fr. Version), Charles Williams (Eng. version). *ph:* Henri Decae. *des:* Jean André. *mus:* Lalo Schiffrin. *ed:* Fedora Zincone.
players: Alain Delon, Jane Fonda, Lola Albright, André Oumansky, Carl Studer, Douking, Sorrell Booke.

PARIS BRULE-T-IL? (1966)
prod: Transcontinental (Paul Graetz)/Marianne Productions.
dir: René Clément. *sc:* (from the book by Dominique Lapierre & Larry Collins). *adapt:* Gore Vidal & Francis Coppola. *Fr. dial:* Marcel Moussy. *Germ. dial:* Beate von Molo *ph:* Marcel Grignon. *des:* Willy Holt. *mus:* Maurice Jarre.
ed: Denis Chardin & Robert Lawrence.
players: Jean-Paul Belmondo, Charles Boyer, Leslie Caron, Jean-Pierre Cassel, George Chakiris, Bruno Cremer, Claude Dauphin, Alain Delon, Kirk Douglas, Pierre Dux, Glenn Ford, Gert Froebe, Joachim Hansen, Felix Marten, Hannes Messemer, Harry Meyen, Yves Montand, Anthony Perkins, Michel Piccoli, Sacha Pitoëff, Wolfgang Preiss, Albert Rémy, Claude Rich, Simone Signoret, Robert Stack, Jean-Louis Trintignant, Pierre Vaneck, Marie Versini, Skip Ward, Orson Welles.

Bibliography:
(a) André Farwagi: "René Clément". (Seghers, Paris, 1967).
(b) "Jeux Interdits" *(Avant-Scène 15.* May 1962).
"Monsieur Ripois" (*Avant-Scène 55.* Jan. 1966).

HENRI-GEORGES CLOUZOT

b. 20 Nov. 1907 at Niort. Author of several unpublished plays (three of them produced in the forties) and a travel book on Brazil: "Le Cheval des Dieux" (1950). Began career as assistant director, directed a short *La Terreur des Batignolles* (1931) and went to Berlin in 1932-3 to direct French versions of various German productions.

1931-41 scriptwriter: *Ma Cousine de Varsovie & Un Soir de Rafle* (Carmine Gallone — 1932), *Le Révolté* (Léon Mathot — 1938), *Le Duel* (Pierre Fresnay — 1939), *Le Monde Tremblera* (Richard Pottier — 1939), *Le Dernier des Six* (Georges Lacombe — 1941) & *Les Inconnus dans la Maison* (Henri Decoin — 1941). Dogged by ill-health throughout his career, he spent the years 1934-8 in various sanitoria, was prevented from directing his script of *Si Tous les Gars du Monde* (made by Christian-Jaque in 1956) and had to abandon *L'Enfer* in 1964 after several days shooting.

Films:

L'ASSASSIN HABITE AU 21 (1942)
prod: Continental Films. *dir:* Henri-Georges Clouzot. *sc:* (from the novel by S. A. Steeman) *adapt:* Clouzot & Steeman. *dial:* Clouzot. *ph:* Armand Thirard. *des:* André Andreyew. *mus:* Maurice Yvain. *ed:* Christian Gaudin.
players: Pierre Fresnay, Suzy Delair, Jean Tissier, Pierre Larquey, Noël Roquevert, René Génin, Jean Despeaux.

LE CORBEAU (1943)
prod: Continental Films. *dir:* Henri-Georges Clouzot. *sc:* Louis Chavance. *adapt.* & *dial:* Clouzot & Chavance. *ph:* Nicolas Hayer. *des:* André Andreyew. *mus:* Tony Aubin. *ed:* Marguerite Beaugé.
players: Pierre Fresnay, Pierre Larquey, Noël Roquevert, Ginette Leclerc, Micheline Francey.

QUAI DES ORFÈVRES (1947)
prod: Majestic — Films. *dir:* Henri-Georges Clouzot. *sc:* (from S. A. Steeman's novel "Légitime Défense"). *adapt.* & *dial:* Clouzot & Jean Ferry. *ph:* Armand Thirard. *des:* Max Douy. *mus:* Francis Lopez. *ed:* Charles Bretonneiche.
players: Louis Jouvet, Simone Renant, Bernard Blier, Suzy Delair, Charles Dullin.

MANON (1949)
prod: Alcina (Paul-Edmond Decharme) *dir:* Henri-Georges Clouzot. *sc:* (from the novel "Manon Lescaut" by the Abbé Prévost) *adapt.* & *dial:* Clouzot & Jean Ferry. *ph:* Armand Thirard. *des:* Max Douy. *mus:* Paul Misraki. *ed:* Monique Kirsanoff.
players: Cécile Aubry, Michel Auclair, Serge Reggiani, Gabrielle Dorziat, Henri Gilbert, Raymond Souplex.

sketch **LE RETOUR DE JEAN** in **RETOUR À LA VIE** (1949)
prod: Jacques Roitfeld/Films Marceau. *dir:* Henri-Georges Clouzot. *sc.* & *dial:* Clouzot & Jean Ferry. *ph:* Louis Page. *des:* Max Douy. *mus:* Paul Misraki. *ed:* Monique Kirsanoff.
players: Louis Jouvet, Noël Roquevert, Jo Dest.

MIQUETTE ET SA MÈRE (1949)
prod: Alcina/C.I.C.C./Silver Films (Paul-Edmond Decharme) *dir:* Henri-Georges Clouzot. *sc:* (from the comedy by Flers & Caillavet). *adapt:* Clouzot & Jean Ferry. *dial:* Clouzot. *ph:* Armand Thirard. *des:* Georges Wakhévitch. *mus:* Albert Lasry.
players: Louis Jouvet, Bourvil, Danièle Delorme, Saturnin Fabre.

LE SALAIRE DE LA PEUR (1953)
prod: C.I.C.C./Filmsonor/Vera Film/Fono Roma. *dir:* Henri-Georges Clouzot. *sc:* (from the novel by Georges Arnaud) *adapt.* & *dial:* Clouzot & Jérôme Géronimi. *ph:* Armand Thirard. *des:* René Renoux. *mus:* Georges Auric. *ed:* Henri Rust, Madeleine Gug, E. Muse.
players: Yves Montand, Charles Vanel, Véra Clouzot, Folco Lulli, Peter Van Eyck, William Tubbs.

LES DIABOLIQUES (1955)
prod: Filmsonor. *dir:* Henri-Georges Clouzot. *sc:* (from the novel "Celle qui n'était plus" by Boileau & Narcejac). *adapt.* & *dial:* Clouzot, Jérôme Géronimi, René Masson & Frédéric Grendel. *ph:* Armand Thirard. *des:* Léon Barsacq. *mus:* Georges Van Parys. *ed:* Madeleine Gug.
players: Simone Signoret, Véra Clouzot, Paul Meurisse, Charles Vanel, Pierre Larquey.

LE MYSTÈRE PICASSO (1956)
prod: Filmsonor. *dir.* & *sc:* Henri-Georges Clouzot. *ph:* Claude Renoir. *mus:* Georges Auric. *ed:* Henri Colpi.
player: Pablo Picasso.

LES ESPIONS (1957)
prod: Filmsonor. *dir:* Henri-Georges Clouzot. *sc:* (from the novel by Egon Hostovsky). *adapt.* & *dial:* Clouzot & Jérôme Géronimi. *ph:* Christian Matras. *des:* René Renoux. *mus:* Georges Auric. *ed:* Madeleine Gug.
players: Curt Jurgens, Peter Ustinov, O. E. Hasse, Sam Jaffe, Véra Clouzot, Martita Hunt, Gérard Séty.

LA VÉRITÉ (1960)
prod: Iéna Productions/C.E.I.A.P. (Raoul Lévy). *dir:* Henri-Georges Clouzot. *sc. adapt.* & *dial:* Clouzot, *with collab.* of Simone Drieu, Jérôme Géronimi, Michèle Perrein & Véra Clouzot. *ph:* Armand Thirard. *des:* Jean André. *mus:* Beethoven & Stravinsky. *ed:* Albert Jurgensen.

players: Brigitte Bardot, Marie-José Nat, Sami Frey, Charles Vanel, Paul Meurisse.

LA PRISONNIERE (1968)
prod: Films Corona/Véra Films (Paris)/Fono (Rome). *dir. sc. & dial:* Henri-Georges Clouzot. *ph:* Andréas Winding. *des:* Jacques Saulnier. *mus:* classics. *ed:* Noëlle Balenci.
players: Laurent Terzieff, Elisabeth Wiener, Dany Carrel, Bernard Fresson, Dario Moreno, Daniel Rivière.

Bibliography:

(a) François Chalais: "Henri-Georges Clouzot" (Ed. Jacques Vautrin, Paris, 1950).

Francis Lacassin & Raymond Bellour: "Le Procès Clouzot" (Le Terrain Vague, Paris, 1964).

Interview in *Cinéma 65* No. 96.

(b) "Quai des Orfèvres" *(Avant-Scène 29.* Sept. 1963).

"Le Salaire de la Peur" *(Avant-Scène 17.* July 1962).

JEAN COCTEAU

b. 5 July 1889 at Maisons – Lafitte nr. Paris. d. 10 Oct. 1963. One of the dominant figures of French intellectual life in the years between the wars: author of numerous novels, plays, poems and ballets as well as painter. He has collaborated with many of the great figures in the world of the arts.

Work as scriptwriter:

dial:	*La Comédie du Bonheur* (Marcel L'Herbier, 1939).
adapt. & dial:	*Le Baron Fantôme* (Serge de Poligny, 1943).
sc. & dial:	*L'Eternel Retour* (Jean Delannoy, 1943).
dial:	*Les Dames du Bois de Boulogne* (Robert Bresson, 1944).
adapt. & dial:	*Ruy Blas* (Pierre Billon, 1947).
commentary:	*Noces de Sable* (André Zwobada, 1949).
sc. adapt. & dial:	*Les Enfants Terribles* (Jean-Pierre Melville, 1950).
adapt. & dial:	*La Princesse de Clèves* (Jean Delannoy 1960).
adapt. & dial:	*Thomas l'Imposteur* (Georges Franju 1965).

Amateur films in 16 mm.:
Coriolan (1950)
Villa Santo-Sospir (1952).

Work as director:

LE SANG D'UN POÈTE (1930-32)
prod: Vicomte de Nouailles. *dir. sc. & ed:* Jean Cocteau. *ph:* Georges Périnal. *des:* Jean D'Eaubonne. *mus:* Georges Auric.
players: Lee Miller, Pauline Carton, Odette Talazac, Enrique Rivero, Jean Desbordes, Fernand Dichamps, Lucien Jager, Féral Benga, Barbette.

LA BELLE ET LA BÊTE (1946)
prod: André Paulvé. *dir. sc. & dial:* Jean Cocteau (from the fairy tale by Mme. Leprince de Beaumont) *ph:* Henri Alekan. *art. dir:* Christan Bérard. *des:* René Moulaert & Lucien Carré. *mus:* Georges Auric. *ed:* Claude Ibéria.
players: Josette Day, Jean Marais, Mila Parély, Nane Germon, Michel Auclair, Marcel André.

L'AIGLE À DEUX TÊTES (1947)
prod: Ariane Films/Sirius. *dir. sc. & dial:* Jean Cocteau (from his own play). *ph:* Christian Matras. *art. dir.* Christian Bérard. *des:* Georges Wakhévitch. *mus:* Georges Auric. *ed:* Claude Ibéria.
players: Edwige Feuillère, Jean Marais, Jean Debucourt, Sylvia Monfort, Jacques Varennes, Gilles Quéant, Abdallah, M. Mazyl, E. Stirling, Yvonne de Bray.

LES PARENTS TERRIBLES (1948)
prod: Ariane (Alexandre Mnouchkine & Francis Cosne). *dir. sc. & dial:* Jean Cocteau (from his own play). *ph:* Michel Kelber. *art. dir.* Christian Bérard. *des:* Guy de Gastyne. *mus:* Georges Auric. *ed:* Jacqueline Sadoul.
players: Josette Day, Jean Marais, Yvonne de Bray, Marcel André, Gabrielle Dorziat.

ORPHÉE (1950)
prod: André Paulvé/Les Films du Palais Royal. *dir. sc. & dial:* Jean Cocteau. *ph:* Nicolas Hayer. *des:* Jean d'Eaubonne. *mus:* Georges Auric. *ed:* Jacqueline Sadoul.
players: Jean Marais, Maria Casarès, François Périer, Marie Déa, Juliette Gréco, Edouard Dermit, Pierre Bertin, Jacques Varennes.

LE TESTAMENT D'ORPHÉE (1959)
prod: Editions Cinématographiques (Jean Thuillier). *dir. sc. & dial:* Jean Cocteau. *ph:* Roland Pontoizeau. *des:* Pierre Guffroy. *mus:* Jacques Metehan. *ed:* Marie-Josèphe Yoyotte.
players: Jean Cocteau, Edouard Dermit, Henri Crémieux, Maria Casarès, François Périer, Jean-Pierre Léaud, Yul Brynner, Claudine Oger, Jean Marais.

Bibliography:

(a) Jean Cocteau: "La Belle et la Bête: Journal d'un Film" (J.- B. Janin, Paris, 1946).

* (translated as "Diary of a Film" (Dobson, London 1950).

Jean Cocteau: "Entretiens autour du Cinématographe" (Ed. André Bonne, Paris, 1951).

* (translated as "Cocteau on the Film" (Dobson, London, 1954).

† K. G. Simon: "Jean Cocteaus Filme" (Rembrandt Verlag, Berlin, 1958).

* chapter in Neal Oxenhandler: "Scandal & Parade" (Constable, London, 1958).

Roger Pillaudin: "Jean Cocteau tourne son dernier film". (Table Ronde, Paris, 1960).

René Gilson: "Jean Cocteau". (Seghers, Paris, 1964).

Claude Beylie: "Cocteau" (*Anthologie du Cinéma 12*. Paris. 1966) Interview in *Cahiers du Cinéma* No. 109.

(b) "Le Sang d'un Poète" (Ed. du Rocher, Monaco, 1957).

* (translated as "Blood of a Poet" (Bodley Press, New York, 1949).

"Orphée" (Ed. André Bonne, Paris, 1950).

† "Orphée" (Marion von Schröder Verlag, Hamburg, 1963).

"Le Testament d'Orphée" (Ed. du Rocher, Monaco, 1960).

JEAN GRÉMILLON

b. 3 Oct 1901 at Bayeux. d. 25 Nov 1959 at Paris. Studied music. Meeting with photographer Georges Périnal aroused interest in cinema. Large Number of Shorts 1923-28:

CHARTRES: LE REVETEMENT DES ROUTES (1923); LA FABRICATION DU FIL; DU FIL À L'AIGUILLE; LA FABRICATION DU CIMENT ARTIFICIEL; LA BIÈRE; LE ROULEMENT À BILLE; LES PARFUMS; L'ÉTIRAGE DES AMPOULES ÉLECTRIQUES; LA PHOTOGÉNIE MÉCANIQUE (1924); L'ÉDUCTION PROFESSIONNELLE DES CONDUCTEURS DE TRAMWAY; L'ÉLÉCTRIFICATION DE LA LIGNE PARIS-VIERZON; L'AUVERGNE; LA NAISSANCE DES CIGOGNES; LES ACIERIES DE LA MARINE ET D'HOME-COURT (1925); LA VIE DES TRAVAILLEURS ITALIENS EN FRANCE; LA CROISIÈRE DE L'"ATALANTE' (1926); GRATUITES (1927); BOBS (1928).

In *PHOTOGÉNIE MÉCHANIQUE* he edited material from some of these works.

Silent feature films:

UN TOUR AU LARGE (1926)
prod: Le Synchronisme Cinématique. *dir. sc. & ed:* Jean Grémillon.
ph: Lucien Lesaint.
MALDONE (1927)
prod: Les Films Charles Dullin. *dir:* Jean Grémillon. *sc:* Alexandre Arnoux. *ph:* Georges Périna & Christian Matras. *des:* André Barsacq. *mus:* Jacques Brillouin & Marcel Delannoy.
players: Charles Dullin, Genica Athanasiou, Roger Karl, Annabella, André Bacque.
GARDIENS DE PHARE (1929)
prod: Société des Films du Grand-Guignol. *dir. & ed:* Jean Grémillon. *sc:* (from a play by Pierre Autiers & Cloquemont). *adapt:* Jacques Feyder. *ph:* Georges Perinal. *des:* André Barsacq.
players: Génica Athanasiou, Geymond Vital, Fromet, Gabrielle Fontan.

Sound feature films:

LA PETITE LISE (1930)
prod: Pathé-Nathan. *dir:* Jean Grémillon. *sc. & dial:* Charles Spaak. *ph:* Jean Bachelet & René Colas. *des:* Guy de Gastyne. *mus:* Roland Manuel.
players: Nadia Sibirskaia, Alcover, Julien Bertheau, Raymond Cordy, Alex Bernard.
DAINAH LA MÉTISSE (1931)
prod: G. F. F. A. *dir:* Jean Grémillon. *sc:* (from a story by Pierre Daye). *adapt & dial:* Charles Spaak. *ph:* Georges Périnal & Louis Page. *des:* Jacques Lafitte.
players: Charles Vanel, Habib Benglia, Laurence Clarius, Gaston Dubosc, Lucien Gérard, Gabrielle Fontan.

POUR UN SOU D'AMOUR (1931)
prod: Jacques Haik. *dir:* Jean Grémillon. *sc:* (from an idea by Alfred Machard). *adapt:* Henri Falk & Pierre Maudru. *dial:* Maudru. *ph:* Paul Coteret. *des:* Jean D'Eaubonne. *mus:* Albert Chaulnier.
players: André Beaugé, Noël Grahame, Jean Diéner, Henri de Livry, André Carnège, Charles Deschamps.

LE PETIT BABOUIN (1932)
prod: S.E.P.I.C. *dir. & mus:* Jean Grémillon. *sc. & dial:* A. Mycho. *ph:* Rudy Maté.
players: Armand Bernard, François Vibert, Gabrielle Fontan.

GONZAGUE OU L'ACCORDEUR (1933)
prod: S.E.P.I.C. *dir. sc. & dial:* Jean Grémillon (from a play by Pierre Veber). *ph:* Nicolas Farkas. *mus:* Jacques Brillouin.
players: Julien Carette, Charles Deschamps, Geo Tréville, Paul Olivier, le Gallo, Germaine Aussey.

LA DOLOROSA (1934 in Spain)
prod: Falco y Compania. *dir:* Jean Grémillon. *sc. dial. & mus:* from the comic opera by José Serrano. *adapt:* M. Montorio. *ph:* Jacques Monthéraud & José-Maria Beltran. *des:* José-Maria Torrès.
players: Rosita Diaz, Maria Amparo Bosch, Pilar Garcia, Agustin Godoy, Ramon Cebrian, José-Maria Linares-Rivas, Luis Moreno.

CENTINELLA! ALERTA! (1935 in Spain).
prod: Filmofono. *dir:* Jean Grémillon. *sc:* (from the play 'Le alegria del batallon' by Carlos Arniches). *adapt:* Eduardo Ugarte. *ph:* José-Maria Beltran. *mus:* Daniel Montorio.
players: Ana-Maria Custodio, Angel Sampredo, Angelillo, Luis Heredia, José-Maria Linares-Rivas, Emilio Portes.

LA VALSE ROYALE (1936 in Germany)
prod: Raoul Ploquin for U.F.A. *dir:* Jean Grémillon. *sc. & dial:* Henri Falk. *ph:* Konstantin Irmen Tschett. *des:* Rudolf Herleth & Walter Rohrig. *mus:* Franz Doelle. *ed:* Klaus Stapenhorst.
players: Henri Garat, Renée Saint-Cyr, Mila Parély, Alla Donnell, Christian Gérard, G. Gallet, le Gallo.

PATTES DE MOUCHES (1936 in Germany)
prod: Raoul Ploquin for U.F.A. *dir:* Jean Grémillon. *sc:* (from Victorien Sardou's play). *adapt:* Grémillon & Roger Vitrac. *dial:* Vitrac. *ph:* E. Daub. *des:* Herman & Butow. *mus:* Lothar Bruhne.
players: Renée Saint-Cyr, Pierre Brasseur, Claude May, Mila Parély, Charles Deschamps, Jean Aymé, Lucien Dayle.

GUEULE D'AMOUR 1937 in Germany)
prod: Raoul Ploquin for U.F.A. *dir:* Jean Grémillon. *sc:* (from the novel by André Baucler). *adapt. & dial:* Charles Spaak. *ph:* Gunther Rittau. *mus:* Lothar Bruhne.
players: Jean Gabin, Mireille Balin, René Lefevre, Marguerite Deval, Henri Poupon.

L'ÉTRANGE MONSIEUR VICTOR (1938 in Germany)
prod: Raoul Ploquin for U.F.A. *dir:* Jean Grémillon. *sc:* Albert Valentin. *adapt:* Charles Spaak. *dial:* Spaak & Marcel Achard. *ph:* Walter Kriene. *des:* Shiller. *mus:* Roland Manuel. *ed:*
players: Raimu, Madeleine Renaud, Pierre Blanchar, Viviane Romance, Marcelle Géniat, Vincent Hyspa.

REMORQUES (1939-41)
prod: S.E.D.I.F. *dir:* Jean Grémillon. *sc:* (from the novel by Roger Vercel). *adapt. & dial:* Jacques Prévert & André Cayatte. *ph:* Armand Thirard. *des:* Alexandre Trauner. *mus:* Roland Manuel. *ed:* Louisette Hautecoeur.
players: Jean Gabin, Michèle Morgan, Madeleine Renaud, Fernand Ledoux, Jean Marchat.

LUMIÈRE D'ÉTÉ (1943)
prod: Discina (André Paulvé). *dir:* Jean Grémillon. *sc. & dial:* Jacques Prévert & Pierre Laroche. *ph:* Louis Page. *des:* Max Douy. *mus:* Roland Manuel & Roger Desormières. *ed:* Louisette Hautecoeur.
players: Madeleine Renaud, Paul Bernard, Pierre Brasseur, Madeleine Robinson, Georges

Marchal.

LE CIEL EST À VOUS (1944)
prod: Les Films Raoul Ploquin. *dir:* Jean Grémillon. *sc:* Albert Valentin & Charles Spaak. *dial:* Spaak. *ph:* Louis Page. *des:* Max Douy. *mus:* Roland Manuel. *ed:* Louisette Hautecoeur. *players:* Madeleine Renaud, Charles Vanel, Jean Debucourt, Léonce Corné, Raoul Marco, Anne Vendenne, Raymonde Vernay.

PATTES BLANCHES (1949)
prod: Majestic Films (Roger de Venloo). *dir:* Jean Grémillon. *sc:* Jean Anouilh & Jean Bernard Luc. *dial:* Anouilh. *ph:* Philippe Agostini. *des:* Léon Barsacq. *mus:* Elsa Barraine. *ed:* Louisette Hautecoeur.
players: Paul Bernard, Suzy Delair, Fernand Ledoux, Arlette Thomas, Michel Bouquet, Jean Debucourt.

L'ÉTRANGE MADAME X (1951)
prod: Claude Dolbert. *dir:* Jéan Grémillon. *sc:* Marcelle Maurette. *adapt:* Albert Valentin. *dial:* Pierre Laroche. *ph:* Louis Page. *des:* Raymond Druart. *mus:* Vincent Scotto. *ed:* Madeleine Gug.
players: Michèle Morgan, Henri Vidal, Maurice Escande, San Jual, Arlette Thomas.

L'AMOUR D'UNE FEMME (1954)
prod: L.P.C./Costellazione. *dir. & sc:* Jean Grémillon *adapt:* Grémillon, René Wheeler & René Fallet. *dial:* Wheeler & Fallet. *ph:* Louis Page. *des:* Robert Clavel. *mus:* Elsa Barraine. *ed:* Louisette Hautecoeur.
players: Micheline Presle, Massimo Girotti, Gaby Morlay, Carette, Marc Cassot, Roland Lesaffre.

Documentaries

LE SIX JUIN À L'AUBE (1945)
prod: Coopérative du Cinéma Français. *dir. sc. comm. & mus:* Jean Grémillon. *ph:* Louis Page, Alain Douarinou, Maurice Pecqueux, André Bac & Henri Ferrand. *ed:* Louisette Hautecoeur.
LES CHARMES DE L'EXISTENCE (1950)
prod: Les Films Saint-Germain-des-Prés. *dir. & sc:* Jean Grémillon & Pierre Kast. *comm. & mus:* Grémillon. *ph:* Maurice Pecqueux.

Music & commentary for Kast's *"Les Désastres de la Guerre"* (1951).

ALCHIMIE part of the **ENCYCLOPÉDIE FILMÉE** (1952)
prod: Le Trident. *dir. sc. comm:* Jean Grémillon. *ph:* Henri Ferrand. *mus:* Grémillon & Pierre Henry. *ed:* Léonide Azar.
ASTROLOGIE (1952)
prod: Le Trident. *dir. & sc:* Jean Grémillon. *ph:* Henri Ferrand. *mus:* Marius Constant & Pierre Henry.
AU COEUR DE L'ILE DE FRANCE (1954)
prod: Les Films du Dauphin. *dir. sc. & comm:* Jean Grémillon. *ph:* Henri Ferrand. *mus:* Roland Manuel & Grémillon. *ed:* Renée Lichtig.
prod: United Europe Films. *dir. sc. & comm.* Jean Grémillon. *ph:* Henri Ferrand. *mus:* Roland Manuel & Grémillon. *ed:* Renée Lichtig.
LA MAISON AUX IMAGES (1956)
prod: Les Films du Dauphin. *dir. sc. comm. & mus:* Jean Grémillon. *ph:* Louis Page & Henri Ferrand. *ed:* J. L. Lévi-Alvarès.
HAUTE LISSE (1957)
prod: Les Films du Dauphin (Christiane Grémillon). *dir. sc. comm. & mus:* Jean Grémillon. *ph:* Louis Page. *ed:* J. L. Lévi-Alvarès.
ANDRÉ MASSON ET LES QUATRE ÉLÉMENTS (1958)
prod: Les Films du Dauphin (Christiane Grémillon). *dir. sc. comm. & mus:* Jean Grémillon. *ph:* Louis Page. *ed:* Suzanne Baron.

Bibliography:

(a) Pierre Kast: "Jean Grémillon" *(Premier Plan* 5, Lyon, 1960).

Pierre Billard: "Grémillon" (*Anthologie du Cinéma 20*. Paris. 1966) Articles and texts in *Cinéma 60* No. 44 (March 1960).

(b) Script of unfilmed "Le Printemps de la Liberté" (Bibliothèque Française, Paris, 1948). Commentary of "André Masson et les quatre Eléments" (*Avant-Scène 18*. Sep. 1962).

ROGER LEENHARDT

b. 23 Aug 1903 in Paris. Reporter. Influential film critic on a number of magazines. Producer as well as director of short films (Les Films du Compas and Les Films Roger Leenhardt). Wrote scripts for *L'Amour autour de la Maison* (Pierre de Hérain — 1946) and *Aubusson* (Jean Lods — 1946). In 1964 he directed *La Fille de la Montagne* for French television and appeared as an actor in Jean-Luc Godard's *Une Femme Mariée*.

Most of Leenhardt's postwar shorts were scripted by himself and produced by Les Films du Compas. His regular collaborators include cameramen Pierre Levent and Daniel Sarrade, composer Guy Bernard and editor Suzanne Gaveau.

Shorts:

LE VRAI JEU (1934); *L'ORIENT QUI VIENT* (with René Zuber — 1934); *R.N. 37* (1938); *REVÊTEMENTS ROUTIERS* (1938); *PAVAGE MODERNE* (1938); *LE REZZOU* (with René Zuber — (1938); *FÊTES DE FRANCE* (1940); *À LA POURSUITE DU VENT* (1943); *LE CHANT DES ONDES* (1943).

LE CHANTIER EN RUINES (1945); *LETTRE DE PARIS* (1945); *LE BARRAGE DE L'AIGLE* (1946); *NAISSANCE DU CINÉMA* (1946); *LA CÔTE D'AZUR* (1948); *LE PAIN DE BARBARIE* (1948); *ENTREZ DANS LA DANSE* (1948).

MÉTRO (1950); *LA FUGUE DE MAHMOUD* (1950); *VICTOR HUGO* (with Yvonne Gerber — 1951); *DU CHARBON ET DES HOMMES* (1953); *LA FRANCE EST UN JARDIN* (1953); *FRANÇOIS MAURIAC* (1954); *LOUIS CAPET* (with Jean-Pierre Vivet — 1954).

LA CONQUÊTE DE L'ANGLETERRE (1955); *NOTRE SANG* (1955); *LES TRANSMISSIONS HYDRAULIQUES* (1955); *LE BRUIT* (1955); *PARIS ET LE DÉSERT FRANÇAIS* (1957); *JEAN-JACQUES* (with Jean-Pierre Vivet — 1958); *BÂTIR À NOTRE AGE* (with Sidney Jezequel — 1958); *EN PLEIN MIDI* (with Sidney Jezequel — 1958); *DAUMIER* (1959).

PAUL VALÉRY (1960); *LE MAÎTRE DE MONTPELLIER* (1960); *ENTRE SEINE ET MER* (1960); *L'HOMME À LA PIPE* (1962). *DES FEMMES ET DES FLEURS* (1963); *1989* (1964). COROT (1965). NAISSANCE DE LA PHOTO (1965). LE COEUR DE LA FRANCE (1966). LE BEATNIK ET LE MINET (1966).

Features:

LES DERNIÈRES VACANCES (1947)
prod: L.P.C. *dir. & sc:* Roger Leenhardt. *adapt. & dial:* Leenhardt & Roger Breuil. *ph:* Philippe Agostini. *des:* Léon Barsacq. *mus:* Guy Bernard. *ed:* Myriam.
players: Berthe Bovy, Pierre Dux, Jean d'Yd, Odile Versois, Michel François, Renée Devilliers.
LE RENDEZ-VOUS DE MINUIT (1962)
prod: Editions Cinématographiques/Argos/Les Films Roger Leenhardt. *dir:* Roger Leenhardt.
sc. adapt. & dial: Leenhardt & Jean-Pierre Vivet. *ph:* Jean Badal. *des:* Bernard Evein. *mus:* Georges Auric. *ed:* Henri Lanoé.
players: Lilli Palmer, Michel Auclair, José-Luis de Villalonga, Maurice Ronet, Jean Galland, Alexandra Stewart.

Bibliography:

(a) No full study exists. Best introduction is the interview published in *Cahiers du Cinéma* No. 137.
(b) —

MAX OPHULS

b. 6 May 1902 at Saarbrucken.d. 26 March 1957 in Hamburg. real name: Max Oppenheimer. Began career as an actor at age of 17; 1924-30 theatrical producer (over 200 plays). 1930 engaged by UFA as assistant to Anatole Litvak, feature début same year.

Features:

DANN SCHON LIEBER LEBERTRAN (1930 in Germany)
prod: U.F.A. *dir:* Max Ophuls. *sc:* Erich Kästner (from his own novel) *adapt:* Emeric Pressburger & Ophuls. *ph:* Eugen Schufftan.
players: Käte Haak, Hannelore Schroth, Heinz Günsdorf, Paul Kemp.
DIE VERLIEBTE FIRMA (1931 in Germany)
prod: D.L.S. *dir:* Max Ophuls. *sc:* Fritz Zeckendorf & Hubert Marischka. *adapt:* Bruno Granich-städten & Ophuls. *ph:* Karl Puth. *mus:* Bruno Granichstädten, Grete Walter, Ernst Hauke.
players: Anny Ahlers, Gustav Fröhlich, Lien Deyers, Ernst Verebes, José Vedorn, Hubert von Meyerinck.
DIE VERKAUFTE BRAUT (1932 in Germany)
prod: Reichsliga Film (Munich). *dir:* Max Ophuls. *sc:* (from the opera by Friedrich Smetana) *adapt:* Curt Alexander, Jaroslav Kvapil & Ophuls. *ph:* Reimar Kuntze, Franz Koch, Herbert Illig & Otto Wirsching. *mus:* Smetana.
players: Willy Domgraf-Fassbender, Karl Valentin, Liesl Karlstadt, Anita Sörensen, Max Nadler, Jarmila Novotna, Otto Wenike, Paul Kemp.
DIE LACHENDEN ERBEN (1932 in Germany)
prod: U.F.A. *dir:* Max Ophuls. *sc:* Trude Herka. *adapt:* Felix Joachimson & Ophuls. *ph:* Eduard

Hoesch. *mus:* Clemens Schmalstich & Hans-Otto Borgmann.
players: Lien Deyers, Lizzi Waldmüller, Heinz Rühmann, Max Adalbert, Julius Falkenstein.
LIEBELEI (1932 in Germany)
prod: Elite Tonfilm Prod. (Fred Lissa). *dir:* Max Ophuls. *sc:* (from the play by Arthur Schnitzler)
adapt: Hans Wilhelm, Curt Alexander & Ophuls. *ph:* Franz Planer. *des:* G. Pellon. *mus:* Theo
Mackeben. *ed:* Friedel Buchott.
players: Wolfgang Liebeneiner, Magda Schneider, Luise Ullrich, Willy Eichberger, Paul Hörbiger,
Gustaf Gründgens, Olga Tschechowa, Lotte Spira, Walter Steinbeck.
(On his arrival in France in 1933 Ophuls directed a French version of this, *Une Histoire d'Amour)*
ON A VOLÉ UN HOMME (1933 in France)
prod: Fox-Europa (Erich Pommer). *dir:* Max Ophuls. *sc:* René Pujol. *adapt:* Pujol & Hans
Wilhelm. *dial:* Pujol. *ph:* René Guissart. *mus:* Brontislav Kapper & Walter Jurman. *ed:* Ralph
Baum.
players: Henri Garat, Lili Damita, Fernand Fabre, Charles Fallot, Nina Myral, Pierre Labry.
LA SIGNORA DI TUTTI (1934 in Italy)
prod: Novella Film (Rizzoli) *dir:* Max Ophuls. *sc:* (from the novel by Salvator Gotta) *adapt:*
Hans Wilhelm, Curt Alexander & Ophuls. *ph:* Ubaldo Arata. *des:* Giuseppe Capponi. *mus:*
Daniele Amfitheatrof. *ed:* Fernandino Poggioli.
players: Isa Miranda, Memo Benassi, Tatiana Pawlova, Nelly Corradi, Federico Benfer.
DIVINE (1935 in France)
prod: Eden Productions (Paul Bentata). *dir:* Max Ophuls. *sc:* Colette. *adapt:* Jean-Georges
Auriol & Ophuls. *dial:* Colette. *ph:* Roger Hubert. *des:* Jacques Gotko & Robert Gys. *mus:*
Albert Wolff. *ed:* Léonide Moguy.
players: Simone Berriau, Georges Rigaud, Gina Manès, Philippe Hériat, Sylvette Fillacier.
AVE MARIA (OF SCHUBERT) & LA VALSE BRILLANTE (OF CHOPIN) (1936 in France)
two five minute shorts, the first featuring Elisabeth Schumann (singer) & the second Alexander
Brailowski (pianist). *prod:* Compagnie des Grands Artistes Internationaux. *dir:* Max Ophuls.
ph: Franz Planer.
LA TENDRE ENNEMIE (1936 in France)
prod: Eden Productions. *dir:* Max Ophuls. *sc:* (from the play by André-Paul Antoine). *adapt:*
Curt Alexander & Ophuls. *dial:* André-Paul Antoine. *ph:* Eugen Schufftan. *des:* Jacques Gotko.
mus: Albert Wolff. *ed:* Pierre de Hérain.
players: Simone Berriau, Georges Vitray, Jacqueline Daix, Maurice Devienne, Marc Valbel,
Lucien Nat, Catherine Fonteney, Germaine Reuver.
KOMEDIE OM GELD (1936 in Holland)
prod: Novella Film (Rizzoli). *dir:* Max Ophuls. *sc:* Walter Schlee. *adapt:* Schlee, Alex de Haas
& Ophuls. *dial:* de Haas. *ph:* Eugen Schufftan. *des:* Heinz Fenschel. *mus:* Max Tak. *ed:* Noël
van Ess & Gérard Bensdorp.
players: Herman Bowber, Rini Otte, Matthew van Eysden, Cor Ruys.

YOSHIWARA (1937 in France)
prod: Milo-Films-Excelsior. *dir:* Max Ophuls. *sc:* (from the novel by Maurice Dekobra). *adapt:*
& *dial:* Arnold Lippschutz, Wolfgang Wilhelm, Jacques Companeez & Ophuls. *ph:* Eugen
Schufftan. *des:* André & Léon Barsacq. *mus:* Paul Dessau. *ed:* P. Meguerian.
players: Pierre-Richard Willm, Sessue Hayakawa, Michiko Tanaka, Roland Toutain, Lucienne
Lemarchand, Gabriello, Camille Bert, Foun Sen.

WERTHER (1938 in France)
prod: Nero Films. *dir:* Max Ophuls. *sc:* (from the novel "Die Leiden des jungen Werthers" by
Goethe) *adapt:* Hans Wilhelm & Ophuls. *dial:* Fernand Crommelynck. *ph:* Eugen Schufftan.
des: Eugène Lourié & Max Douy. *mus:* Paul Dessau. *ed:* Gérard Bensdorp & Jean Sacha.
players: Pierre-Richard Willm, Annie Vernay, Jean Galland, Paulette Pax, Henri Guisol.

SANS LENDEMAIN (1939 in France)
prod: Gray Film (Gregor Rabinovitsch). *dir:* Max Ophuls. *sc:* Hans Wilhelm. *adapt:* Hans
Jacobi, André-Paul Antoine & Ophuls. *dial:* Antoine. *ph:* Eugen Schufftan. *des:* Eugène Lourié.
mus: Allan Gray. *ed:* L. Sejourne & Jean Sacha.
players: Edwige Feuillère, Georges Rigaud, Daniel Lecourtois, Paul Azais, Gabriello, Georges
Lannes, Michel François, Jeanne Marken, Mady Berry, Pauline Carton.

DE MAJERLING À SARAJEVO (1940 in France)
prod: B.U.P. Française (Eugène Tuscherer). *dir:* Max Ophuls. *sc:* Carl Zuckmayer. *adapt:* Marcelle Maurette, Jacques Natanson, Curt Alexander & Ophuls. *dial:* Natanson. *ph:* Curt Courant & Otto Heller. *des:* Jean d'Eaubonne. *mus:* Oscar Straus. *ed:* Myriam & Jean Oser.
players: Edwige Feuillère, John Lodge, Aimé Clariond, Jean Worms, Gabrielle Dorziat, Aimos Jean Debucourt, Jean Paul Dreyfus (= le Chanois).
In Switzerland in 1940, Ophuls worked very briefly on an unfinished version of Molière's *L'Ecole des Femmes* starring Jouvet. From 1941 to 1946 he was in Hollywood unable to find work. In 1946 he began work on *Vendetta* but was replaced by others.

THE EXILE (1947 in U.S.A.)
prod: Universal-International-Douglas Fairbanks Jnr. *dir:* Max Ophuls. *sc:* (from the novel "His Majesty the King" by Cosmo Hamilton) *adapt.* & *dial:* Douglas Fairbanks & Ophuls. *ph:* Franz Planer. *des:* Russell Gansmann & Ted Offenbecker. *mus:* Frank Skinner. *ed:* Ted J. Kent.
players: Douglas Fairbanks, Maria Montez, Paule Croset, Henry Daniell, Nigel Bruce, Robert Coote, Otto Waldis, Eldon Gorst, Milton A. Owen.

LETTER FROM AN UNKNOWN WOMAN (1948 in U.S.A.)
prod: Universal-International (John Houseman). *dir:* Max Ophuls. *sc:* (from the story by Stefan Zweig) *adapt.* & *dial:* Howard Koch & Ophuls. *ph:* Franz Planer. *des:* Alexander Golitzen. *mus:* Daniele Amfitheatrof. *ed:* Ted. J. Kent.
players: Joan Fontaine, Louis Jourdan, Mady Christians, Marcel Journet, Art Smith, Howard Freeman, John Good, Leo P. Pessin.

CAUGHT (1948 in U.S.A.)
prod: Enterprise Studios (Wolfgang Reinhardt). *dir:* Max Ophuls. *sc:* (from Libbie Block's story "Wild Calendar") *adapt.* & *dial:* Arthur Laurents. *ph:* Lee Garmes. *des:* Frank Sylos. *mus:* Friedrich Hollländer. *ed·* Robert Parrish.
players: Barbara Bel Geddes, James Mason, Robert Ryan, Frank Ferguson, Curt Bois, Marcia Mae Jones, Ruth Brady, Nathalie Schaefer, Art Smith.

THE RECKLESS MOMENT (1949 in U.S.A.)
prod: Columbia (Walter Wanger). *dir:* Max Ophuls. *sc:* (from the story "The Black Wall" by Elisabeth Holding): Henry Garson & R. W. Soderberg. *adapt.* & *dial:* Mel Dinelli & Robert E. Kent. *ph:* Burnett Guffey. *des:* Cary Odell & Frank Tuttle. *mus:* Hans Salter. *ed:* Gene Havlick.
players: James Mason, Joan Bennett, Geraldine Brooks, Henry O'Neill, David Blair, Roy Roberts, Frances Williams, Shepperd Studwick.

LA RONDE (1950 in France)
prod: Sacha Gordine. *dir:* Max Ophuls. *sc:* (from the play "Reigen" by Arthur Schnitzler) *adapt:* Jacques Natanson & Ophuls. *dial:* Natanson. *ph:* Christian Matras. *des:* Jean d'Eaubonne. *mus:* Oscar Strauss. *ed:* Léonide Azar.
players: Anton Walbrook, Simone Signoret, Serge Reggiani, Simone Simon, Daniel Gélin, Danielle Darrieux, Fernand Gravey, Odette Joyeux, Jean-Louis Barrault, Isa Miranda, Gérard Philipe.

LE PLAISIR (1952 in France)
prod: Stera Films — C.C.F.C. *dir:* Max Ophuls. *sc:* (from 3 stories by Guy de Maupassant) *adapt:* Jacques Natanson & Ophuls. *dial:* Natanson. *ph:* Christian Matras (1 & 2), Philippe Agostini (3). *des:* Jean d'Eaubonne. *mus:* Joe Hajos & Maurice Yvain. *ed:* Léonide Azar.
players: (1) *Le Masque* Claude Dauphin, Gaby Morlay, Jean Gallard, Gaby Bruyère.
(2) *La Maison Tellier* Madeleine Renaud, Danielle Darrieux, Ginette Leclerc, Mila Parély, Jean Gabin, Pierre Brasseur.
(3) *Le Modèle* Daniel Gélin, Jean Servais, Simone Simon.

MADAME DE . . . (1953 in France)
prod: Franco-London Films/Film Indus/Rizzoli. *dir:* Max Ophuls. *sc:* (from the novel by Louise de Vilmorin) *adapt:* Marcel Achard, Annette Wademant & Ophuls. *dial:* Achard. *ph:* Christian Matras. *des:* Jean d'Eaubonne. *mus:* Oscar Strauss & Georges Van Parys. *ed:* Boris Lewin.
players: Danielle Darrieux, Charles Boyer, Vittorio de Sica, Jean Debucourt, Lia de Léa, Mireille

Perey.
LOLA MONTÈS (1955 in France & Germany)
prod: Gamma Films/Florida Films (Paris)/Union Films (Munich). *dir:* Max Ophuls. *sc:* (from the novel "La Vie Extraordinaire de Lola Montès" by Cécil Saint-Laurent.) *adapt:* Jacques Natanson, Annette Wademant, Max Ophuls & (German version) Franz Geiger. *dial:* Natanson. *ph:* Christian Matras. *des:* Jean d'Eaubonne. *mus:* Georges Auric. *ed:* Madeleine Gug. *players:* Martine Carol, Peter Ustinov, Anton Walbrook, Ivan Desny, Will Quadflieg, Oscar Werner.

Bibliography:

(a) * Richard Roud: "Max Ophuls. An Index" (B.F.I., London, 1958).
Georges Annenkov: "Max Ophuls" (Le Terrain Vague, Paris, 1962).
Claude Beylie: "Max Ophuls" (Seghers, Paris, 1963).
Claude Beylie: "Max Ophuls" *(Anthologie du Cinéma*, Paris, 1965).
† Max Ophuls: "Spiel im Dasein" (Henry Goverts Verlag. Stuttgart. 1959).
Interview in *Cahiers du Cinéma* No. 72. Memoirs in eleven issues of *Cahiers du Cinéma* (Nos. 117 to 134).
b) "La Ronde" *(Avant-Scène 25.* Apr. 1963).
† "Lola Montès" (in "Spektakulum: Texte moderner Filme". Suhrkamp Verlag, Frankfurt, 1961; and *Avant-Scène 88,* Jan. 1969).

JEAN RENOIR

b. 15 Sept 1894 in Paris, younger son of the Impressionist painter Auguste Renoir. First interest was ceramics. Early work in the cinema includes the script *Une Vie sans Joie* which was directed as *Catherine* (1924) by Albert Dieudonné and starred Renoir's wife Catherine Hessling. He also appeared with the latter in two films by Alberto Cavalcanti: *Le Petit Chaperon Rouge* (1929) and *La P'tite Lili* (1929). In later life Renoir has written a number of works, including three plays "Orvet" (1953), "The Heirs" and "Carola" (1957), as well as adapting "The Big Knife" by Clifford Odets. In 1958 he published the biography of his father, on which he had worked for many years.

Films:

LA FILLE DE L'EAU (1924)
prod. dir. & des: Jean Renoir. *sc:* Pierre Lestinguez. *ph:* Jean Bachelet.

players: Catherine Hessling, Pierre Philippe (= Lestringuez), Pierre Champagne, Harold Lewingston, Maurice Touzé.
NANA (1926)
prod. & dir: Jean Renoir. *sc:* (from the novel by Zola) *adapt:* Pierre Lestringuez. *ph:* Jean Bachelet. *des:* Claude Autant-Lara.
players: Catherine Hessling, Jean Angelo, Werner Krauss, Pierre Philippe, André Cerf, Raymond Guérin, Waleska Gert.
CHARLESTON (1927)
prod. & dir: Jean Renoir. *sc:* Pierre Lestringuez (from an idea by André Cerf). *ph:* Jean Bachelet. *mus:* Clément Doucet.
players: Johnny Huggins, Catherine Hessling.
MARQUITTA (1927)
prod: Artistes Réunis (Films Renoir) *dir:* Jean Renoir. *sc:* Pierre Lestringuez. *ph:* Jean Bachelet. *des:* Robert-Jules Garnier.
players: Marie-Louise Irribe, Jean Angelo, Henri Debain, Mancini.
LA PETITE MARCHANDE D'ALLUMETTES (1928)
prod. & dir: Jean Renoir & Jean Tedesco. *sc:* (from Hans Andersen) *adapt:* Renoir. *ph:* Jean Bachelet. *des:* Eric Aes. *mus:* Manuel Rosental (classical arrangements).
players: Catherine Hessling, Manuel Raaby, Jean Storm, Amy Wells.
TIRE AU FLANC (1928)
prod: Néo-Films/Braunberger. *dir:* Jean Renoir. *sc:* (from farce by Mouezy-Eon & Sylvane) *adapt:* Renoir & Claude Heymann. *ph:* Jean Bachelet. *des:* Eric Aes.
players: Georges Pomiès, Michel Simon, Jean Storm, Félix Oudart, Paul Velsa, Jeanne Helbing, Manuel Raaby, Fridette Faton.
LE TOURNOI (1929)
prod: Société des Films Historiques. *dir. & sc:* Jean Renoir (from story by Henry Dupuy-Mazuel). *ph:* Marcel Lucien & Maurice Desfassiaux. *des:* Mallet Stevens. *ed:* André Cerf.
players: Aldo Nadi, Jackie Monnier, Enrique Rivero, Blanche Bernis, Suzanne Després, Manuel Raaby, Gérard Mock, Viviane Clarens.
LE BLED (1929)
prod: Société des Films Historiques. *dir:* Jean Renoir. *sc:* Henry Dupuy-Mazuel & Jager-Schmidt. *ph:* Marcel Lucien.
players: Arquillière, Manuel Raaby, Enrique Rivero, Jackie Monnier, Diana Hart.

ON PURGE BÉBÉ (1931)
prod: Braunberger/Richebé. *dir. sc. & dial:* Jean Renoir (from Georges Feydeau's comedy) *ph:* Theodore Sparkuhl & Roger Hubert. *des:* Gabriel Scognamillo. *ed:* Jean Mamy.
players: Louvigny, Michel Simon, Sacha Tarride, Fernandel, Marguerite Pierry.
LA CHIENNE (1931)
prod: Braunberger/Richebé. *dir. sc. & dial:* Jean Renoir (from the novel by Georges de la Fouchardière). *ph:* Theodore Sparkuhl & Roger Hubert. *des:* Gabriel Scognamillo. *ed:* Marguerite Renoir.
players: Michel Simon, Janie Marèze, Georges Flament, Madeleine Bérubet, Jean Gehret, Alexandre Rignault.
LA NUIT DU CARREFOUR (1932)
prod: Europa Film. *dir. sc. & dial:* Jean Renoir (from the novel by Simenon). *ph:* Marcel Lucien. *des:* William Aguet. *ed:* Marguerite Renoir.
players: Pierre Renoir, Winna Winfried, Georges Koudria, Georges Térof, Dignimont, Jean Gehret, Michel Duran, Jean Mitry.
BOUDU SAUVÉ DES EAUX (1932)
prod: Michel Simon & Jean Gehret. *dir. & sc. & dial:* Jean Renoir (from the play by René Fauchois). *ph:* Marcel Lucien. *des:* Laurent & Jean Castanier. *mus:* Raphaël *ed:* Suzanne de Troeye.
players: Michel Simon, Charles Grandval, Marcelle Hainia. Jean Gehret, Max Dalban, Jean Dasté, Jacques Becker.
CHOTARD ET CIE (1933)
prod: Société R.F. *dir. sc. & dial:* Jean Renoir (from the play by Roger Ferdinand). *ph:* J. L. Mundwiller. *des:* Jean Castanier. *ed:* Marguerite Renoir.
players: Charpin, Jeanne Lory, Pomiès, Jeanne Boitel, Max Dalban, Louis Seigner, Dignimont,

Louis Tunc, Mme. Treki.

MADAME BOVARY (1934)

prod: Nouvelle Société de Films. *dir. sc. & dial:* Jean Renoir. (from the novel by Gustave Flaubert). *ph:* Jean Bachelet. *des:* Eugène Lourié. *mus:* Darius Milhaud. *ed:* Marguerite Renoir. *players:* Valentine Tessier, Pierre Renoir, Max Dearly, Daniel Lecourtois, Fernand Fabre, Alice Tissot, Pierre Larquey, Jean Gehret, Héléna Manson.

TONI (1934)

prod: Films d'Aujourd'hui (Marcel Pagnol). *dir:* Jean Renoir. *sc:* Renoir & Carl Einstein (from an idea by J. Levert). *dial:* Einstein. *ph:* Claude Renoir. *des:* Bourelly. *mus:* Eugène Bozza. *ed:* Marguerite Renoir & Suzanne de Troeye.
players: Charles Blavette, Célia Montalvan, Jenny Hélia, Edouard Delmont, Andrex, Max Dalban.

LE CRIME DE MONSIEUR LANGE (1936)

prod: Obéron. *dir:* Jean Renoir. *sc. & dial:* Jacques Prévert (from an idea by Renoir & Jean Castanier). *ph:* Jean Bachelet. *des:* Jean Castanier & Robert Gys. *mus:* Jean Wiener. *ed:* Marguerite Renoir.
players: René Lefèvre, Jules Berry, Florelle, Nadia Sibirskaia, Sylvia Bataille, Marcel Levesque, Henri Guisol, Maurice Bacquet, Odette Talazac.

LA VIE EST À NOUS (1936)

prod: French Communist Party. *dir:* Jean Renoir. *sc:* Renoir & P. Vaillant-Couturier. *ph:* Jean-Serge Bourgoin, Alain Douarinou, Claude Renoir & Jean Isnard.
players: Julien Bertheau, Marcel Duhamel, O'Brady, Jean Dasté, Emile Drain.

UNE PARTIE DE CAMPAGNE (1936, released 1946)

prod: Pierre Braunberger. *dir. sc. & dial:* Jean Renoir (from the story by Guy de Maupassant). *ph:* Claude Renoir. *mus:* Joseph Kosma. *ed:* Marguerite Renoir.
players: Sylvia Bataille, Georges Darnoux, Gabriello, Jeanne Marken, Paul Temps, Jacques Brunius, Jean Renoir, Pierre Lestringuez, Marguerite Renoir.

LES BAS-FONDS (1936)

prod: Albatros. *dir:* Jean Renoir. *sc:* (from the novel by Gorki): E. Zamiatine & Jacques Companeez. *adapt. & dial:* Charles Spaak & Jean Renoir. *ph:* Fedote Bourgassof. *des:* Eugène Lourie & Hugues Laurent. *mus:* Jean Wiener. *ed:* Marguerite Renoir.
players: Jean Gabin, Louis Jouvet, Suzy Prim, Wladimir Sokolov, Robert le Vigan, Junie Astor, René Génin, Gabriello.

LA GRANDE ILLUSION (1937)

prod: R.A.C. *dir:* Jean Renoir. *sc. & dial:* Charles Spaak & Renoir. *ph:* Christian Matras. *des:* Eugène Lourié. *mus:* Joseph Kosma. *ed·* Marguerite Renoir.
players: Jean Gabin, Pierre Fresnay, Erich von Stroheim, Dalio, Carette, Gaston Modot, Jean Dasté.

LA MARSEILLAISE (1938)

prod: financed by public subscription. *dir. sc. & dial:* Jean Renoir. *ph:* Jean Bourgoin & Alain Douarinou. *des:* Léon Barsacq & Georges Wakhévitch. *mus:* Classiscs, Joseph Kosma, & Sauveplane. *ed:* Marguerite Renoir.
players: Pierre Renoir, Louis Jouvet, Aquistapace, Spinelly, Jaque Catelain, Aimé Clairond, Maurice Escade, Andrex, Carette, Gaston Modot.

LA BÊTE HUMAINE (1938)

prod: Paris Films Production. *dir. sc. & dial:* Jean Renoir (from the novel by Emile Zola) *ph:* Curt Courant *des:* Eugène Lourié. *mus:* Joseph Kosma. *ed:* Marguerite Renoir.
players: Jean Gabin, Simone Simon, Fernand Ledoux, Carette, Blanchette Brunoy.

LA RÈGLE DU JEU (1939)

prod: Nouvelle Edition Française. *dir:* Jean Renoir. *sc. & dial:* Renoir & Cart Koch. *ph:* Jean Bachelet. *des:* Eugène Louriè & Max Douy. *mus.* classics arranged by Roger Desormières & Joseph Kosma. *ed:* Marguerite Renoir.
players: Marcel Dalio, Nora Gregor, Jean Renoir, Roland Tutain, Mila Parely, Paulette Dubost, Julien Carette, Gaston Modot.

Renoir worked briefly on *Tosca* in Italy in 1940, completed by his assistant Carl Koch.

SWAMP WATER (1941 in U.S.A.)

prod: 20th Cent. Fox. (Irving Pichel). *dir:* Jean Renoir. *sc:* (from a story by Vereen Bell). *adapt. & dial:* Dudley Nichols. *ph:* Peverell Marley. *des:* Thomas Little. *mus:* David Buttolph. *ed:* Walter Thompson.

players: Walter Brennan, Walter Huston, Dana Andrews, John Carradine, Anne Baxter, Virginia Gilmore.

THIS LAND IS MINE (1943 in U.S.A.)

prod: R.K.O. Radio. *dir:* Jean Renoir. *sc:* Dudley Nichols. & Renoir. *dial:* Nichols. *ph:* Frank Redman. *des:* Eugène Lourié. *mus:* Lotar Perl.

players: Charles Laughton, Maureen O'Hara, Georges Saunders, Walter Slezak, Una O'Connor.

THE SOUTHERNER (1945 in U.S.A.)

prod: David J. Loew & Robert Hakim. *dir. sc. & dial:* Jean Renoir (from the novel "Hold Autumn in your hand" by George Perry). *ph:* Lucien Andriot. *des:* Eugène Lourié. *mus:* Werner Janssen. *ed:* Gregg Tallas.

players: Zachary Scott, Betty Field, J. Carrol Naish, Beulah Bond, Perry Killbride, Blanche Yurka.

THE DIARY OF A CHAMBERMAID (1946 in U.S.A.)

prod: Benedict Bogeaus & Burgess Meredith. *dir:* Jean Renoir. *sc:* (from the novel by Mirabeau). *adapt. & dial:* Renoir & Meredith. *ph:* Lucien Andriot. *des:* Eugène Lourié. *mus:* Michel Michelet.

players: Paulette Godard, Burgess Meredith, Hurd Hatfield, Reginald Owen, Francis Lederer, Judith Anderson, Florence Bates, Irene Ryan.

THE WOMAN ON THE BEACH (1946 in U.S.A.)

prod: Jack Gross. *dir:* Jean Renoir. *sc:* (from the novel "None so Blind" by Michael Wilson) *adapt. & dial:* Frank Davis, Renoir & Michael Hogan. *ph:* Leo Tover & Harry Wild. *des:* Darrell Silvera, John Sturtevant. *mus:* Hanns Eisler. *ed:* Roland Gross & Lyle Boyer.

players: Joan Bennett, Robert Ryan, Charles Bickford, Nan Leslie, Walter Sande, Irene Ryan, Glenn Vernon, Frank Darien, Jay Morris.

THE RIVER (1950 in India)

prod: Theater Guild. *dir:* Jean Renoir. *sc.* (from the novel by Rumer Godden). *adapt. & dial:* Renoir & Godden. *ph:* Claude Renoir. *des:* Eugène Lourié & Basi Chandra Gupta. *mus:* traditional Indian. *arr.* M. -A Parata Sarati. *ed:* Georges Gale.

players: Nora Swinburne, Esmond Knight, Arthur Shields, Thomas E. Breen, Patricia Walters, Radha, Adrienne Corri.

LE CARROSSE D'OR (1952 in Italy)

prod: Panaria Film/Hoche Production. *dir:* Jean Renoir. *sc:* (from the play "Le Carrosse du Saint-Sacrement" by Mérimée). *adapt. & dial:* Renoir, Jack Kirkland, Renzo Avanzo, Giulio Macchi & Ginette Doynel. *ph:* Claude Renoir. *des:* Mario Chiari. *mus:* Vivaldi. *ed:* Mario Serandrei & David Hawkins.

players: Anna Magnani, Duncan Lamont, Riccardo Rioli, Paul Campbell, Jean Debucourt, Odoardo Spadaro.

FRENCH CANCAN (1954)

prod: Franco-London Films/Jolly Films. *dir. sc. & dial:* Jean Renoir (from an idea by André-Paul Antoine). *ph:* Michel Kelber. *des:* Max Douy. *mus:* Georges Van Parys. *ed:* Boris Lewin.

players: Jean Gabin, Françoise Arnoul, Maria Félix, Jean-Roger Caussimon, Gianni Esposito, Franco Pastorino, Dora Doll, Jean Parédès.

ELENA ET LES HOMMES (1956)

prod: Franco-London Films/Films Gibé/Electra Compania Cinematografica. *dir. & sc:* Jean Renoir. *adapt. & dial:* Renoir & Jean Serge. *ph:* Claude Renoir. *des:* Jean André. *mus:* Joseph Kosma. *ed:* Boris Lewin.

players: Ingrid Bergman, Jean Marais, Mel Ferrer, Pierre Bertin, Elina Labourdette, Jean Richard, Magali Noel, Juliette Gréco.

LE TESTAMENT DU DOCTEUR CORDELIER (1959)

prod: R.T.F. — Sofirad/Compagnie Jean Renoir. *dir. sc. & dial:* Jean Renoir (inspired by the novel by Robert Louis Stevenson.) *ph:* Georges Leclerc. *des:* Marcel Louis Dieulot. *mus:* Joseph Kosma. *ed:* Renée Lichtig.

players: Jean-Louis Barrault, Michel Vitold, Teddy Bilis, André Certes, Jacques Dannoville, Jean Topart, Jacqueline Morane, Micheline Gary.

LE DÉJEUNER SUR L'HERBE (1959)
prod: Compagnie Jean Renoir. *dir. sc. & dial:* Jean Renoir. *ph:* Georges Leclerc. *des:* Marcel Louis Dieulot. *mus:* Joseph Kosma. *ed:* Renée Lichtig.
players: Paul Meurisse, Catherine Rouvel, Jacqueline Mourane, Fernand Sardou, Jean-Pierre Grandval, Charles Blavette.

LE CAPORAL ÉPINGLÉ (1962)
prod: Films du Cyclops. *dir. sc. & dial:* Jean Renoir & Guy Lefranc (from the novel by Jacques Perret.) *ph:* Georges Leclerc. *des:* Wolf Witzmann. *mus:* Joseph Kosma. *ed:* Renée Lichtig.
players: Jean-Pierre Cassel, Claude Brasseur, Claude Rich, O. E. Hasse, Jean Carmet, Conny Froboess, Mario David.

Bibliography:

(a) Armand-Jean Cauliez: "Jean Renoir" (Ed. Universitaires, Paris, 1962).

Bernard Chardère (ed): "Jean Renoir" *(Premier Plan 22 — 24, Lyon, 1962).*

* Jean Renoir' "Renoir my Father" (Collins. London. 1962)

* Jean Renoir: "The Notebooks of Captain Georges" (Collins. London. 1966).

Pierre Leprohon: "Jean Renoir" (Seghers. Paris. 1967).

Interviews in *Cahiers du Cinéma* Nos. 34–5, 78 & 155 and in *Cinéma 67.* Nos. 116–7.

(b) "Une Partie de Campagne" *(Avant-Scène 21.* Dec. 1962).

"La Grande Illusion" *(Avant-Scène 44.* Jan. 1965).

* translated into English (Lorrimer. London. 1967).

"La Règle du Jeu" *(Avant-Scène 52.* Oct. 1965).

"Le Testament du Docteur Cordelier" *(Avant-Scène 6.* Jul. 1961).

GEORGES ROUQUIER

b. 23 June 1909 at Lunel-Viel (Hérault). Worked as linotype operator. In 1929 he produced, scripted, directed, photographed and edited a documentary *VENDANGES*. Recently has worked in television.

Shorts:

LE TONNELIER (1942)
prod: Films Etienne Lallier. *dir. & sc:* Georges Rouquier. *ph:* André Dantan. *mus:* Henri Sauguet.
LE CHARRON (1943)
prod: Célia Films. *dir. & sc:* Geoges Rouquier. *mus:* Henri Sauguet.

L'ÉCONOMIE DE MÉTAUX (1943)
prod: Films Etienne Lallier. *dir.* & *sc:* Georges Rouquier. *mus:* Roger-Roger.

LA PART DE L'ENFANT (1943)
prod: Films Etienne Lallier. *dir.* & *sc:* Georges Rouquier.

L'OEUVRE SCIENTIFIQUE DE PASTEUR (1947)
prod: Ciné-France. *dir.* & *sc:* Georges Rouquier & Jean Painlevé. *ph:* Marcel Fradetal, Daniel Sarrade & Painlevé. *mus:* Guy Bernard. *ed:* Suzanne Sandberg.
player: Roland Tirat.

LE CHAUDRONNIER (1949)
prod: Films Étienne Lallier. *dir.* & *sc:* Georges Rouquier. *ph:* Marcel Fradetal. Daniel & Henri Sarrade. *mus:* Guy Bernard. *ed:* Monique Rousseau.

LE SEL DE LA TERRE (1950)
prod: Intermondia Film. *dir.* & *sc:* Georges Rouquier. *ph:* Marcel Fradetal, Daniel & Henri Sarrade. *mus:* Guy Bernard.

MALGOVERT (1952)
prod: Intermondia Film. *dir.* & *sc:* Georges Rouquier. *comm.* & *ed:* Daniel Lecomte. *ph:* Antoine Dumaître & R. Picon-Borel. *mus:* Guy Bernard.

LE LYCÉE SUR LA COLLINE (1953)
prod: Intermondia Film. *dir:* Georges Rouquier. *sc. dial.* & *comm:* Maurice Barry. *ph:* Marce Fradetal.

UN JOUR COMME LES AUTRES (1953)
dir: Georges Rouquier.

LOURDES ET SES MIRACLES (1954)
prod: Productions du Parvis. *dir.* & *sc:* Georges Rouquier. *ph:* Albert Viguier.

ARTHUR HONEGGER (1955)
prod: Intermondia Film. *dir:* Georges Rouquier. *sc:* René Delange. *ph:* René Colas. *mus:* Honegger.

LA BÊTE NOIRE (1958)
prod: U.G.C. *dir.* & *sc:* Georges Rouquier.

UNE BELLE PEUR (1958)
dir. & *sc:* Georges Rouquier.

LE BOUCLIER (1960)
dir. & *sc:* Georges Rouquier.

SIRE LE ROY N'A PLUS RIEN DIT (France/Canada 1964)
prod: Films Amorial/O.N.F. Canada. *dir.* & *sc:* Georges Rouquier. *ph:* Philippe Brun. *mus:* Maurice Blackburn.

Features:

FARREBIQUE (1946)
prod: Écran Français/Films Étienne Lallier. *dir. sc.* & *dial:* Georges Rouquier. *ph:* André Dantan & Daniel Sarrade. *mus:* Henri Sauguet. *ed:* Madeleine Gug. ●

SANG ET LUMIÈRES (1953)
prod: Cité Films (Jacques Bar)/Cocinor/Joachim Reig. *dir:* Georges Rouquier (French version) & Ricardo Munoz-Suay (Spanish version). *sc:* (from the novel by Joseph Peyré). *adapt:* Maurice Barry & Michel Audiard. *dial:* Audiard. *ph:* Maurice Barry. *des:* Jean Mandaroux. *ed:* Christian Gaudin.
players: Daniel Gélin, Zsa-Zsa Gabor, Henri Vilbert, Christiane Carrère.

SOS NORONHA (1957)
prod: U.G.C./Joly Film/Pallas Film. *dir:* Georges Rouquier. *sc:* (from the novel by Pièrre Viré) *adapt.* & *dial:* Rouquier, Pierre Boileau & Thomas Narcejac. *ph:* Henri Decae. *des:* Eugène Pierac. *mus:* Jean-Jacques Grunenwald. *ed:* Germaine Arthuis.
players: Jean Marais, Daniel Ivernel, Yves Massard, Ruy Guerra, Jose Lewgoy, Vanja Orico.

Bibliography:

(a) There is no extensive article or interview. A good introduction to Rouquier's place in the documentary is Claude Goretta: "Aspects of French Documentary" *(Sight & Sound.* Winter. 56-7).
(b) "Album de Farrebique" (Ed. Fortuny, Paris, 1947).

JACQUES TATI

b. Jacques Tatischeff, 9 Oct. 1908 at Le Pecq (Seine et Oise). Early interest in sport, esp. rugby which he played for the Racing Club de France. From sport he went to sporting mimes and hence to the music halls (from about 1933).

At the same time, during the thirties, he wrote and appeared in a number of short comic films:

OSCAR, CHAMPION DE TENNIS (1932)
Scripted and acted by Tati.

ON DEMANDE UNE BRUTE (1934)
dir: Charles Barrois. *sc:* Tati & Alfred Sauvy. *acting:* Tati.

GAI DIMANCHE (1935)
prod: Atlantic Films (O. M. de Andria) *dir:* Jacques Berr. *sc. & acting:* Tati & the clown Rhum.

SOIGNE TON GAUCHE (1936)
prod: Cady Films (Fred Orain). *dir:* René Clément. *mus:* Jean Yatove. *sc. & acting:* Tati.

RETOUR À LA TERRE (1938)
sc. & acting: Tati.

After the war Tati had small roles in two films by Claude Autant-Lara, *Sylvie et le Fantôme* (1945) and *Le Diable au Corps* (1947). Subsequently Tati made the short film which he later elaborated into the first of his feature films:

L'ÉCOLE DES FACTEURS (1947)
prod: Cady Films (Fred Orain). *dir. sc. & dial:* Jacques Tati. *ph:* Louis Félix. *mus:* Jean Yatove. *player:* Jacques Tati.

Feature films:

JOUR DE FÊTE (1949)
prod: Cady Films (Fred Orain). *dir:* Jacques Tati. *sc. & dial:* Jacques Tati & Henri Marquet

with *collab. of* René Wheeler. *ph:* Jacques Mercanton. *des:* René Moulaert. *mus:* Jean Yatove.
ed: Marcel Moreau.
players: Jacques Tati, Guy Decomble, Paul Frankeur, Santa Relli, Maine Vallée, Roger Rafal,
Beauvais, Delcassan.

LES VACANCES DE MONSIEUR HULOT (1953)
prod: Cady Films/Discina/Eclair Journal. *dir:* Jacques Tati. *sc. & dial:* Jacques Tati & Henri
Marquet *with collab. of* P. Aubert & Jacques Lagrange. *ph:* Jacques Mercanton & Jean Mousselle.
des: Roger Briaucourt & Henri Schmitt. *mus:* Alain Romans *ed:* Suzanne Baron, Charles
Bretoneiche & Grassi.
players: Jacques Tati, Nathalie Pascaud, Louis Perrault, Michèle Rolla, Suzy Willy, André
Dubois, Valentine Camax, Lucien Frégis.

MON ONCLE (1958)
prod: Specta Films/Gray Film/Alter Film (Paris)/Film del Centauro (Rome). *dir. sc. & dial:*
Jacques Tati *with collab. of* Jacques Lagrange & Jean L'Hôte. *ph:* Jean Bourgoin. *des:* Henri
Schmitt. *mus:* Franck Barcellini & Alain Romans *ed:* Suzanne Baron.
players: Jacques Tati, Jean-Pierre Zola, Alain Bécourt, Lucien Frégis, Dominique Marie, Betty
Schneider, André Dino.

PLAYTIME (1967)
prod: Specta Films. *dir:* Jacques Tati. *sc:* Jacques Tati, *with collab. of* Jacques
Lagrange. *Eng. dial:* Art Buchwald. *ph:* Jean Badal & Andreas Winding. *des:*
Eugène Roman. *mus:* Francis Lemarqne. *ed:* Gérard Pollicand.
players: Jacques Tati, Barbara Dennek, Jacqueline Lecomte, Léon Doyen, François
Viaur, Reinhart Kolldehoff, Michel Francini.

Bibliography:

(a) Geneviève Agel: "Hulot parmi nous" (Ed. du Cerf, Paris, 1955).

Armand-Jean Cauliez: "Jacques Tati" (Seghers, Paris, 1962).

Interviews in *Cahiers du Cinéma* Nos. 83 & 199, and *Cinéma 65*
No. 99.

(b) —

Monsieur Hulot paints his canoe. Jacques Tati in his own LES VACANCES DE MONSIEUR HULOT.

INDEX OF PRINCIPAL FILM REFERENCES

(ordinary type indicates reference in the text, **heavy type** shows location of filmographical details).